TEACHING
Gifted Kids
IN
Today's Classroom

**Updated
Fourth Edition**

Strategies and Techniques Every Teacher Can Use

Susan Winebrenner, M.S.,
with contributing author Dina Brulles, Ph.D.

free spirit
PUBLISHING®

Library of Congress Cataloging-in-Publication Data

Winebrenner, Susan.
 Teaching gifted kids in today's classroom : strategies and techniques every teacher can use / Susan Winebrenner, Dina Brulles. — Rev. & updated third ed.
   p. cm.
 Rev. ed. of: Teaching gifted kids in the regular classroom, c2001.
 Summary: "Fully revised and updated for a new generation of educators, this is the definitive guide to meeting the learning needs of gifted students in the mixed-abilities classroom—seamlessly and effectively with minimal preparation time. For years, teachers have turned to this book daily to ensure their gifted students are getting the opportunities they need and deserve. Included are proven, practical, classroom-tested strategies and step-by-step instructions for how to use them. The new edition of *Teaching Gifted Kids in Today's Classroom* provides information on using technology for accelerated learning, managing cluster grouping, increasing curriculum rigor, improving assessments, boosting critical and creative thinking skills, and addressing gifted kids with special needs. Already a perennial best seller, this guide's third edition is sure to be welcomed with open arms by teachers everywhere."—Provided by publisher.
 ISBN 978-1-57542-395-1 — ISBN 1-57542-395-2
 1. Gifted children—Education—United States. I. Brulles, Dina. II. Winebrenner, Susan, Teaching gifted kids in the regular classroom. III. Title.
 LC3993.9.W56 2012
 371.95—dc23

2012024020

Updated Fourth Edition ISBN: 978-1-63198-372-6

The Compactor form introduced in chapter 2 and used throughout the book is adapted from a document originally published in 1978 by Creative Learning Press. Used with permission from Creative Learning Press.

Edited by Meg Bratsch
Cover and interior design by Michelle Lee Lagerroos

10 9 8 7 6 5 4 3 2
Printed in the United States of America

Free Spirit Publishing Inc.
6325 Sandburg Road, Suite 100
Minneapolis, MN 55427-3674
(612) 338-2068
help4kids@freespirit.com
freespirit.com

Dedication

This book is dedicated to all the educators who have found its previous editions so helpful, and who have consistently spread the word to colleagues far and wide. We are forever in your debt!

Acknowledgments

Sincere thanks go to:

Contributing author, Dr. Dina Brulles, for her helpful perspectives on the realities of current educational best practices, and for her significant contributions to the third and fourth editions.

Our editor, Meg Bratsch, for her patience and dedication in working tirelessly to confirm that the ideas expressed in the book are clearly communicated to you, its readers.

Our publisher, Judy Galbraith, whose diligent efforts over the years continue to ensure that all kids get the understanding and support they deserve.

Teachers Karen L. Brown, Karen Mensing, Erica Bailin, Alys Carnesi, and David Graham in the Paradise Valley Unified School District in Arizona, for their contributions in the areas of technology and assessment.

And last, but certainly not least, to Susan's husband, Joe, whose amazing patience with the demands of this most time-consuming task surely demonstrates how fortunate she is to share her life with him.

Contents

Digital Content

See page 245 for instructions for downloading this content and digital versions of all reproducible forms.

Chapter 10: Parenting Gifted Children
Additional Extension Menus
PDF Presentation for Professional Development
Reproducible Pages from the Book

List of Reproducible Pages

Chapter 1

Chapter 2

Chapter 6

Chapter 9

List of Figures

Foreword
by Bertie Kingore, Ph.D.

Is the word "classic" overused? Not when referencing this book. *Teaching Gifted Kids in the Regular Classroom* (its original title) is a true classic in gifted education. Susan Winebrenner's first and second editions transformed how gifted children are perceived and nurtured in mixed-ability classrooms. At the university level, both my undergraduate and graduate in-service teachers were enriched by the content and spirit of this book and perceived immediate connections that influenced their interactions with gifted students.

With Dina Brulles, the impact continues with a third, and now fourth, edition: *Teaching Gifted Kids in Today's Classroom*. The title change is most appropriate, as this work explores applications in contemporary education and more authentic learning initiatives, including the changes implied by the required standards that are integrated throughout the book.

This new edition continues the tradition of excellence with updated content, new topics, expanded resources, and the addition of Dr. Brulles's field experience and research in school systems. The book is a pleasure to read. It is well-crafted with practical applications that demonstrate how to address the two crucial needs of gifted students: compacting and differentiation. The discussion and applications of curriculum compacting and differentiation techniques are succinct, clear, and absolutely manageable—the best available to teachers. Compacting is particularly crucial for gifted students to enable them to experience continuous learning and avoid the less meaningful repetition of known concepts and skills.

The added chapter and expanded emphasis on assessment and technology is timely and sorely needed. The authors build a solid case for effectively combining the two for increased interest and achievement outcomes. They provide numerous, ready-to-use formative assessment techniques in keeping with required standards and the increased emphasis on continual assessments by most schools. Educators must use preassessment and formative assessment to document that gifted students have changed as learners as a result of classroom learning. Assessment is also vital to ensure that gifted students experience continuous progress in all content areas.

The authors provide a useful and unintimidating set of technology techniques and sample lessons for the classroom. Their choices encourage teachers who are less "techie" than their students to embrace the benefits of technology, while teaching students to be smart internet researchers who understand how to evaluate websites.

In the current educational forum, there are very few guarantees. But Susan Winebrenner and Dina Brulles have provided us strategies and procedures that guarantee effectiveness. There is a good reason why this book has been in continuous publication since 1992: It is a definitive book on teaching gifted kids, and we need it in today's classrooms.

Bertie Kingore, Ph.D.

Introduction

Of all the students you are teaching in a given class, which group do you think will probably learn the least this year? It may surprise you to find that in a class that has a range of abilities (and which class doesn't?), it is the *most* able, rather than the least able, who will make the smallest amount of academic progress. These are the students who are almost never given an opportunity to demonstrate that they already know what is going to be taught.

How does this happen? Mostly it's because each year we are presented with our curriculum content and feel intense pressure and responsibility to teach all the standards assigned to our grade or subject to all of our students. For advanced learners, this creates a situation in which much of their school time is wasted on grade-level work they have already mastered.

As adults, we often have options when we find ourselves in a situation like this. We can leave the class, lecture, or presentation and seek an alternative way to spend that time with something more satisfying and productive. Students do not often get that choice. To some extent, they are confined within a system that will not let them move ahead until they first complete all the grade-level requirements. The frustration faced by these students can be agonizing and maddening, and their wasted time and energy a tragedy.

For example, when a student was interviewed by a national researcher and was asked what it was like to be a gifted student in a heterogeneous classroom, he said it felt like his teacher was "stealing" his learning time by making him sit through so many lessons he already knew.

Can you identify with this student's frustration, impatience, and resentment? Think of the last time you *didn't* have the option to leave a redundant meeting or lecture and were instead forced to sit through it. And vow that now as a teacher you will avoid imposing such a fate on your gifted students.

How can you avoid this? You might want to hold on to something before you read the next sentence. *You are not required to teach all the standards to all of your students.* You are only required to document that the standards assigned to you have been mastered by the students assigned to you. Some of your students are gifted, or very advanced, and they may already

A Note from the Authors About This Update

For this updated fourth edition of *Teaching Gifted Kids in Today's Classroom*, we have refreshed its classic content for a new generation of educators. As the number of gifted programs continues to decrease in schools year after year, teachers in inclusion classrooms need this resource more than ever before to ensure their brightest learners receive the challenges and special attention they seek and need. Likewise, in this age of required standards focused on depth and rigor, gifted education techniques can now benefit many more students than just those formally identified as gifted. In this fourth edition, we include updated information on students with twice-exceptionalities, discuss the implications of MTSS (Multi-Tiered System of Supports) on gifted students, and address debates about some gifted education practices. We also elaborate on our popular Study Guide method to make it even easier for teachers and students to use. And in the spirit of keeping up with technology, we have improved our section on helpful digital tools for teachers, particularly as it relates to Google Classroom and related resources. We hope you enjoy!

know much of what you are planning to teach, or they can often learn new material in much less time than their age peers.

Students are recognized as gifted if they have exceptional abilities in any area of learning that significantly exceed grade-level expectations, and they can understand content designed for students older than them by about two years or more. Since grade-level standards are designed for grade-level learners of a certain age, grade-level curriculum cannot, by definition, be at the instructional level of gifted students. This is essential to understand if we are to ensure that gifted students actually learn something new and challenging every day in school. All other students have that experience daily, so why shouldn't gifted students also enjoy it? As long as mastery is documented, students may experience any of the challenging learning options described in this book.

"But It's Too *Hard!*"

The United States is struggling to maintain a leadership role in the world. One reason is that in the United States we have been unable to provide enough candidates for high-level math and science courses and, consequently, for jobs in technology, science, and engineering. This is not because we lack students who are gifted in math and science. It is because these students often rebel from the tedium of spending so much time being taught what they've already learned that they likely come to assume that if someone is gifted, he or she must just "know" what is required without having to work hard to learn it. Hence, it is understandable that by the time these kids have an opportunity to take advanced courses, they are out of practice at working hard and may have lost the courage to put forth effort without the promise of easy success. When asked why they opt not to take advanced math courses in high school, for example, a common response from students is simply, "Because it's too *hard!*" This—from some of the smartest kids in the country.

The research of Dr. Carol Dweck at Stanford University validates these ideas. Her study, described in chapter 1 of this book (see page 18), demonstrates that in order for students to be

motivated to progress to advanced and challenging levels of learning, they must have the mindset that hard work is absolutely necessary for learning success and the perception that effort is the key factor to seeking new challenges throughout one's lifetime. They must believe, from their own experience, that smart people can work very hard—and even struggle, sweat, and fail sometimes—and *still* be considered smart and gifted. In short, when gifted students discover early on that they can get high praise and grades for tasks they complete with little or no effort, they may conclude that being gifted means being able to do things without really trying. And the longer they are allowed to believe this, the harder it is for them to rise to the challenge when one is finally encountered.

We should be seriously concerned about the plight of gifted students in most classrooms today. Many consistently bring home perfect report cards and sail from grade school through high school, graduating in the top five percent of their class, while rarely being required to work hard. When they are accepted into prestigious colleges and universities, where everyone in the freshman class was *also* in the top five percent of their high school graduating class, the competition for A's is fierce and learning requires a lot of time, effort, and intensive study skills. Many gifted students have never learned these skills and are at a loss about how to effectively study, manage their time, handle intense competition and pressure, or deal with less-than-stellar grades and test scores—all of which can lead to a sense of discouragement, severe anxiety, eating disorders, depression, and other harmful outcomes.

Where do we want these kids we care about to be when they realize that success is not always easy and that it is perfectly natural for all students to have to work hard in order to learn new things? Surely not alone in a freshman dorm, miles away from home. We want them to experience challenges in their local school environment, so we can help them celebrate their first B and demonstrate that life goes on—and often improves!—even when one's grades are not perfect.

One fourth-grade teacher who attended a gifted workshop series Susan presented had an eye-opening experience that you may relate to. She started thinking about how happy she had felt the day before, when all of her most capable readers got A's on the end-of-the-unit test. But then she wondered whether their grades reflected what they had actually learned from her. Was it possible that these students knew the material before the unit even began?

Since there were two weeks between each workshop, she decided to find the answer to her question. The next day, with no advance warning, she gave these same students the end-of-the-unit test for the following unit. They were tested on the skills and the vocabulary only, not on the content of the stories, which they had not yet read. Again, they all got A's. This experience was one of the most startling of the teacher's career. She began to consider alternate methods of teaching her most capable readers to make sure they were not simply going through the motions of learning, but they were making measurable forward progress.

When gifted students realize that they already know a lot of the subject matter, they usually have little choice but to dutifully go through the assigned curriculum, waiting and hoping for the rare times when there will be something new or challenging for them to learn. Since very few teacher training programs require candidates to take even one course in gifted education, you are not to blame as a teacher for not knowing how to handle this situation effectively. We are confident that this book will help you teach gifted students in ways that can empower them for a lifetime of challenge, hard work, and achievement.

Author and educator Dr. Sylvia Rimm has expressed this eloquently when she says: "The surest path to high self-esteem is to be successful at something you perceived would be difficult." It is therefore possible that each time we take away students' opportunity to struggle by insisting they do work that is too easy for them, we steal their opportunity to have an esteem-building experience. Unless kids are consistently engaged in challenging work, they will lose their motivation to work hard.

A related self-esteem issue is that, especially in grades preK–8, students' self-esteem is usually a goal of the school. When atypical learners conclude that their specific learning needs are not being attended to, they may worry that other students and even teachers do not approve of them the way they are and wish they were more "average" or "normal." There are few challenges to one's self-esteem as painful as knowing you have to try to hide your real self on a daily basis. Many gifted students realize from an early age that it is safer for them to pretend to be average than to demonstrate their exceptional learning abilities. This leads to serious disenfranchisement issues. However, this entire situation is fixed when their teachers provide appropriate compacting and differentiation opportunities daily in their classes for students who need them. Gifted students interpret these options as evidence that it is okay to be themselves. Their classmates come to the same conclusion and are more likely to follow the teacher's example and demonstrate acceptance behaviors toward any students with significant learning differences.

Why Gifted Students Need Differentiation

Many educators believe there is no need to do anything special for gifted kids. "After all," they reason, "most gifted students get good grades and high scores on standardized tests. They do just fine without extra help or attention. They will 'make it' on their own." In fact, this idea is causing discreet gifted programs to disappear in districts across the country. Some states have even reallocated funds formerly earmarked for gifted education to the "general fund," leaving decisions about where that money should be spent up to individual districts. To understand why gifted students *do* need special attention, let's look at the bell curve on page 5. Rest assured that we use this model only to demonstrate reasons why differentiating for gifted students is required as much as it is for students who are struggling.

When we teach a class of students, we usually differentiate content, pacing, amount of work, and activities based on what we know about typical students at that age. Let's call those kids the Twos, because they are in the middle of the three groups represented on the bell curve and are usually students of average abilities. Many students enter a grade level missing many of the basic

A Question of Terms

Perhaps we should consider the question of whether to continue to call advanced students gifted. This term has caused decades of hard feelings between children and families when some students are deemed "chosen" and others are rejected. Even worse, the implied opposite of "gifted" is "un-gifted." This has not been intentional, but the label "gifted" resonates with many as a prize that some people win and some people lose. Some argue for a more judgment-free term such as "advanced learners" to clarify the advanced level at which students are able to work. Other terms used for these students are "high-ability," "accelerated," and "high-potential"—all perhaps less divisive and less emotional terms than "gifted." However, no matter the word used to describe it, giftedness itself remains the same, identified through careful testing and observation. It is, after all, a *learning difference,* not a label.

competencies they were supposed to acquire in earlier grades. They are often children with learning differences or special needs, or children of poverty, and may have lacked the early learning experiences that prepare kids for kindergarten. These kids are far to the left on the bell curve (see page 5); let's call them the Ones. These children are described as students with exceptional educational needs because they are not typical learners, nor do their abilities and performance fall into the middle range of the bell curve.

We also have some students who are ahead of their age peers in what they know and can do. We'll call them the Threes. On the bell curve, the Threes are the same distance to the far right as the Ones are to the far left. Hence, they can also be described as students with exceptional educational needs. Therefore, they are entitled to all the same differentiation opportunities our system makes available for the Ones—not because the Threes are specially privileged, but because they are *equally as atypical in their learning needs*.

Now ask yourself, "What do I do differently for students who are having trouble keeping up with the grade-level standards (the Ones)?" Your answer might include these interventions:

- **Adjust the amount of work** they have to do. You may require them to do less work than the typical learner for equivalent credit.

- **Change the pacing of the lesson** and adjust the amount of time they have to work. You might slow down your rate of instruction or provide more time for them to complete their work.

- **Change the content** in order to teach them what they are missing. If they are missing material they were supposed to master in a previous grade, you provide learning time on standards from other grade levels even though they are not part of your assigned standards.

- **Teach to their learning modalities and preferences,** and allow students to express what they have learned in ways that are compatible with those modalities.

- **Find topics in which they are highly interested**, so you can entice them to learn some of the standards through those high-interest topics.

- **Change the peer interactions** they have with their classmates, taking special care to pair them with students who can support them and with whom they can work comfortably.

- **Seek out their parents and former teachers** to get information that might empower you to help them learn more successfully. You may even invite their parents to come to school beyond the regular conference times, because you know that these students' achievement often improves with parental interest and assistance.

Many of us make most or all of these adjustments daily for the benefit of the Ones in our classes. Do you feel that these adjustments are unnecessary or unfair to the other students? Do you refrain from making them because of the extra work that is required of you? Probably not.

Just like the Ones, the Threes on the other end of the bell curve are deserving of differentiated instruction and interventions. Not because they are gifted, but because, like the Ones, they are not average. The level, pacing, amount of work, and type of learning activities that benefit average learners are just as inappropriate for above-average learners as they are for students who are working below grade-level expectations. For the Threes, the following adjustments are often necessary to improve their attitudes and willingness to do their schoolwork:

- **Lessen the amount of grade-level work** they must do because they can demonstrate mastery with less practice.

- **Increase the pace of a lesson** and allow them to spend considerable class time working on extensions or independent study.

- **Adjust the content** so it extends beyond the grade-level parameters, fuels students' passion for learning all they can about an interesting topic, and gives them opportunities for acceleration as part of their regular school experience.

- **Allow them to work with each other** on extension tasks and limit our expectations for them to assist other students who need help.

- **Change our style of interaction with them** from being a provider of information, or "sage on the stage," to being a learning "guide on the side."

- **Welcome their parents as important partners** in their learning. After all, every adult's goal for his or her kids is the same—for kids to love school and love learning for the rest of their lives.

Building Lifelong Learners

Becoming an enthusiastic lifelong learner is, arguably, the most important goal for success in the 21st century. Many experts predict that all the students we currently teach will be required throughout their work lives to change careers numerous times before they retire, due to economic situations and advances in technology.

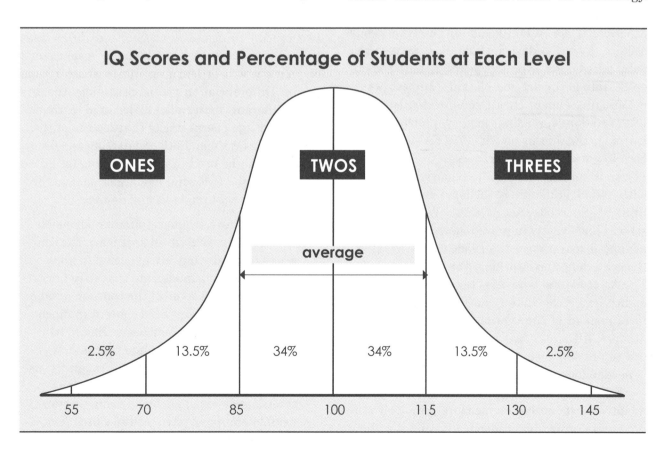

IQ Scores and Percentage of Students at Each Level

ONES　　TWOS　　THREES

average

2.5%　13.5%　34%　34%　13.5%　2.5%

55　70　85　100　115　130　145

Thus, many students will need to go back to some sort of schooling to be retrained for another career. In order for them to welcome that reality, they must have had positive experiences in school when they were young.

Look again at the bell curve on page 5. Which two groups of students do you predict are the *least* likely to be happy about returning to school later in life? If you predicted the Ones and the Threes, you would be correct. Why? Because school for many of them was stressful most of the time. The Twos usually have more positive experiences because much of what happens in school is geared toward them, the typical learners. The Ones feel stressed to meet standards and pass tests, while the Threes feel frustrated about feeling unchallenged so often in school.

Gifted Education Techniques Benefit Everyone

When students have had access to gifted education, it has significantly improved learning experiences for all students in heterogeneous classes. Every pedagogical method we've used with gifted kids over the years is now considered state-of-the-art for all kids. Project work, meaningful student choice, self-directed learning, literature-based reading, inquiry, problem-based learning, and a focus on STEM/STEAM—all were born in gifted education practices.

Another methodology previously used only with gifted students is included in the Every Student Succeeds Act (ESSA). Within ESSA, schools have vastly improved methods for testing advanced learners in the grade levels at which these students are working. For instance, under ESSA, students who are taking geometry in eighth grade can take a math test at their own level instead of the typical state test for eighth graders. All states are now required by federal law to provide such "out-of-level" testing when it is needed for any advanced learner.

ESSA also encourages the use of computer-adaptive tests to better measure how well students are growing academically and to show whether students need advanced math classes to take their work beyond their actual grade levels. All states are now required to describe how they plan to provide all students with the opportunity to take advanced math. This is another example of how attention to the needs of advanced learners can positively impact entire schools.

When we provide what gifted kids need—namely, a consistently challenging curriculum—other students are likely to benefit as well. Teachers who are trained for cluster classes learn that the differentiation opportunities are always offered to all students—not just those formally identified as gifted. This practice demonstrates high expectations for all students and most students react very positively to those expectations.

What Gifted Students Need

A good definition of learning might be "forward progress from a student's entry level at the beginning of each school year to her or his achievement levels at the end of the school year." So what do gifted students need in order to learn? They need two crucial things: *compacting* and *differentiation*. Compacting means condensing a semester's or year's worth of learning into a shorter time period. Differentiation means providing students with different materials, tasks, and activities than their age peers—tasks that lead to authentic learning for them. Both compacting and differentiation can be used to tailor learning for gifted students in the following five areas: *content, process, product, environment,* and *assessment*.

1. **Content.** As a teacher, you are responsible for making sure that all kids learn the content standards they are expected to know. Students who demonstrate that they have already learned some of the content, or who are able to learn required content in much less time than their age peers, should be provided with differentiated content.

   Content is differentiated through the use of curriculum compacting, learning contracts, accelerated pacing, learning centers, flexible grouping, advanced resource materials, independent study, and mentorships. The focus of differentiated content should be on students attaining a deeper, more nuanced understanding of the issues and viewpoints connected to a specific topic.

2. **Process.** This defines the methods students use to make sense of concepts, generalizations, and the required learning standards. It encompasses learning modality considerations, creative and productive thinking and conceptualizing, focus on open-ended and problem-solving tasks, opportunities for meaningful research, and the skills to share what they are learning.

   Gifted students should spend most of their learning time using learning processes that are more complex and abstract than is suitable for their age peers. They should collect and analyze knowledge and data as though they are professionals in a given field, assuming an attitude of inquiry rather than one of information gathering. And they should be expected to support their findings with valid evidence.

   Process is differentiated through the use of flexible grouping, approaches based on learning modalities or multiple intelligences, opportunities for learning at more complex levels, sophisticated research practices, and adjustable time limits.

3. **Product.** This describes the ways in which students choose to demonstrate their understanding of the content and process. Some gifted students resist assignments that require a written product, as their brains may move much faster than their hands. They may be more willing to produce a unique artifact, exhibit, independent study, or performance. Gifted students should be guided to produce what Dr. Joseph Renzulli calls "real-life products for appropriate audiences." These go beyond the typical research papers or reports to include alternatives that develop individual students' talents and curiosities.

   Product is differentiated by steering students to exciting and unusual resources and to people who can help them mine and use them, and by encouraging students to use available technology to its best advantage.

4. **Environment.** This describes the physical setting where learning takes place, as well as the expectations and attitudes present in the classroom and other learning locales. Gifted students typically spend more time in independent study than their classmates, and they sometimes may work outside the classroom or school as part of their differentiated learning. They thrive in a challenging atmosphere in which individuality is valued and nurtured.

   Learning environment is also differentiated by adjusting your expectations as a teacher to require higher level responses to more challenging lessons, establishing a positive attitude toward individual differences, allowing flexible time limits, providing opportunities for in-depth research, and arranging mentorships.

5. **Assessment.** Assessment practices have changed dramatically. They now are coming much closer to the attributes of assessment we have always used with gifted students. Gifted learners should experience consistent opportunities to demonstrate previous mastery before a particular unit is taught or to experience differentiated pacing. They should be encouraged to develop their own scoring rubrics and other methods to assess their independent study projects. We should strive to be certain that the manner in which we set up the assessments for their advanced work avoids simple extrinsic reward systems such as special stickers or extra credit. When we do that, students are working for the points or grades, rather than the intrinsic desire to learn all they can about a particular topic. To quote Karen Brown, a highly effective teacher of the gifted, "It's not just about the grades, it's about the *learning*." In a perfect world, that should be the goal for all students and teachers.

   Assessment is differentiated for advanced learners by setting up classroom conditions that allow them to get full credit for required standards without necessarily being expected to do all the activities that have been designed to lead to mastery.

We understand the uncertainty, and even fear, you might be feeling as you contemplate the tasks of finding out what your gifted students already know, giving them credit for it before you teach it, and providing alternate activities for them to work on instead. You may be asking yourself, "How will I gather the materials and resources I need? Won't differentiating content, process, product, environment, and assessment take a lot of time and add more to my teaching load? Will I lose control of my classroom?" We assure you this book will ease your doubts and fears and make your efforts to teach your gifted students—and consequently *all* your students—more successful and rewarding. As in all new learning, you will be less stressed if you choose one strategy to use in one subject area, and concentrate on that until you and your students have reached a comfort level. At that time, you might choose to use the same strategy with another subject area or try out another strategy in the same subject area. The catchphrase is *"start slowly,"* as you build toward successful implementation of several strategies from this book.

About This Book and Digital Content

Formerly titled *Teaching Gifted Kids in the Regular Classroom,* this book has been in constant publication since 1992, during which time hundreds of thousands of educators have shared, discussed, dog-eared, highlighted, and, most importantly, *used* it. The feedback from teachers, administrators, and parents has been dramatically positive and readers often state, "I wish I would have known the things in this book years ago—I might have avoided a lot of heartache and frustration for myself and the gifted kids I have taught and parented." No guilt intended! Simply begin today to make your own forward progress in your quest to have gifted students (and their parents) feel happy that you are their teacher.

In creating the third and fourth editions, we chose a slightly different title to more clearly state its mission: *Teaching Gifted Kids in Today's Classroom.* It's a guide written for educators of gifted kids in all grades, kindergarten through high school, in a variety of present-day learning environments—be they "regular" classrooms, gifted cluster classes, full-time gifted classes, school- or district-wide gifted programs, or at home. The design has undergone a complete face-lift, and extensive content has been updated, revised, and added to such topics as technology and assessment to make the book resonate with current teaching and learning realities.

Each chapter presents proven, practical, easy-to-use teaching and classroom management strategies, which are listed in a box at the start of each chapter. These strategies have been used by many teachers for over more than two decades. Scenarios profile students with whom the strategies have been successfully used, so you'll be able to draw parallels to the characteristics, needs, and responses of your own students. The strategies are described in step-by-step detail, frequently asked questions about the strategies are answered, and chapter summaries review the main points of each chapter. Of course, you are free to adjust any of the strategies as you use them as long as you never lose sight of these students' critical need for consistent compacting and differentiation that are essential parts of their total school program. The references and resources for all chapters appear together at the end of the book, listed by chapter.

Chapter 1 describes the learning and behavioral characteristics of gifted students. Special attention is given to populations that have been underserved in the past, including young gifted children, nonproductive students, gifted students from multicultural and low socioeconomic populations, and those considered "twice-exceptional" (possessing both gifted abilities and learning challenges). The chapter concludes with a discussion of the qualities needed by teachers of gifted students.

The strategies in **chapter 2** are designed to be used with curriculum that is skill-based and lends itself to pretesting, because some of your students will already know much of what you plan to teach. These strategies will help you meet the needs of your gifted students in any skill work related to reading, math, language arts, or other subject areas. Chapter 2 also contains information about creating and using extension activities.

The strategies in **chapter 3** are designed to be used with subject areas in which most of the content is new to students, such as science, social studies, literature, problem-based learning, and interdisciplinary or thematic units. Methods other than pretests and learning contracts are often necessary for these types of curriculums. **Chapter 4** describes appropriate reading and writing instruction for gifted students, and **chapter 5** explains how to plan differentiated curriculum for all of your students at the same time. Chapters 3 through 5 use many similar principles and methods, so you may want to read and use these chapters together.

Chapter 6 shows you how to help gifted kids manage independent study based on personal interests. **Chapter 7** describes issues to consider when grouping gifted students for instruction and learning. Strategies for making cooperative learning fair for gifted students, and methods for grouping gifted students in homerooms or self-contained classes—including cluster grouping—are explained.

Chapter 8 includes discussions of assessment and grading practices for gifted students and strategies for using technology to challenge gifted students. There are also many references to technology throughout the book. Technology is becoming integrated in students' learning, facilitates our easy location of extension activities, and can transform pretesting and formative assessment.

Chapter 9 discusses issues related to gifted education programming, such as acceleration, schoolwide cluster grouping, and International Baccalaureate programs; record-keeping for differentiation experiences; the roles of gifted education specialists; and how to interact with parents and colleagues.

Chapter 10 (available in the digital content) is intended to be read by parents of gifted kids. Teachers should read it, too, so they can anticipate parents' questions and expectations. Sharing this section with the parents of gifted students before you conference with them is often very productive.

Finally, the **conclusion** pulls all of the book's content together, while the **references and resources** section lists research and information materials, arranged by chapter, which can assist you in keeping your gifted students motivated to move forward in their learning.

The **digital content** included with the book contains all the reproducible forms from the book. Many of the digital forms are customizable, which means you can alter them and print out your own versions. The digital content also includes chapter 10 on parenting, 20 additional extension menus, and a PDF presentation that provides an overview of concepts and strategies described in the book and can be used for professional development. For information on how to access the digital content, see page 245.

How to Use This Book and Digital Content

The chapters presented here flow the best if the book is examined from start to finish. However, if you decide to study one or two chapters ahead of the others or to read the chapters in a different order, that's perfectly fine as well.

The book is intended for educators of gifted students. It is an essential resource for every classroom teacher and every building principal, and even for some parents. All classes have some overlooked gifted kids, and we want this book to be a resource for all teachers, whether or not they have any identified gifted students in their classes. As districts restructure the way they deliver gifted education services, administrators often tell parents that although self-contained and/or pull-out classes have been cancelled, the "gifted program" will now take place in the regular classroom. That promise cannot be kept unless those regular classroom teachers know how to challenge gifted students. As a teacher of gifted students in any setting, you can use this book as your guide to meeting those students' unique needs. Administrators promising to meet gifted students' needs can fulfill that commitment by sharing this book with all classroom teachers and allowing them time to study its contents and plan for differentiation. An ongoing book study will ensure that you implement the strategies successfully.

This book is also useful in PLCs (professional learning communities) studying issues regarding differentiation, keeping families enrolled in your school or district, and gifted education issues in general. The PDF presentation included in the accompanying digital content can be used at grade-level or department meetings, and for coaching teachers toward optimum success with all their students.

Overall, we must remember: *Gifted kids are gifted 24 hours a day,* not just during those times they spend in separate classes or on challenging projects or activities. Our goal must be to provide conditions that allow gifted kids to experience consistent opportunities to truly enjoy school and be as challenged and productive as possible. With that in mind, make this *your* book. It's written for you to use without much fuss. All methods have been field-tested with educators like yourself who have found them to work very effectively and who have found through this book the confidence and capability to inspire positive attitudes toward school in gifted students and to keep them on the path to being enthusiastic lifelong learners.

Here are our promises to you, our readers:

- We promise you that the strategies presented here will work in your heterogeneous classes as well as in gifted cluster classes and open-enrollment Honors and AP programs.

- We promise you that these strategies and techniques will also be useful for many students besides those formally identified as gifted.

- We promise you that there will be little or no resentment on the part of your other students as they see gifted students "doing their own thing."

- We promise that you won't have to spend long hours preparing extension materials.

- Finally, we promise you the following results for your gifted students:

  ◆ They will be more motivated.

  ◆ They will be more productive—they will actually get their work done.

  ◆ They will feel safe to demonstrate their advanced abilities.

  ◆ They will have more positive feelings about school.

  ◆ Their parents will be pleased with what's happening in your class and will be content to allow their children to continue their education at your school.

  ◆ Their teacher (you) will be pleased with their attitude and productivity and with the professionally satisfying results of your efforts.

To make sure your gifted students never feel like you are stealing their learning time, make use of the strategies presented in this book. Everything you need to know to be able to teach them well is inside these covers.

Most importantly, don't spend any time or energy feeling guilty about what you should have done differently in the past. If you had known what to do, you would have done it. This book will help you learn how to teach gifted kids well, starting now. Watch these students become more motivated to work, less sullen and hostile, less driven to always be perfect, and more likely to enjoy school and your teaching. Listen to their parents thank you for making their children's school experience so enjoyable and rewarding. Notice the positive feelings you experience as you realize you are truly meeting the exceptional learning needs of *all* your students.

For the many years we have been presenting this content to educators and parents, one question is always asked: "Aren't the strategies you've been teaching us good for all kids, not just gifted ones?" Our hearty answer is *yes!* Good teaching is good teaching, regardless of labels. So you have our blessing to apply the strategies in this book to any students who might benefit from them. Let's get started!

As always, we invite you to share your stories, questions, or concerns with us at help4kids@freespirit.com.

Susan Winebrenner and Dina Brulles, 2018

CHAPTER 1
Characteristics of Gifted Students

⭐ STRATEGIES

- The Name Card Method, page 14

Being gifted in schools today is not necessarily a positive experience. Gifted students and their parents experience a lot of rejection from an educational system in which conformity is valued and most kids are expected to work along with the group without resistance or complaint. We have long wondered why educators spend considerable time and effort teaching students to appreciate diversity in ethnic and cultural terms but don't extend that mindset to differences in learning ability. Gifted children do not ask to be born that way; it just happens. We need to consider giftedness as simply another difference and make gifted children as welcome in our classrooms as any other student.

In terms of classroom teaching, gifted students may be defined as those who have ability that exceeds grade- or age-level expectations by two years or more. Some gifted students have the potential to exceed expectations, but need teachers who understand their innately different learning needs to develop that potential. By this definition, the regular curriculum and standard instructional strategies can't possibly provide the challenge these students need to continually move forward in their learning.

Some fascinating insights into giftedness have emerged from the work of Polish psychiatrist and psychologist Kazimierz Dabrowski (1902–1980). When Dabrowski studied a group of gifted children and teens, he found that they displayed what he called "overexcitabilities." They perceived all kinds of stimuli more intensely than others did, they were super-sensitive to everything in their environment, and they felt the joys and sorrows of life more extremely than other children. Today, overexcitability, or OE, is considered a marker of giftedness, one of the many things to look for when identifying a gifted child. Dabrowski believed that OE can lead to a series of "positive disintegrations," or developmental crises, during which the individual rejects the status quo and questions everything. When things go well, the person emerges from this process as an autonomous, authentic human being with carefully thought-out values and beliefs. When things don't go well, the person may get stuck in antisocial behavior, disharmony, and despair. Dabrowski's theories help us understand why living with and teaching gifted kids can be such an incredible challenge.

In order to help identify those who might need an alternative approach to learning, people often ask for a short list of common characteristics of gifted children. Students who possess most or all of the following five characteristics may be gifted, and may benefit from differentiated instruction and compacted curriculum.

1. They learn new material faster and at an earlier age than their age peers.

2. They remember what they have learned for a very long time, making review unnecessary.

3. They are able to deal with concepts that are too complex and abstract for their age peers.

4. They have a passionate interest in one or more topics and would spend all available time learning more about those topics if they could.

5. They do not need to watch the teacher to understand what is being said, and they can process more than one task at a time.

Other characteristics are described throughout this chapter. All gifted children do not possess all of these characteristics. However, when you observe students consistently exhibiting many of these behaviors, the possibility that they are gifted is very strong. Trust your own observations more than how they perform on criterion-referenced standardized test scores or grades. Listen respectfully to parents whose descriptions of their children at home match some of the information presented here. Sometimes, gifted kids do not appear gifted at school but demonstrate gifted characteristics at home.

It's rare to find a child who is gifted across all academic areas. Most gifted kids are more likely to be advanced in one or two specific areas. Asynchronous development is common with gifted kids. This is seen when children are highly advanced in one or more areas and average in other areas. For example, highly verbal children may appear emotionally immature or deficient in bodily kinesthetic abilities (as seen in physical education classes). Sometimes their physical abilities are developmentally appropriate for their age but seem glaringly outpaced by their intellectual abilities. Compacting and differentiation opportunities are just as appropriate for children who show evidence of giftedness in one or two areas as they are for those who are gifted in several areas.

You might never be asked to formally identify gifted students. In fact, as you'll learn later in this chapter, gifted students often informally "identify" themselves by showing their readiness for compacting and differentiation. The characteristics are included here in case you need guidelines for recognizing behaviors associated with giftedness.

Learning and Behavioral Characteristics of Gifted Students

Gifted students might:

- Learn at a much earlier age than their age peers and make much more rapid progress in certain areas of learning.

- Be high achievers and motivated by high grades.

- Delight in completing work with precision and excellence.

- Exhibit asynchronous development. (Be highly precocious in some areas while demonstrating age-appropriate or delayed behaviors in other areas.)

- Have advanced vocabularies and verbal abilities for their age level.

- Have outstanding memories, possess lots of information, and be able to process it in sophisticated ways.

- Learn some things very easily with little help from others and seek to master certain topics of study.

- Operate on higher levels of thinking than their age peers, be comfortable with abstract and complex thinking tasks, and need a minimum of concrete experiences for complete understanding.

- Perceive subtle cause-and-effect relationships, and see patterns, relationships, and connections that others do not see.

- See better ways for doing things and suggest them to others, not always in positive or appreciated ways.

- Prefer complex and challenging tasks to basic work and may change simple tasks or directions to more complex ones to stay interested.

- Transfer concepts and learning to new situations.

- Make intuitive leaps toward understanding without being able to, or caring to, explain how they got there.

- Want to share all they know and love to know reasons for everything.

- Like to be noticed and appreciated for their advanced abilities.

- Be curious about many things and ask endless questions.

- Be keen observers who don't miss a thing.

- Be very intense and extremely emotional and excitable.

- Have a tendency to become totally absorbed in activities and thoughts and lose awareness of what's going on around them.

- Have difficulty making transitions and be reluctant to move from one subject area to another.

- Have many (sometimes unusual) interests, hobbies, and collections, and have a passionate interest that has lasted for many years.

- Be strongly motivated to do things of interest in their own way, like making discoveries and solving problems.

- Prefer to work alone.

- Have a very high energy level, seem to require little sleep, and have difficulty calming down or falling to sleep because they are so busy thinking, planning, problem solving, and creating.

- Be very sensitive to beauty and other people's feelings, emotions, and expectations.

- Have an advanced sense of justice, morality, empathy, and fairness, especially about global issues that many of their age peers aren't interested in.

- Have sophisticated senses of humor that can be inappropriate at times.

- Like to be in charge and are natural leaders.

NOTE Not all gifted kids learn to read before starting school and not all kids who learn to read before starting school are gifted. One significant indication of giftedness is the child who teaches himself or herself to read, with little or no help from an adult.

While many of these characteristics can be considered in a positive light, many pose inherent challenges in the classroom. Some challenges associated with having outstanding talents are often perceived as problems with behavior, motivation, or attitude. In addition to the characteristics previously listed, gifted children whose learning needs are not met in school might:

- Resist doing schoolwork or homework, or work in a sloppy, careless manner.

- Become frustrated with the pace of the class and what they perceive as stagnant or mundane progress.

- Rebel against routine and predictability.

- Ask embarrassing questions and demand good reasons for why things are done a certain way.

- Resist taking direction or orders.

- Daydream.

- Monopolize class discussions.

- Be bossy with peers and teachers.

- Become intolerant of their own imperfections and those of others.
- React in a super-sensitive way to any form of criticism or cry easily.
- Refuse to conform.
- Resist cooperative learning.
- Act out or disturb others.
- Be the "class clowns."
- Become impatient when they're not called on to recite or respond; blurt out answers without raising their hands.

When you notice these problems, don't panic! Before trying to "fix" the child, fix the curriculum and instruction by following the suggestions in this book. More often than not, an understanding of the academic, social, and emotional needs of gifted students, while differentiating instruction and compacting curriculum for them, can noticeably diminish negative behaviors and enhance their more positive behaviors.

More often than not, an understanding of the academic, social, and emotional needs of gifted students can noticeably diminish negative behaviors and enhance their more positive behaviors.

 ⭐ STRATEGY

The Name Card Method[1]

If there's one thing many gifted kids have in common—except those who have given up on school and retreated into full-time daydreaming—it's the tendency to blurt out answers and dominate class discussions. Even students whose learning needs are being met by compacting and differentiation have a hard time controlling these impulses. Conversely, there are also those gifted students who are shy or insecure and choose not to show their advanced intelligence by participating in class discussions. A method is needed to ensure that all students are fully engaged in discussions at all times. Sounds like a tall order, but it's really not.

An alternative to hand raising, the Name Card method is a great solution. Teachers who use this method claim they simply cannot teach without it, because its benefits are numerous. The Name Card method:

- Minimizes blurting and other attention-getting, discussion-controlling behaviors.
- Ensures nearly total participation in all discussions by all students; makes it impossible for anyone to "hide."
- Greatly improves listening behaviors. Students feel the need to hear every word said by the teacher and by other students.
- Eliminates teaching behaviors that may inadvertently communicate ethnic, cultural, socioeconomic, or gender bias.

Start by trying this method in one subject area or class period. Don't add other subjects or classes until you feel comfortable with the method and can see evidence of its positive outcomes.

1. Write each student's name on a 3" x 5" card. (Some teachers prefer using tongue depressors or Popsicle sticks.)

2. Tell your students that when you use the cards, instead of calling on people who raise their hands, you will call on the person whose name is on the card you've drawn randomly from the stack. Explain that you'll ignore any hand-waving, noise-making gestures, deep sighs, rolling eyes, and other behaviors they use to attempt to get your attention.

3. Group students in "discussion buddy" pairs. Explain that they will stay in their pairs for a specific period of time, perhaps two to

---

[1] Adapted from "Think-Pair-Share, Thinktrix, Thinklinks, and Weird Facts" by Frank T. Lyman Jr., in *Enhancing Thinking through Cooperative Learning,* edited by Neil Davidson and Toni Worsham. Columbia, NY: Teachers College Press, 1992. Used with permission of Frank T. Lyman Jr.

three weeks, after which you'll match them with other partners. Make it clear that you'll choose the pairs, and that you'll change them on a regular basis.

Each pair should consist of students who are at different levels of competency. *Exception:* Students who are highly capable in that subject or content area should be grouped with each other—especially the blurters. They will be less likely to blurt and more likely to participate when their partners are similar to them in learning ability and understand and appreciate their passion for knowing everything.

If you have a student no one wants to partner with, privately ask a particularly sensitive and helpful student if he or she will be that student's partner for this period. ("Future teacher/social worker" types are usually glad to oblige.)

4. Use the Think-Pair-Share method created by Dr. Frank Lyman. Ask an open-ended question. Give students a few seconds to think about their response, and tell them they can jot down their ideas if they like.

5. Tell students you are going to give them time to talk with their discussion buddies and come up with several more responses to the question. Demonstrate the signal you will use to indicate when pair time is over. When you give the signal, they should stop talking to each other and redirect their attention to you. Some teachers find it helpful to practice this in advance.

6. Let students know that when you call on them after pair time using the name cards, they will have to give an answer. It could be their own idea or their buddy's idea; they don't have to declare whose idea it is. The goal is simply to have everyone engaged.

Explain that they should answer loudly enough for the whole class to hear, since you won't be repeating anyone's answer. Tell them also that they cannot repeat what others have said, and that no one can say, "I pass." Since they will have time to confer with their partners, it's highly likely they will have an answer when you call on them.

7. Give the students 30–45 seconds of pair time. Tell them to use soft voices. Like before, they can jot down their ideas.

You may be worrying that your kids will get off-task during pair time. If you consistently keep the allotted time to under a minute, and use the name cards, they will stay on task.

8. Using the name cards, call on students to share what they have discussed. When you call on a student, he may share any response he and his partner came up with, as long as no one else has already given that answer.

To enjoy all the benefits of the Name Card method, it's important to follow these guidelines when calling on kids:

- Don't look at the cards before asking a question. If you do, you'll try to match the question's level of difficulty with your perception of the student's ability. This sends a clear message of your expectations for that student, whether high or low. Since you have paired struggling students with supportive partners, it's okay to ask challenging questions of all students.

- Don't show the cards to the students. Every now and then, you may want to call on someone other than the person whose name card you pull—such as a student who's getting very impatient to participate.

- Once you call on a student, stay with him or her until you get a response. Don't ask the class to help. Wait 10 seconds (no more), and if the student hasn't responded by then, start to coach him or her. Provide a clue or hint, give a choice between two alternatives, or allow the student more time to consult with the partner while you call on other kids. Always be certain to return to the student for a response within 60 seconds, so the student will know you have confidence that he or she is a capable learner. *Important*: Don't call on someone other than the partner to help. This is embarrassing and counterproductive to the goal of total participation.

* When you finish with a name card, put it somewhere inside the stack, never on the bottom. Shuffle the stack often. This way, kids won't stop paying attention once they've been called on, because they know they might be called on again at any time. Of course, some students will get more chances than others to respond, but that's okay, since all students actually answer every question anyway with their partners.

* If you use tongue depressors instead of cards, use only one can. Never put the used ones in another can, or you run the risk of losing the students' attention.

9. Using the name cards, call on several students to share before commenting or giving your input. Simply "receive" their responses in a noncommittal way. You might nod or say "Thank you" or "Okay."

   When you show that you'll receive multiple responses to the same question, students don't stop thinking about the question even after someone else has answered it. They know their name card might be next and they'll have to come up with a reasonable response as well.

10. Before moving on to the next question, for the benefit of students who enjoy sharing their deep wealth of knowledge, ask, "Does anyone have anything to add that hasn't already been said? Raise your hand if you do."

    Make it very clear that they may only *add* to the discussion; they may not repeat what has already been said. If they do repeat, they forfeit their right to add anything more to the rest of that particular discussion. (This encourages students to listen carefully to the contributions of their classmates.) They can continue to participate in the activity, however, because their name card stays in the stack.

Kids who have tended to dominate discussions in the past are now in a very satisfying situation. They get to tell the answers to all of the questions to their partners, and they always have the opportunity to add to a discussion.

Perfectionism

In addition to dominating class discussions, many gifted kids also exhibit characteristics of perfectionism. In the primary grades, these perfectionists are easy to spot. They work ever so slowly to create a perfect product, constantly asking you, "Is this okay? Is this what you want me to do?" In the upper grades, perfectionism becomes harder to identify, since it may look more like procrastination. Gifted kids begin avoiding assignments, reasoning that, "Since I probably can't do this perfectly because I don't have the right materials or the teacher hasn't given us enough time, I may as well not bother doing it at all." This handy defense mechanism hides an underlying anxiety that if they do give the assignment their best shot, and it isn't good enough to earn the top grade, they might not be able to handle the consequences.

Perfectionist Characteristics

Perfectionists often:

* Believe that what they can do is more important and valuable than who they are.

* Believe that their worth as human beings depends on being perfect.

* Set impossible goals for themselves.

* Have been praised consistently for their "greatness" and exceptional ability; fear they will lose the regard of others if they can't continue to demonstrate that exceptionality.

* May suffer from the "Impostor Syndrome"—the belief that they aren't really very capable and don't deserve their success.

* Resist challenging work for fear that their struggle will be seen by others.

* Work very slowly in the hope that their products will be perfect.

- Discover a mistake in their work; erase until there is a hole in the paper, or crumple up the paper and throw it away—sometimes accompanied by tears.

- Limit their options and avoid taking risks.

- Procrastinate to the point at which work never gets done or even started. In this way, they ensure that no one can ever really judge their work, and they don't have to face the possibility that their best may not be good enough.

- May cry easily in frustration when their work at school doesn't seem to reach a state of being perfect. (This is often misjudged as immaturity or the result of too much pressure from home.)

- Ask for lots of extra time to complete their work.

- Ask for lots of help and reassurance from the teacher. ("Is this all right? Please repeat the directions.")

- Can't take criticism or suggestions for improvement without being defensive, angry, or tearful. Criticism proves that they aren't perfect, and suggestions imply that they aren't perfect. Imperfection is intolerable.

- Expect other people to be perfect—especially classmates, teammates, and teachers.

- Are never satisfied with their successes.

Parents and teachers unwittingly contribute to the need of these students to be perfect at all times. In their early years at home, these children notice how the adults in their life make a pleasant fuss when they exhibit precocious behaviors. Well-meaning teachers add fuel to the fire when they call attention to a student's exceptional work, holding it up as a model for the other students without knowing whether any true effort was involved.

Meanwhile, capable students who just didn't feel like doing their best on a particular assignment get it back for revision, with some comment like, "C'mon, Amy, you can do better than this! I'll give you another chance to earn an A." To these students, the message is clear: "Adults like me more when I'm the best—when my work is perfect and deserves an A." Since most adults have been known to goof off occasionally and do a less than perfect job on some project that doesn't interest them, perhaps those same adults should lighten up on their expectations for gifted kids. We need to teach kids how to struggle to learn, not how to keep completing tasks without true effort.

Starting in kindergarten, it becomes the teacher's responsibility to communicate to students that authentic learning involves struggle, and that what one already knows represents memory, not learning. The way to communicate these important concepts is by consistently providing gifted students with challenging, possibly even slightly frustrating work. Furthermore, these students need to learn that the best grade possible represents a long-term goal of mastery, and that lower grades are not a reflection of inadequacy, but an indication that mastery has not yet been achieved.

Students need to learn that the best grade possible represents a long-term goal of mastery, and that lower grades are not a reflection of inadequacy, but an indication that mastery has not yet been achieved.

Teachers can support this risk-taking behavior by refraining from always expecting perfect work and grades from gifted students, and by encouraging them to try tasks that are truly difficult for them. Gifted students need to develop an appreciation for the values that accompany the struggle to learn. They need to replace their self-talk that says, "I must make it appear that the work is effortless so no one questions my intelligence" with a message that says, "True intelligence is reflected in my willingness to stay with a frustrating and difficult task until mastery is achieved."

The Problem with Praise

It's also possible that praising a child too much can contribute to perfectionism, especially if the praise is for the child's natural abilities or products that didn't require much effort. High praise can make a child believe that if you're smart, all learning should come easily.

Research by Dr. Carol Dweck at Stanford University has affirmed this fact.[2] Dweck conducted an experiment with 400 fifth graders of varying ability levels to see what really motivated them to welcome difficult learning tasks. Students were divided at random into three groups, and all students were given a puzzle task that was challenging but attainable. Upon completion of the task, a third of the students were praised for their intelligence, with phrases such as, "You must be really smart—you got a really good score." Another third of the students were praised for their effort: "Your answer was correct—I can tell you worked very hard on this task. Good for you." The final third were praised only for the outcome they got, with no comment on why they had been successful.

The same students were then told another task was to follow. They were asked if they wanted to try a more challenging task from which they could learn a lot, or an easier task on which they were sure to do well. Can you guess which of the three groups chose the more challenging task? Yes, the students who took the most risk and chose the difficult task were *not* those who had previously been praised for "being smart," but rather those who had been praised for their effort. Those praised for their innate ability wanted the easier task, because they were afraid to do anything that might cause others to question their smarts.

This is an important lesson for parents and teachers. When we praise our gifted kids for their abilities with comments like, "You are really very smart," they are likely to choose the safe path that is guaranteed to allow them to continue to think they are smart. These kids conclude that adults prefer to observe them in situations where they are easily successful. But when we instead praise young people for their effort and hard work, they are more likely to want to remain engaged in the activity, believing that hard work will lead to better outcomes.

> When we praise our gifted kids for their abilities, they are likely to choose the safe path that is guaranteed to allow them to continue to think they are smart.

Attribution theory, or what Dweck calls "mindset theory," can be used to explain why this happens. People who attribute their success to their inborn ability live in fear that one day their fixed ability will not be sufficient for some required task; they have a "fixed mindset." But people who attribute their success to hard work are in complete control of the outcome; they have a "growth mindset." All they have to do is work harder to grow. When we instill that essential knowledge in the children we care about, they are on the road to lifetime achievement.

Teachers and parents who implement effort-based praise are often astonished at how quickly they observe a difference in their kids—sometimes in a week or less! They are delighted to observe a much higher motivation to learn and to work hard on appropriately challenging schoolwork.

Ways to Help the Perfectionistic Child

Our most important job as teachers of gifted students is to help them understand that it's perfectly all right to struggle to learn, and that the world will not think less of them because that struggle is apparent. You need to make sure that all of your students, including those who are gifted, are always working on tasks that require real effort. In order to do that, you must be willing to assess and give full credit for previous mastery each time an instructional unit begins. Once you discover that some students have already mastered what you are about to teach, their class

[2] Dweck, 2008.

time should be spent on alternate activities that challenge them.

- Help perfectionists learn that success with long-term goals is merely an accumulation of successes with short-term goals. The Goal-Setting Log on page 21 is a very effective tool you can use to teach this concept. Once students form the habit of taking pride in their ability to set and reach a goal during today's work period, they can worry less about whether the final product, due two weeks later, will be perfect.

- Teach them how to use creative problem solving (CPS). In CPS, sometimes the best or most useful ideas come later in the brainstorming process. This relieves kids of some of the pressure to get the "right answer" quickly.

- Avoid the phrase "Always do your very best." When you want to encourage your students to work their hardest, say, "Put forth your *best effort*." This shifts the emphasis from the product to the learning process.

How to Use the Goal-Setting Log

The Goal-Setting Log is designed to be used by students who have trouble getting started with a task, who work too slowly, or who never seem to be able to finish long-term tasks. It's especially helpful for perfectionists. You'll find a reproducible Goal-Setting Log on page 21.

1. At the beginning of each work period, have students enter the date in the left column. In the center column, they should write a brief description of the work they predict they can accomplish *during that single work period.*

2. Five minutes before the end of the work period, have students complete the right column by recording how much work they have actually accomplished. If they accomplished less than they predicted, they should move down a line, record tomorrow's date (or the date of the next work period), and briefly describe the work they have left to do.

Always keep the logs in the classroom—in the students' folders, their compacting folders (see page 39), or a community folder if necessary. Have all students who use the logs sit in the same general area. Work with them as a group to set and review their goals.

For some students, old habits die hard, and they may have trouble letting go of their perfectionism. Guide them through this review:

If the goal has been met, ask:

- What was your goal?

- Did you accomplish your goal?

- Who is responsible for your success in reaching your goal? (It may take patience and prodding, but the student must respond, "I am responsible for my success in accomplishing my goal.")

- How does it feel to be successful? (Again, you may have to prompt the student to say, "It feels good to be successful.")

- How can you congratulate yourself or give yourself some recognition for a job well done? (Offer suggestions if necessary.)

If the goal has not been met, ask:

- What was your goal?

- Did you accomplish your goal?

- Who is responsible for the fact that you didn't reach your goal? (The student may blame some external source. Don't ask how it feels not to accomplish the goal. Instead, prompt until the student can say, "I am responsible for not reaching my goal.")

- What plan can you make for tomorrow to prevent the same problem from happening again? (Have the student write his or her plan on the back of the Goal-Setting Log.)

- Never reprimand students who don't reach their goals. The best way to get kids on track is to help them learn to set realistic goals and feel satisfaction from reaching them. The inability to earn positive feedback (from themselves and from you) is all the reprimanding they need.

- If you must grade students' work under this arrangement, we recommend he or she earns:
  - a C for reaching a goal that is well below the work you expect from the rest of the class.
  - a B when the goal gets into the grade-level range.
  - an A only for exceptional work that either meets most of the "Above Proficiency" standards or exceeds grade-level standards altogether.

Have students work on one area or subject at a time until progress is apparent and success feels comfortable to them. If you add other areas or subjects too quickly, students may develop a "fear of success." (As in: "Adults always expect more of you if you show them what you can do. I guess I should stop working so hard.")

Creative Thinkers

Creative thinkers often aren't identified as gifted because their behavior tends to annoy teachers, and their apparent "fooling around" often results in incomplete work. Many creative thinkers don't do well in school. They get poor grades, refuse or forget to hand in work on time, and constantly argue for things to be done differently. They are so challenging that we sometimes forget that the people who have made the most significant contributions to humankind throughout history generally exhibit many characteristics of creative thinkers. It's the nonconformists who are the problem-solvers, artists, dreamers, and inventors, thinking "outside the box" in ways that profoundly affect our lives. Some people who come to mind are Thomas Edison, Steve Jobs, Mahatma Gandhi, Oprah Winfrey, and Steven Spielberg, to name a few.

> Sometimes we forget that the people who have made the most significant contributions to humankind throughout history generally exhibit many characteristics of creative thinkers.

Creative thinkers often:

- Display original ideas and products. Are sometimes characterized as thinking up "wild and crazy ideas."

- Are fluent in idea generation and development. Notice endless possibilities for situations or ways objects may be used.

- Are able to elaborate on ideas. Add details others don't think of.

- Demonstrate flexibility of ideas and points of view. Can see merit in looking at things and situations from numerous perspectives.

- Experiment with ideas and hunches.

- Have outstanding senses of humor. Love to play with words and ideas.

- Are impatient with routine and predictable tasks. Add or change directions given by the teacher to make assignments more interesting.

- Have a tremendous capacity for making unexpected connections.

- Challenge accepted assumptions.

- Say what they think without regard for consequences. Are capable of great independence and autonomy.

- Have a great imagination; daydream often. Enjoy pretending; may have one or several imaginary playmates.

- Dress or groom in nonconformist ways.

- Can persist at one task to the total exclusion of others.

- Are brilliant, but absentminded about details.

- Are passionately interested in a particular topic or field of endeavor.

text continues on page 22

Student's Name: _____

Date	Goal for This Work Period	Work Actually Accomplished

- May be talented in the fine arts.

- May do much better on standardized tests than their classwork leads you to expect.

Ways to Nurture Creative Thinking

- Encourage children to observe and explore their environment and universe from many perspectives.

- Encourage children's natural curiosity and accompanying need to ask zillions of questions. Remember that you're not expected to know all the answers. Help the children predict their own answers or locate resources where they might find the answers themselves.

- Provide numerous open-ended learning experiences—those without a single right answer, solution, or method of exploration.

- Provide many opportunities for children to engage in meaningful decision making.

- Provide regular opportunities for daydreaming or reflection. In the creative thinking process, this is called *incubation*—the time when great ideas synthesize and emerge.

- Group creatively gifted kids together with others like themselves on projects and other activities. This experience validates their sense of self-worth and gives them courage to continue in their talent and interest areas.

- Help creative children find outlets and audiences for their creative products. Example: Pair them with adult mentors who can help them explore their creative interests.

Creativity Inhibitors

Creative thinkers may be blocked and frustrated when:

- They perceive they must succeed at everything they do, or that every product must be perfect.

- They feel pressured to conform in order to be accepted. Some of this pressure may come from peers; some may come from parents, teachers, and the media.

- They lack opportunities to work alone.

- They are told to "stop daydreaming" and don't understand the importance of daydreaming in the creative process.

- They spend too much time with highly structured toys and games and not enough time playing with ordinary objects in creative ways.

- Their creativity is met with misunderstanding, suspicion, or disdain from adults in their lives.

- Their creativity clashes with gender-related expectations.

- They are told that creativity is a waste of time when compared to more important endeavors.

- Their parents and teachers are authoritarian ("Do this because I say so").

Students Who Are Twice-Exceptional

Some gifted students exhibit behaviors that confuse their parents and teachers and frustrate the students themselves. They have exceptionally high ability in one or more areas of learning while simultaneously exhibiting significant weaknesses in others. Their strengths are often evident in the arts and in their ability to think and speak creatively. But when you ask them to write down their thoughts, they may claim they "can't write."

Scenario: Elizabeth

Elizabeth had a serious learning disability and didn't appear to be very gifted. But she also had an avid interest in geography, maps, and national parks. During the year she was in Susan's sixth-grade class, Susan took a class period to introduce an upcoming review unit on map skills. At the end of the period, Elizabeth came up to her, and they had the following conversation.

Elizabeth: "You know, Mrs. Winebrenner, I know a lot about maps."

Susan: "You do? How did that happen?"

Elizabeth: "I don't know. I just love maps. I've always loved maps. Maps are just really interesting things to me."

Susan: "What do you do with this love of maps?"

Elizabeth: "Well, when my family goes on a trip, I get to plan the trip on the map."

Susan: "No kidding! Where did you go last year?"

Elizabeth (proudly): "Yellowstone National Park."

Susan: "And how did you get there?"

Then Elizabeth told Susan how she had gotten her family to Yellowstone—remembering all the highways, states, time zone changes, national monuments, and national and state parks!

Susan: "Pretty impressive. Where did you go the year before?"

Elizabeth (happily): "Great Smoky Mountains."

Susan: "How did you get there?"

Once again, the same breadth of details emerged.

Susan: "Hmmm. I bet the prospect of spending several weeks reviewing basic map skills is not very appealing to you."

Elizabeth: "I've thought about that."

Susan: "I'll tell you what. I'll bring in the end-of-the-unit test tomorrow, and if you pass it with the equivalent of an A, you won't have to do the map work we're doing. You'll be able to spend your social studies time on a different activity of your choice."

Elizabeth (smiling): "Thanks!"

Next, Susan did something every teacher should do routinely when offering "special consideration" to gifted students: Offer the same opportunity to *everyone* in the class. Sixteen of Susan's 27 students volunteered to take the pretest she offered them, which they did during the next day's social studies period. Students who opted not to take the test watched a video about the national parks.

Students were told beforehand that if they didn't get an A, their tests wouldn't count. Six students completed the test. Two passed with A's—Elizabeth and another student.

When Susan discovered Elizabeth's superior competency in map concepts, she faced a dilemma. Should Elizabeth be allowed to experience compacting and differentiation in the map work? Or should her social studies time instead be used to help shore up her inadequate skills in sentence structure, handwriting, number facts, and most other areas of the sixth-grade curriculum?

The dilemma was solved when Susan asked herself two critical questions: "When compared to her classmates, is Elizabeth clearly advanced in this particular content?" Yes. "By virtue of her exceptional ability, is she as entitled to compacting and differentiation as any other student who demonstrated mastery on the pretest?" Clearly, yes again. Therefore, Susan chose to allow her to work on differentiated activities during social studies. (For more about Elizabeth, see page 48.)

The Meaning of Twice-Exceptional

Although there are several reasons why gifted students fail to achieve at a level compatible with their potential (see page 29), many students in this group are now recognized as "twice-exceptional." Their giftedness coexists with a learning challenge of some sort, most commonly a learning difficulty, behavioral problem, attention deficit disorder (with or without hyperactivity), or autism spectrum disorder.

These kids have some noticeable academic learning strengths but may never be recognized as gifted. Their learning challenge may mask their strengths. Since most schools usually stop looking for exceptional educational abilities once a learning deficiency has been identified, their giftedness will probably go unidentified.

As many as 30 percent of gifted kids may have some form of learning disability, difference, or difficulty.

As many as 30 percent of gifted kids may have some form of learning disability, difference, or difficulty. A study of twice-exceptional students led to these conclusions[3]:

1. Many high-ability students who have learning disabilities are not recognized for their giftedness and may have negative school experiences.

2. Traditional remediation techniques like special education classification, tutoring, and/or retention offer little challenge to high-ability students with learning difficulties and may perpetuate a cycle of underachievement.

3. High-ability students with learning differences need support to understand and effectively use their strengths.

4. Lack of understanding by school personnel, peers, and self may cause emotional and academic problems for students struggling to cope with learning differences and giftedness.

5. Parents are often the only ones to offer support to their high-ability children who also have learning differences. Parents can increase their effectiveness by exploring all available options and advocating for their children from an early age.

Twice-exceptional children may demonstrate one or more of these learning challenges:

■ On tests of ability, their scores may show significant discrepancies of 12 points or more between verbal and nonverbal subtests.

■ They have large vocabularies, which may be deficient in word meanings and the subtleties of language.

■ They may be reading significantly below grade level but have a large storehouse of information on some topics.

■ They may have the ability to express themselves verbally but an apparent inability to write down any of their ideas, organize their thoughts, write legibly, and spell accurately.

■ They may have difficulty following multistep directions.

■ They may excel at abstract reasoning but seem unable to remember small details or follows steps sequentially.

■ They may seem bright and motivated outside of school but have difficulty with traditional school tasks.

■ Their slow reaction speed may result in incomplete work and low test scores on timed tests.

■ Their general lack of self-confidence may manifest itself as inflexibility, inability to take risks, super-sensitivity to any type of criticism, helplessness, socially inadequate behaviors, stubbornness, and other behaviors designed to distract others from their learning inadequacies.

■ They may lack effective organization and study skills and may have difficulty estimating the amount of time it will take to complete a task.

■ Some of these children may have vision problems related to scotopic sensitivity that interfere with their reading ability. Colored overlays or lenses (try gray or yellow first) may help.

■ They may be sensitive to ridicule and become embarrassed easily, so they may be reluctant to take academic risks.

Children with ADD/ADHD

When people look for children with ADD/ADHD (attention deficit disorder or attention deficit hyperactivity disorder), they usually expect to see all four of these characteristics:

1. Hyperactivity (high energy).

2. Distractibility (inattention and difficulty with concentrating).

[3] Reis, Neu, and McGuire, 1997.

3. Impulsivity (which may be displayed as blurting or interrupting).

4. Disorganization (difficulty in finding materials and finishing tasks).

However, children who have ADD *without* hyperactivity may:

- Appear lethargic.

- Daydream a lot; seem like "absent-minded professors."

- Be easily distractible and unable to pay attention; have a short attention span.

- Have difficulty listening, following directions, and completing tasks or chores.

- Seem unaware of the risks or consequences of their actions.

- Lack social interaction skills; may be characterized as very quiet or shy.

- Pay little or no attention to details; make careless mistakes.

- Appear completely disorganized and forgetful; lose things; be unable to get homework to or from home and school.

And children who have ADD *with* hyperactivity (ADHD) may:

- Behave as if driven by a motor.

- Be fidgety and squirmy; have difficulty sitting still.

- Run, climb, and move about incessantly.

- Blurt or talk excessively; be unable to wait for the teacher to call on them.

- Have trouble sharing; be unable to wait their turn.

- Intrude on other people's conversation and play.

CAUTION These behaviors can often appear very similar to behaviors exhibited by gifted students who are not being challenged by the regular curriculum. If a child who possesses some characteristics of giftedness appears inattentive or frequently speaks out of turn, try compacting and differentiation before pursuing a diagnosis of ADD/ADHD. When ADD/ADHD behaviors are present, accommodating the student's learning modality and preferences and teaching compensation techniques can often reduce the need to place the child on medication.

According to Deirdre V. Lovecky, Ph.D., director of the Gifted Resource Center of New England:

Misdiagnosis of ADD/ADHD can occur in two directions. Highly energetic gifted children can be seen as ADD/ADHD, and some gifted children who can concentrate for long periods of time on areas of interest may not be seen as ADD/ADHD even when they are. Thus, knowledge about what is giftedness and what is ADD/ADIID is vital in assessing ADD/ADIID, and in ensuring that gifted children are not misdiagnosed.[4]

Colleen Willard-Holt suggests these questions to ask in differentiating between giftedness and ADD/ADHD[5]:

- Could the behaviors be responses to inappropriate placement, insufficient challenge, or lack of intellectual peers?

- Is the child able to concentrate when interested in the activity?

- Have any curricular modifications been made in an attempt to change inappropriate behaviors?

- Has the child been interviewed? What are his or her feelings about the behaviors?

- Does the child feel out of control? Do the parents perceive the child as being out of control?

- Do the behaviors occur at certain times of the day, during certain activities, with certain teachers, or in certain environments?

[4] Lovecky, 2004.
[5] Willard-Holt, 1999.

Sources of help for living with and treating children with ADD/ADHD may be found on the internet and are always being updated. See the references and resources on page 233 for suggestions.

Children with Autism Spectrum Disorder

According to the fifth edition of the *Diagnostic and Statistical Manual of Mental Disorders (DSM-5)*, the categories formerly referred to as "Asperger's syndrome" and "pervasive developmental disorder not otherwise specified (PDD-NOS)" are no longer described as separate disorders. "Autism spectrum disorder (ASD)" is a new umbrella term that includes autism, Asperger's syndrome, and PDD-NOS. ASD is characterized first by persistent deficits in social communications and interactions across many contexts. For example, some people on the autism spectrum exhibit difficulty making or maintaining eye contact, show very limited facial expression, and demonstrate no apparent interest in their peers. The second criterion describes restricted, repetitive behaviors that may include hand-flapping, insistence on a strict routine, or an unusual fixation on a single topic.

Children with ASD often tend to:

- Avoid direct eye contact with others.

- Have trouble forming relationships with peers; cannot read social cues that age peers understand instantly.

- Crave social acceptance but don't know how to get it.

- Lack empathy for others.

- Have repetitious and monotonous speech patterns.

- Be unable to engage in small talk.

- Focus on a single topic and have very one-sided conversations.

- Appear to lack enjoyment in certain situations.

- Exhibit repetitive motor mannerisms, such as tics or hand flapping, which may lead to a misdiagnosis of Tourette's syndrome.

- Have an unusual but passionate interest in one topic.

- Rarely show emotion except during a meltdown; have a short fuse for flight or fight.

- Take words very literally; follow rules precisely as they are written or stated.

- Have difficulty understanding differing viewpoints.

- Focus on details and rarely see the big picture.

- Be hypersensitive to sensory extremes in noise, light, and touch.

- Become upset by commotion and may hide when things become overwhelming.

- Dislike being the center of attention.

- Be devoted to their routines and grow extremely upset over changes.

- Demonstrate anxiety-provoked behaviors— bouncing their knees or walking in circles talking to themselves.

- Have food issues such as gluten and casein allergies.

- Be focused on their own self-preservation.

- Exhibit other characteristics associated with autism.

Some gifted children who exhibit characteristics of ASD may not be properly identified. And some children who are perceived as odd or eccentric may in fact have ASD and benefit from appropriate interventions.

Ways to Help Twice-Exceptional Students Succeed in School

Twice-exceptional children cannot improve simply by "trying harder." They must be taught specific compensation strategies. They must know and appreciate the fact that they have above-average intelligence. They and the adults in their lives need to understand that their brains possess certain physiological factors that influence their ability to learn.

Twice-exceptional children cannot improve simply by "trying harder." They must be taught specific compensation strategies.

Following are ways you can help the twice-exceptional kids in your classroom:

- Provide a nurturing environment in which individual differences are valued. Teach all kids to respect learning differences in all areas of learning.

- It's unrealistic to expect anyone to be equally capable in all learning areas. Strengths should be recognized and weaknesses compensated for. *Example:* Learning number facts through song and rhythm is much easier for some students with learning challenges than through rote memorization with flash cards.

- Before concluding that a gifted child is lazy or has an attitude problem, consider that poor performance may indicate a learning difficulty. Look for significant discrepancies in ability subtests and for evidence of glaring strengths accompanied by equally glaring weaknesses.

- Provide materials that will help students understand their learning difficulties and find ways to compensate. For suggestions, see page 233 in the references and resources.

- Assess each student's learning modality and preferences and create tasks that capitalize on them. *Examples:* Kids with certain learning difficulties often work better in low light, while listening to soothing music through headphones. They may prefer working in more relaxed positions and must be allowed to move about at regular intervals. Eating, chewing, or movement may also increase their concentration. Kids with ADD/ADHD are more likely to stay focused on a task if it's hands-on or related to a passionate interest. *Tip:* Ask parents to tell you about times at home when their child stays on-task for long periods.

- Allow and encourage students to demonstrate their learning in ways that are compatible with their learning modality and preferences.

Avoid traditional remediation techniques (special education classification, tutoring, retention) until alternate approaches have been thoroughly explored. Instead, teach compensation strategies directly. Compensation enables one part of the brain to take over a function that another part of the brain is unable to do. Be aware that a child's ability to compensate can be threatened by anxiety, fatigue, illness, or finding himself or herself in a totally new situation.

- For global, holistic learners, make sure they see and understand the "big picture" of a unit or story before asking them to learn about it in sections. Graphic organizers can help.

- If students have difficulty writing, give them other options. *Examples:* Instead of reading something and writing about it, they might record their learning audiovisually by using a smartphone or computer with a built-in video camera.

- When students have significant reading problems, texts and other information should be read aloud to them. A company called Learning Ally provides audio recordings of most texts and literature books used in schools, from elementary through post-graduate and professional levels. (See references and resources on page 234 for more information.)

- Provide clear, concise written directions, and don't give too many directions at one time. Use colors and shapes to help communicate what is expected. Ask students to describe what they think they are supposed to do before they begin any task.

- Teach organizational and executive functioning skills directly to students who need them. Mastering these skills is as important as learning required content. Use the Goal-Setting Log (page 21) to teach students to set short-term, realistic goals, starting with things they can accomplish during the next 30 minutes. Coach them to take pride in these accomplishments. Emphasize that accumulating short-term goals eventually leads to accomplishing longer-term goals.

- Whenever possible, provide students with two sets of books and learning materials—one to use at school and one to take home.

- Recognize that twice-exceptional students, along with all students with learning differences, need longer time periods for completing assignments and tests. Also, some students do much better on tests if they can read the test items aloud (or if someone else reads them aloud).

- Whenever possible, design learning experiences for individual students around their interests. Most standards can be taught in almost any context.

- Understand that gifted children with learning difficulties can experience and enjoy many of the same opportunities we offer to gifted students without difficulties. This includes interaction with complex and abstract thinking concepts and project work around areas of intense interest.

> **NOTE** School is designed for students of average ability, and so twice-exceptional students sometimes feel doubly cursed. They know they are smart, but they cannot show it the way that others can. When we treat them as gifted, we are acknowledging that they are very smart and this can be quite motivating. When we ignore their high intelligence, we alienate them from school. This alienation makes them withdraw and eventually give up in school. Focusing on their strengths can help these students become more productive in school.

When working with twice-exceptional students, the *2E Newsletter* recommends to teachers the following approaches[6]:

- Involve teamwork between gifted education and special education teachers.

- Build on students' strengths and interests.

- Challenge the students' intellectual abilities.

- Include hands-on instruction.

- Incorporate the arts to provide outlets for students' creative abilities.

- Provide support for students' areas of weakness in the form of accommodations and compensation strategies.

- Be flexible in the ways you allow students to receive instruction and produce the required work.

- Make provisions for someone to serve in the role of advocate for twice-exceptional students, coordinating services and ensuring that everyone involved in their education is aware of the nature and needs of a twice-exceptional learner.

Dr. Beverly Trail, professor at Regis University, offers the following practical ways that teachers can support their twice-exceptional students:

- Provide extra time to complete work and tests.

- Encourage effort. Help them develop a "can do" attitude.

- Emphasize that mistakes are part of learning.

- Promote the use of learning tools and assistive technology, such as graphic organizers and special keyboards, to help them be successful.

- Teach them the skills and strategies they need to succeed: problem solving and study skills, and test-taking, learning, and coping strategies.

- Help students learn how to plan and how to set realistic goals.

- Give them the flexible structure they need to be successful.

- Help them accept responsibility and seek support (i.e., self-advocate).

In summary, twice-exceptional students should receive actual advanced learning opportunities in both their areas of strength and their areas of weakness. Instruction and activities in their weaker areas should focus on their visual and tactile-kinesthetic strengths. And time should never be taken away from their strength areas to increase the amount of time they spend daily in their weaker areas.[7]

[6] See 2enewsletter.com.
[7] Winebrenner and Kiss, 2014.

Please see the references and resources on pages 233–234 for our recommendations of excellent sources of information about twice-exceptionality.

The Mystery of the Gifted Underachiever

As noted earlier, some so-called gifted under-achievers are actually twice-exceptional. But some of them don't have a learning difference or challenge . . . except the challenge of getting through another endless day at school.

Underachievement, a discrepancy between capability and achievement, can be caused or affected by a variety of factors including:

- Perfectionism
- Work that is too easy or too difficult
- The lack of opportunity for students to demonstrate what they know in ways that are compatible with their learning modality or preference
- Students' perception that what they are learning does not have any meaningful, relevant, and/or useful real-life application
- The lack of opportunity to learn about areas of interest
- Fear of being rejected for being different
- The lack of dreams or goals, or the sense that dreams or goals are unattainable
- Family interaction patterns that may interfere with achievement

It can be difficult to understand how children with high intelligence can get into a situation in school in which they are not "doing their work." However, in reality, we have rarely met gifted kids who won't do *their* work. Yet we know scores of gifted kids who won't do the *teacher's* work—in other words, the work their teacher asks them to do so a checkmark can be entered in the grade book. This is the basis of most power struggles between gifted kids, their parents, and their teachers. When gifted students are forced to do work related to content they have already mastered, they resist (a.k.a. underachieve), and the power struggle is on. In truth, they are not underachieving, they are under-challenged. They need to be given their *own* work to do—work that is challenging and meaningful to them—and be motivated to welcome these rigorous learning experiences.

> We have rarely met gifted kids who won't do *their* work. Yet we know scores of gifted kids who won't do the *teacher's* work.

Children also need to feel good about themselves. Our schools often focus on the importance of all students enjoying high self-esteem, yet all too often, gifted kids experience low self-esteem. This is partly because high intelligence is not always respected in school, and partly because gifted students fear that one day people will see them working hard to learn and will perceive that they aren't really very smart after all. To avoid ridicule, some students might pretend that they are not highly intelligent or that they do not need to work hard to learn material that may be challenging for them. Bragging also is a sign of low self-esteem. The student who is bragging is trying to keep others aware of his or her advanced abilities, so any deficiencies will not be noticed. And there are few situations more likely to diminish self-esteem than coming to school each day and pretending to be someone different from who you really are. Only in classrooms where individual differences in ability level and learning behaviors are recognized and accepted will all students' self-esteem truly flourish.

Because of these reasons—lack of appropriate learning challenges and low self-esteem—many gifted kids are working significantly below their potential. Throughout this book, you'll find strategies that will help you avoid and remedy the school-related factors that inhibit achievement while motivating your highly capable students to demonstrate their advanced abilities in productive ways.

NOTE To provide gifted services to students who have dual exceptionalities such as those described here, consider using an inclusive approach such as cluster grouping. The Schoolwide Cluster Grouping Model (SCGM) is one method for enfranchising gifted students who have exceptional learning needs. When included in a gifted cluster group, these students learn with other gifted students and have more opportunities to build on their areas of strength and develop their potential. See chapter 7, pages 194–198, for more information about cluster grouping.

Students from Diverse Populations

The current federal definition of giftedness includes "students, children, or youth who give evidence of high achievement capability in areas such as intellectual, creative, artistic, or leadership capacity, or in specific academic fields, and who need services and activities not ordinarily provided by the school in order to fully develop those capabilities."[8] Yet many gifted children from ethnically and culturally diverse backgrounds, minority cultures, and economically disadvantaged families continue to fall through the cracks when children are identified for gifted programs and other learning opportunities. There are four main reasons why this happens:

1. Some standardized tests are culturally biased. They assume that all students have had similar life experiences, which many of the children in these groups might not have had.

2. The tests use language and idioms with which many of these children might not be familiar. Although nonverbal tests of ability such as the *Naglieri Nonverbal Ability Test* (NNAT) can remedy this situation, they are not always available in every school district, or are misunderstood in that people think the test identifies only students who are

gifted in nonverbal ways. This is inaccurate: the NNAT is a nonverbal method to identify general intelligence.

3. Many of these children attend schools in which gifted education is not a priority. Gifted program opportunities may simply be unavailable, and therefore, the gifted students remain unidentified.

4. Many teachers do not recognize the gifted characteristics and behaviors in nonproductive students or students from cultures other than their own.

Identifying Gifted Students from Diverse Populations

Examine your school's gifted identification process. Check to make certain that one assessment is a nonverbal test of intelligence, such as the NNAT. Except for an individual intelligence test administered by a trained psychologist, no single test will identify all gifted students. Therefore, schools should use multiple measures, which include both verbal and nonverbal ability tests. At the very least, when administering any type of assessment to kids, it's imperative to first give them practice items or activities that will familiarize them with the format of the assessment and help them know what to expect.

Other options are available for identifying these students, and we encourage you to look into them. Here are some examples:

- The Entrada Scholars Program at Calvin College in Grand Rapids, Michigan, offers ethnic minority high school students an opportunity to participate in a college program accompanied by various levels of support, including financial.

- In Dade County, Florida, a program called T.E.A.M. for Success (Teaching Enrichment Activities for Minorities) uses specific criteria to identify students from diverse populations and retain them in gifted programs. Retention is what separates this program from others of its kind, since it has historically been easier to identify gifted kids in minority populations

---

[8] Elementary and Secondary Education Act, Title IX, Section 9101 (22).

than to keep them in programs for more than one year. The T.E.A.M. program is so successful that teachers of the gifted usually can't tell the difference between kids who entered gifted education via the program and those who entered through more traditional pathways.

Several nonverbal standardized tests have successfully been used for this purpose, including the NNAT previously mentioned. The results of these tests should be combined with teacher observations over time that look for evidence of particular strengths in any area of learning, especially in open-ended tasks that require creative, visual, and spatial thinking and the ability to solve real problems.

You can also watch for students who:

* Exhibit unusual fluency or advanced use of their native language.

* May develop fluency in English more quickly than others (if English isn't their native language).

* Can maintain their unique cultural identity while functioning well in the dominant culture.

* Assume responsibilities maturely.

* Display leadership qualities.

* Absorb information quickly.

* Demonstrate a highly developed sense of humor.

* Have an intuitive grasp of situations; are highly able to adapt to changes.

* See cause-and-effect relationships.

* Show interest in how and why things work.

* Indicate intense interest in one or more topics.

* Display originality.

* Exhibit fluency in creative thinking activities.

* Make intuitive leaps in thinking and problem solving.

* Exhibit many of the characteristics described earlier on pages 12–13.

In *Teaching Young Gifted Children in the Regular Classroom,* Joan Franklin Smutny, Sally Yahnke Walker, and Elizabeth A. Meckstroth propose two basic guidelines when looking at children from diverse populations:

1. Use the broadest definition of giftedness to include diverse abilities.

2. Find and serve as many children with high potential as possible.

They suggest the following identification strategies:

* Consider every possibility of exceptional skill when seeking to discover a child's outstanding abilities.

* Find a child's "best performance." Look for any sign of exceptional, even isolated, performance that could represent unidentified abilities. If you find an outstanding ability, such as memory for music, you can begin to invite a child's confidence by creating opportunities for him or her to use that talent. A single encouraging experience can often produce a ripple effect on the child's self-assurance and on the competence he or she begins to show in other directions.

* Consider "processing" behaviors, such as risk taking and the ability to hypothesize and improvise.

* Ask other teachers.

* Trust your hunches. If you suspect that a child has exceptional abilities, your hunch will probably be reliable.

* Make classroom observations, especially during multicultural-based activities.

* Interview the child to gain insight into her or his thinking, aspirations, home activities, and sense of self.

* Solicit a parent's views about the child's talents, abilities, and expressions of creative and critical thinking.

A Few Ways to Help Gifted Students from Diverse Populations

1. Seek out information about how cultural values may impact a child's classroom behavior. *Example:* Many students from Latin American cultures prefer working in a communal environment, rather than independently. They enjoy cooperative learning situations and subtle public recognition for their performance and behavior. Many of these students are uncomfortable in competitive situations. Some have been taught at home never to maintain eye contact with an adult, since it is considered disrespectful to do so. Their families and ethnic communities are very important to them.

2. Whenever possible, send messages home in the child's native language. When visiting students' homes, take someone along who can either communicate directly with the family or provide translation assistance. Similar opportunities should be available when these students need counseling or social work services at school. Language and cultural differences can keep parents away and can distance teachers from discovering children's exceptional abilities. One important and very effective way to bridge this gap is by working with your school or district to establish a "cultural liaison," a contact person for parents who are not comfortable speaking English.

3. Integrate curriculum from other cultures in literature, biography, and history activities. This shows students that the school values their uniqueness. It's much more effective than reserving cultural information and experiences for "multicultural fairs."

4. If your school has a gifted program, make sure that those who receive services reflect the ethnic and socioeconomic composition of your school's student population. If it does not, consider creating a more inclusive program that allows culturally and linguistically diverse students to be equally served. By identifying and addressing the learning needs of *all* your gifted students, you will build a school culture that embraces students' differences.

> By identifying and addressing the learning needs of *all* your gifted students, you will build a school culture that embraces students' differences.

5. Accept that culturally and linguistically diverse students who are gifted might not be currently achieving at the same level as their intellectual peers who are native English speakers. When we treat them as gifted, we acknowledge that they are highly capable and we raise our expectations. When provided with the same opportunities as other gifted students, we often see that their achievement increases and they begin working at higher levels.

6. Use instructional tools that minimize the amount of writing needed for students to demonstrate what they have learned. When we rely less on language, these students' level of understanding frequently surprises us. For example, use graphic organizers such as Thinking Maps to visually document main ideas and show connections between ideas. Allowing students to orally discuss an essay question can also help gauge understanding more accurately than writing.

An Overview of Guidelines for Identifying Gifted Students

▪ Use a combination of formal and informal methods. Formal methods include standardized tests of ability and achievement, and other testing results. Informal methods include student observations, parent nominations, nominations from former teachers, and even self-nominations.

- Consider results from both verbal and nonverbal measures, remembering that using only *one* type of test may not identify all students who are gifted.

- Do not use student grades. Many gifted students purposefully choose not to show their advanced abilities in school for various reasons.

- Seek nominations from any teachers the student has had and invite parents to nominate their child for inclusion in the program. Parents and other caregivers are the only people who observe a student in two settings—school *and* home—so their input is often valuable.

- Combine formal test scores with teacher observation methods to create a list of students who may benefit from the program. Match students with available program options. For example, if you are offering an honors-level chorus, you need demonstration of musical abilities rather than just high intelligence test scores. If advanced math classes are available, student candidates should have high scores in math assessments.

- It is often easier to formally identify giftedness in young children versus older children. This is because gifted kids who have experienced frustration and boredom in the primary years may "go underground" in the upper and middle school grades and become more difficult to reach. Some reliable assessment instruments to use with young children:

  - The *Kingore Observation Inventory* (KOI) improves observational skills in teachers of kids in kindergarten to grade 3. Visit kingore.com.

  - The *Cognitive Abilities Test* (CogAT) assesses reasoning and problem-solving abilities of students in grades K–12. Visit www.hmhco.com.

  - The following assessment instruments are available from Pearson at pearsonassessments.com:

- The *Otis-Lennon School Ability Test* (OLSAT) assesses cognitive abilities of students in grades K–12 and is considered reliable for young children.

- The *Naglieri Nonverbal Ability Test* (NNAT) measures general ability without the use of language.

- The *Peabody Picture Vocabulary Test* measures receptive English vocabulary in children as young as age 2.

- For preschool children, investigate the *Gifted Rating Scales*.

For more information on identifying and serving young gifted children and providing for them in your classroom, see our recommendations in the references and resources section on pages 233–235.

Gifted Students Identify Themselves

If you feel unsure about how to identify the gifted students in your class, rest assured that many teachers share your uncertainty. You and your administrators may have had little or no training in gifted education. No wonder you worry about doing the right thing. What if you identify the wrong students and they're not "truly gifted"? What if you fail to identify those kids who are gifted?

Relax! You don't have to formally identify anyone. All you have to do is provide learning opportunities that gifted students will appreciate, and a magical thing happens: The opportunities allow students to identify *themselves*—not necessarily as gifted, but as students who can benefit from working on activities that extend the regular curriculum. Your other students won't resent that some students are working on more challenging work, because all students will have the same opportunities to demonstrate their readiness for extension activities. With these strategies, everyone has the same opportunity to learn at his or her own level of personal challenge.

You don't have to formally identify anyone. All you have to do is provide learning opportunities that gifted students will appreciate.

The Qualities of Teachers Needed by Gifted Students

Do teachers have to be gifted themselves in order to teach gifted students? Rest assured that you don't have to have a superior IQ to teach gifted students. The truth is that many teachers who pursue training in gifted education have some personal connection to gifted students. They may have children who have been identified as gifted, or perhaps they went through gifted programs themselves. In the interest of being able to handle any issue in their class, many teachers seek training in gifted education. Of course, it sure helps to be a wonderful teacher who welcomes the challenge of facilitating academic progress for all students.

Teachers who are successful with gifted kids often possess certain qualities that gifted children respond to positively. They tend to:

- Be enthusiastic about teaching and the joy of lifelong learning.
- Have confidence and competency in teaching their content area(s).
- Have flexible teaching styles and be comfortable with situations in which students are flexibly grouped for learning and some students are doing different activities than others.
- Possess strong skills in listening, leading discussions, and using inquiry-based instruction.
- Be knowledgeable about the unique characteristics and needs of gifted students and willing to accommodate them.

- Be willing and able to create and nurture a learning environment where it's safe to take risks and make mistakes.
- Know how to praise effort more than products.
- Respect students' strengths and weaknesses and have the ability to encourage students to accept both without embarrassment.
- Be eager and willing to expose students to new ideas and provide opportunities for exploring those ideas.
- Have a free-flowing sense of humor and a level of comfort with their personal strengths and weaknesses.
- Be comfortable connecting the curriculum to students' learning profiles, interests, and questions and are good at empowering students to follow their passions.
- Be well organized—though not necessarily neat!
- Be able to multitask and effectively manage their time.
- Provide a wide range of learning materials, including those that are appropriate for older students.
- Network with organizations and local experts who can help gifted kids.
- Be aware that gifted students need less time with practice and more time with complex and abstract learning tasks.
- Understand the importance of communicating with students and their parents about their individual progress.
- Be willing to advocate for what gifted students need.

Chapter Summary

Identifying gifted students has always been a tricky process. Historically, we have identified some kids as gifted who were simply high achievers, and we have failed to identify truly gifted students who were nonproductive in school. Some gifted students have not been identified because they have a learning difficulty or difference that masks their giftedness. Some have not been identified because their performance on standard identification instruments has been hampered by cultural, linguistic, or socioeconomic issues.

We hope this chapter has made you more aware of the various ways in which gifted ability can manifest itself and be identified. Subsequent chapters will demonstrate how your gifted students can actually identify themselves when you provide consistent opportunities for kids to demonstrate and fulfill their learning needs in heterogeneous classrooms.

CHAPTER 2
Compacting and Differentiating for Skill Work

⭐ STRATEGIES

- Most Difficult First, page 42
- Pretest for Volunteers, page 48
- The Learning Contract, page 51

Banishing the "B" Word

"Boring" is a word that has the power to create a very emotional response in us as teachers. When we hear kids and parents use it, our first response is probably to feel defensive. None of us feels good about watching students painfully sit through instruction that is far below their challenge level. We struggle to explain why all students must do the grade-level work before working on material that appropriately challenges them. Yet, we receive very little support or guidance on how to work with these highly capable students in our classes who are ready to learn material beyond the level of what we are currently teaching.

If we personalize the frustration gifted students feel with the regular curriculum, we can better understand their plight. Suppose you sign up for an adult education course. You choose an advanced class that you hope will allow you to expand your skills in a particular area. At the first meeting, you discover that most of the other people in attendance aren't ready for the advanced section. The instructor announces that she will spend several sessions reviewing the basics.

You probably feel immediately frustrated. Your precious time is limited. What will you do? Chances are you'll drop the course and seek a more suitable alternative. We adults are allowed to go elsewhere when it appears that our time will be wasted. Gifted students in our schools don't usually have that option. When they think they are starting a year (or a class) filled with new and exciting content, then discover it's going to begin with four to six weeks of intensive review of material they have already mastered, what they feel may be close to panic. Certainly chagrin; certainly an overwhelming sense of "Oh, no, here we go again!"

Happily, changes to the popular Response to Intervention (RTI) model have made it possible for educators of gifted students to feel comfortable applying the RTI approach to their students, instead of using it solely for the benefit of struggling learners. RTI has been enhanced with a model called Multi-Tiered System of Supports (MTSS), defined as a framework for supporting *both* the academic and behavioral needs of all students within a school in order to improve student outcomes and provide safe school climates. MTSS adds attention to students' social-emotional needs as well as to their behavioral issues, and now specifically includes attention to *all* learners, including those who are gifted. If you examine the MTSS process, you will find that it asks you to:

1. Identify the student's current level of competency with a skill or task.

2. Diagnose an intervention that is likely to move the student forward.

3. Apply the intervention.

4. Evaluate the success of the intervention.

5. Prescribe the next intervention to move the student forward.

6. Repeat the process.

The same teaching approach is beneficial for gifted students. You can identify their current level of mastery with the pre-assessments described in this book. You can diagnose the next step they need to move forward and make academic progress. After that intervention has been applied, you can assess the degree to which it successfully documented academic progress. If it was successful, you prescribe another intervention to move them forward once again, and repeat the process. Since all differentiation opportunities in this book may, from time to time, be available to students beyond those formally identified as gifted, it follows that some of the learning models designed primarily for struggling students should also be available for gifted students.

The concept of teaching all students at their own challenge level is one with which most teachers agree in principle. Yet in today's heterogeneous classrooms, large class sizes and increasing ranges of ability create significant stresses for teachers who must find ways to reach and teach all of their students. Sometimes, when we try to offer gifted kids opportunities for challenge, they refuse to take us up on it. Complacency sets in

when gifted students get high grades and everyone (including the students themselves, their parents, and their teachers) sees this as evidence that real learning is taking place. Why should they work harder if they don't have to?

When we assume that the required standards, curriculum guides, or scope-and-sequence charts must be taught to all students, we are confusing the words "teach" and "learn." There is no state or national assessment that can measure how well you have taught. The only thing such assessments can measure is how much your students have learned.

There are probably students in your class right now who could have taken any end-of-the-year standardized test at the start of the year and scored at or above the 95th percentile. They simply don't need the same type of preparation as students who aren't yet ready for the test. When we insist that all students in a given class learn the total content together, we create a situation that most gifted students find very difficult to cope with. Many of them, because they're teacher-pleasers, will go through the motions, do the work, produce some very respectable products, and easily get A's. Others who are less compliant will do some of the work, but it will be sloppy, messy, and/or careless. (Maybe what they're trying to say is, "I know I've got to do this, but I can't stand wasting all this time!") Still others will give up, reject any more repetition, and refuse to do the work at all. It's just too boring.

Compacting Curriculum and Differentiating Instruction

If gifted students are bored and unchallenged in our classes, it's not because they are not doing their work; it's because the work that we plan for them is really *our* work. It doesn't become their work until it represents true learning for them. We need to find a way to let students "buy back" the school time we planned for them, so they can spend it in ways that extend or accelerate their learning.

Fortunately, this process already exists. Dr. Joseph Renzulli calls it *compacting*. Think of other contexts in which you use this word, and you'll probably come up with images of trash and garbage! Compacting helps students deal with the part of the curriculum that represents "trash" to them because it's expendable. They can throw it away without missing it and without incurring any academic harm, because they already have enough of it to demonstrate mastery.

> **NOTE** When you do a lesson plan, you are actually planning a budget! You are budgeting the amount of time you estimate it will take for the average students in your class to master the content. When struggling students need more time to demonstrate mastery, you usually add more minutes to the budgeted time. When gifted students need less time, they will be happy to hear they can "buy back" some of the time that has been budgeted to spend on choice activities. They will love this option.

The Meaning of Differentiation

The practice of differentiating instruction is integral to the compacting process. According to Dr. Sandra Kaplan, *differentiation* is defined as a response to the cognitive, affective, social, and physical characteristics that distinguish what and how students learn. A differentiated classroom is a place where learners are provided with equal opportunity to learn, but are not expected to learn the same curriculum in the same way at the same time. Respect for individual differences among and between learners is key, as is the belief that heterogeneity rather than homogeneity is the norm in any teaching and learning environment.

Differentiation is defined as a response to the cognitive, affective, social, and physical characteristics that distinguish what and how students learn.

Going even further, we believe that when you practice differentiation with your students throughout the grades, there will be fewer students who will feel like an outcast. And outcasts are typically the students who, later in their school career, might become so fed up with never being accepted for who they really are, they start acting out. When teachers expect everyone to be working together on the same task as one group, students may conclude that their teacher likes them better when they are all the same. The peer pressure in those classes will be to conform to this sameness. Conversely, when teachers differentiate for those who need it, students will feel accepted for their differences and will often demonstrate that acceptance toward their classmates.

That said, following are three key strategies for differentiating instruction and compacting curriculum in any skill-based area of learning. They are: Most Difficult First, Pretest for Volunteers, and the Learning Contract. All of these techniques can be used with skills from math, language arts, reading, vocabulary, or other subject areas. Strategies for compacting and differentiating content that is *new* to students—in subjects such as literature, science, social studies, and problem-based learning—are included in chapter 3. And for strategies that apply specifically to reading and writing, see chapter 4.

You might anticipate some negative attitudes regarding compacting and differentiation, especially from students who don't experience these opportunities. However, the cost of *not* providing these options may include students who "burn out" very quickly from the lack of challenge and become negative, seemingly lazy, and possibly even troublemakers. Furthermore, we know that when you practice differentiation, you send a clear message to students that you accept and accommodate their individual differences. This sometimes makes it more likely that students will then be accepting of differences in kids who are quite different from them. So, rather than give up a practice essential to advanced learners, begin calling the class's attention to ways in which other students are experiencing differentiation. Examples include when you assign fewer make-up items to an advanced student who was absent, when a student who is hearing impaired uses special equipment to comprehend what the teacher is saying, when some students are grouped together because they need different types of technology to maximize their learning, or even when a student with a broken bone is allowed to engage in a different activity in place of physical education class. These are all examples of students' unique needs being met appropriately.

How to Compact Curriculum

To compact the curriculum, we need to determine what competencies certain students have and give them full credit for what they already know. Then we need to decide how to let them use their "choice time" so it doesn't become a burden to them, their classmates, or to you. *Note:* Avoid calling this "free time," as this is likely to concern parents and administrators. It really isn't free, it's choice.

Using the Compactor Form

Joseph Renzulli and Linda H. Smith created a record-keeping form called the Compactor to use with students whose learning is compacted. You'll find a reproducible Compactor on page 41 and samples of compactors created for actual students throughout this chapter and in chapter 6.

1. Use a separate Compactor for each student. You may need to use a new one each month for a student who requires a great deal of compacting.

---

7 Steps to Successful Compacting

1. **Identify the learning objectives** or standards that all students must learn.

2. **Give students time to examine** the content to be tested.

3. **Offer a pretest opportunity to volunteers** after explaining the level of achievement needed to pass the pretest. Tell students they may stop the pretest at any time if they realize they will score below the required level. Make sure all students understand that the pretest results will not be formally entered as grades. The pretest simply allows advanced students to demonstrate that they need less direct instruction than age peers on upcoming content. See the strategy on page 48 for more details.

4. **Have extension activities available** for those who can "compact out" of specific learning activities because they have demonstrated their existing competence with that particular content on a pretest. These extension activities should be connected to the unit of study but not limited to the required standards. As states have pared down the amount and complexity of their required standards so that struggling students have better chances for proficiency, the narrowness of the resulting curriculum can be frustrating for gifted students who desire to intensely explore a topic of interest. Until a time when required standards focus on problem-solving tasks rather than on simple skills, advanced students will spend considerable school time doing extension activities. See page 40 for more on extension activities.

5. **Eliminate all standardized test drill, practice, and review** for students who have already demonstrated advanced levels of mastery.

6. **Decide how you will keep accurate records** of the students' compacting experiences, perhaps using the forms in this book, such as the Compactor (page 41). Then instruct students how to keep their own records of their extension activities.

7. **Devise a method for storing compacting documents.** You might use hanging file folders in a plastic crate so all students have a place to store their extension work. Gifted students will use them more often, but all students should have occasional time to work on extension activities so it is helpful to keep them accessible to your whole class. The Compactor, the Daily Log of Extension Work (page 92), and other contract documents should all be dated and kept in this extension folder.

2. Record all curriculum and independent study modifications.

   ▪ In the left column, record the student's areas of strength, one per box.

   ▪ In the center column, describe the methods used to document the student's mastery of a particular skill, competency, chapter, unit, or standard.

   ▪ In the right column, describe the alternate activities the student will be engaged in during "choice time," while the rest of the class is doing grade-level work.

      Some teachers make a copy of the required standards in a subject area, insert them in the left column, and check off and date each item as the student demonstrates mastery on pretests.

      Alternate activities are usually drawn from the same subject area from which the student bought back time. Sometimes, however, they may represent different subject areas, or they may be ongoing projects related to the student's areas of interest.

3. Store the Compactor in the student's extension folder, along with dated pretests and post-tests, Learning Contracts (see chapter 3), any logs of student work, evaluation contracts (see page 93), brief notes about parent or student conferences, and any other pertinent information.

> **IMPORTANT**   Never use the time students buy back from strength areas to remediate learning weaknesses. Always allow students to capitalize on their strengths through activities that extend their exceptional abilities. Remediate their weaknesses only when the whole class is working on those areas of the curriculum.

Compacting and Flexible Grouping

Perhaps you've been expected to teach students in heterogeneous classrooms as one large group, using direct teaching methods that keep the whole group moving along together as one unit. You most likely realize that this style of teaching is almost certain to hold gifted students back from the pace and depth they need.

A practice called flexible grouping provides opportunities for compacting without grouping the entire class in ability-based groups. To group flexibly means to group students together by areas of interest, achievement level, activity preference, learning modality, or special needs. This type of grouping is not in conflict with the philosophy of heterogeneous grouping. As a matter of fact, even when gifted students are grouped with each other, there is quite a range of abilities, interests, strengths, and weaknesses. The strategies described here and in the rest of this book enable you to continually regroup students, unit by unit, who need faster pacing or more complex activities in any area of learning depending on the material being studied. See chapter 7 for more detail on grouping gifted learners.

After reading this chapter, you should be ready to start compacting for several students who will benefit from it. Use it in one subject, unit, or lesson at a time. Do not move on to other content or classes until you are confident you know how to use the strategy very well. If it takes you several weeks to reach your comfort level, reassure yourself that you are doing more compacting than you have done in the past! Always know that you can schedule a "Lunch and Chocolate" meeting (see page 147) to ask for assistance from other teachers who are trying to implement similar strategies.

Extension Activities

The use of extension activities complements successful compacting and differentiation. When students demonstrate previous mastery of an upcoming standard, their first activity should be to engage with that same standard at a higher level of interaction—one that focuses on more depth and complexity—to experience how a particular standard may be *extended* in more challenging ways. This practice may lead to more students scoring "above proficiency" on high stakes tests.

text continues on page 42

The Compactor

Joseph Renzulli and Linda Smith

Student's name: _____

Areas of Strength	How Mastery Was Documented	Alternate Activities

As students work on extension activities, it is acceptable for them to be working with topics that are related to grade-level standards, but not limited to them. The purpose of creating and offering extension activities that broaden the students' experience beyond the exact language of the description of the standard is to accommodate gifted students' desire to learn everything there is to know about a topic in which they are interested. It is reasonable to expect students to choose extension activities in the same subject area in which they now have discretionary time.

You may be wondering how you will monitor the behavior of students who are working on extension activities. Refer to the handouts: How to Work Independently on Extension Activities (page 43) and the Essential Rules for Independent Work (page 44). Either use these forms as is or create one or both with your own expectations on it and explain the responsibilities independent workers will have. For some students, the behavior and productivity expectations might have to be introduced and practiced, one at a time, and cumulatively.

Working on extension activities is beneficial for *all* students.

Working on extension activities is beneficial for *all* students. Gifted students might work on them throughout a unit. Other students can also enjoy some exposure to them in a simpler format from time to time. Or they might be given some time to work on one extension activity throughout the span of a unit, perhaps with a partner or in a small group. All students should keep an accurate log of their extension activities (see the Daily Log of Extension Work on page 92).

STRATEGY

Compacting One Lesson at a Time: Most Difficult First

You probably realize that some highly capable learners don't need the same amount of practice and work as their age peers. However, many teachers are afraid to learn the truth about these kids, believing that once they do, they'll have to scramble to find appropriate extension materials and spend lots of time they don't have supervising the students' work on those activities.

The Most Difficult First strategy is designed to help you overcome that fear. Try it and you'll discover that your gifted kids will sometimes rather work on activities of their own choosing, instead of having you always decide what activities to make available. Take it *one lesson at a time* with this strategy; don't worry about anything beyond that just yet. Once you feel confident that compacting won't create lots of extra work for you to do, you can move on to other strategies in this book that link extension work to the content being studied.

There is a very comforting aspect in using Most Difficult First as your initial attempt at compacting. You still get to teach one lesson to all students in a particular subject area every day. That makes it much less scary than sending students off to work independently and feeling a loss of control regarding their mastery of the day's lesson.

text continues on page 45

What About Grades?

One of the first questions teachers ask us about compacting and extension activities, "How do I grade them?" The answer is that you don't (most of the time!). The only grades you enter for students experiencing compacting are those grades that document their mastery of a topic area at their grade level. For example, if a student scores 90 percent or higher on a pretest, you will enter an "A" in your grade book for that unit, even if 90 percent is not an A in your district. A 90 percent correct result demonstrates mastery, and the letter grade for mastery is A. See chapter 8 for further discussion of grading and assessment.

How to Work Independently on Extension Activities

✔ Listen to the teacher's lesson if you are required to do so.

✔ Ask any questions you have about the lesson while it is being taught.

✔ Do the problems or activities you are asked to do.

✔ When you are allowed to, select an extension activity.

✔ Work on the extension activity for the rest of this period.

✔ Working with a partner is okay; if you need help, ask your partner for help first.

✔ Follow the Essential Rules for Independent Work at all times.

✔ Check the answers if they are available.

✔ If you need to talk to the teacher, let her or him know in an agreed upon way so that you do not interrupt instruction.

✔ If you finish early, either select another activity or make a more difficult version of the one on which you have been working.

✔ If you are working in math, make up some more difficult problems just like the ones the class is working on, or create some word problems for others to solve.

✔ Complete the necessary record keeping.

✔ File your extension work in the required location.

The Essential Rules for Independent Work

1. Do your work without bothering anyone.

2. Work on your extension activity without calling attention to yourself; please don't talk while the teacher is teaching.

3. Refrain from asking the teacher questions while he or she is working with other students.

4. Do the extension activity you have agreed to complete. If you finish it before the class is finished working, choose another extension activity.

5. Keep records of the tasks you are working on in the way your teacher has explained.

Scenario: Benjamin

Benjamin was a seventh grader with very high potential who, according to most of his teachers, had made a career out of "wasting time and not working up to his ability." He had been denied permission to attend the gifted education class because of his poor work habits in all of his subjects.

The gifted specialist at Benjamin's school, Mrs. Lee, offered to come to his class and demonstrate the Most Difficult First strategy for his teacher. Mrs. Lee suspected it might help Benjamin be more productive in math class and hoped that it would convince his teacher to let him attend the gifted program classes.

First, Mrs. Lee taught the day's math lesson to the class, allowing 20 minutes of practice time at the end so students could start their homework. Benjamin was noticeably uninvolved; in fact, he had no work at all on his desk, saying that he had lost his math book. At the end of the instructional time, Mrs. Lee wrote the assignment on the board. It looked like this:

Homework: pages 59–60, problems 3–5, 8 & 9, 11–15, 21–23

★#s: 5, 9, 14, 15, 22

Then Mrs. Lee announced:

"I have assigned these problems for your homework, because I think most of you will need that much practice to master the standards we talked about today. However, I may be wrong, so I have starred the five most difficult problems. Anyone who wants to do the starred problems first, and who can complete them correctly in a way that can be clearly read and understood without getting more than one wrong, is done practicing. The problems must be completed and corrected before this practice section of the math period is over. You have 20 minutes. If you can't finish them in that time period, or if you find the problems to be challenging, that simply means you need more practice than you thought. At that point, just stop your work on the most difficult problems and begin practicing at the beginning of the assignment."

Benjamin had been in his characteristic "I-dare-you-to-make-me-work" slouch. As the explanation was finished, his head shot up, and the following conversation ensued.

Benjamin: "Excuse me, what did you just say?"

Mrs. Lee: "What do you think I said?"

Benjamin: "I think you said that if I get those five problems right, and you can read them, I don't have to do my homework!"

Mrs. Lee: "That's correct."

Benjamin: "Uh, is my regular teacher going to do this tomorrow?"

Mrs. Lee: "I'm not sure, but I'll bet it has something to do with whether or not it works today."

Benjamin: "Yeah, right." (Pause.) "What happens if I get two wrong?"

Mrs. Lee: "Benjamin, how much of the 20 minutes' practice time is left?"

Benjamin: "Oh, yeah. Right. Okay, I'll give it a try."

Benjamin suddenly "found" his math book, a pencil, and some paper in his desk. He got right to work and finished the designated problems accurately and neatly. His classroom teacher had the evidence she needed that he understood the standards, which made her more willing to let him participate in the gifted program. And Benjamin had the joyful feeling that somehow he'd gotten away with something.

How to Use Most Difficult First

1. When giving your class an assignment of skill or practice work, start by determining which items represent the most difficult section of the entire task. These might appear sequentially near the end of the assignment or in various sections of the assignment. Five examples are a reasonable number, but you may choose a few more or less, depending on what seems appropriate for the assignment.

The Compactor
Joseph Renzulli and Linda Smith

Student's name: **Benjamin**

Areas of Strength	How Mastery Was Documented	Alternate Activities
Math computation	Most Difficult First	Attendance in CHALLENGE program

2. Post the assignment and then make note of the Most Difficult First examples. Then give this explanation to the class:

"The regular assignment should give just the right amount of practice for most of you to master the standards we learned today. As a matter of fact, I expect most of you will need this much practice. However, some of you may have learned this material before and don't need as much practice. Instead of doing the regular assignment, you may choose to do just the five starred problems, which I consider to be the most difficult problems in the assignment.

"When you finish, come to me and I'll check your work. The first person who gets four or five correct will become the checker for the rest of the period, if that person wants the job. If he or she prefers not to be the checker I'll wait for someone else to become today's checker. Once I announce who the checker is, anyone else who completes the most difficult problems should stay at your desk, put your thumb up as a signal, and wait for the checker to get to you. If your work is neat and legible and has no more than one wrong, the checker will collect your paper to give to me."

(*Note:* Exceptions to this rule may be made for students with exceptional educational needs. Perhaps you'll want to correct their papers if they might be embarrassed for another student to see it. However, it has been our experience that when a teacher expects neatness and legibility, students

make an honest effort to demonstrate those qualities to the best of their abilities.)

"After the checker has collected your paper, you may use whatever time is left for any activity you choose in the same subject area, as long as you follow the Essential Rules for Independent Work (see page 44). During practice time, I will be helping students who are doing the regular assignment. If you need help, start at the beginning of the regular assignment, and I'll be happy to help you."

3. As you walk around the classroom giving assistance to students who need it, let those who are working on the Most Difficult First problems come to you. Once you identify the checker (the first student who meets the criteria and agrees to be the checker that day), she or he checks the papers of the remaining students working on the Most Difficult First problems, using his or her correct paper as the answer key. When the checker finds papers that meet the criteria, he or she places the papers in a designated place. *Tip:* Finding a checker usually takes less than five minutes. After that, you can devote your full attention to helping your struggling students. It is well worth the time it takes to "train" your checkers. The guidelines in the following box should be discussed with the entire class and posted in a prominent place so each day's checker can consult the guidelines.

4. If you use the beginning of the next period to check homework, the students who met the Most Difficult First requirement may again

have some choice time—as long as they follow the Essential Rules (see page 44). As soon as you begin the new lesson, they should rejoin the rest of the class for instruction.

How to Be a Checker

■ You may be a checker only one time each week. On other days, you may work on extension activities when you meet the requirement for Most Difficult First.

■ As the checker, you may not provide any help to students whose papers you are checking. You may not return to any student more than one time.

■ If the student's paper has zero or one wrong, say, "You can work on extension activities."

■ If the student's paper has more than one wrong, say, "Continue with the practice page."

■ Never discuss any information about a student's correct or incorrect answer with the student or anyone else. You must keep that information confidential.

■ Place all papers you have collected in the designated place after checking the work. Write the word "Checker" and today's date at the top of your paper.

To make the most of this strategy, follow these guidelines:

■ Limit practice time to 10–15 minutes or less.

■ Don't allow students to correct their own papers. Gifted students are very competitive in this type of situation, and values get a little muddled. Students wondering how their buddies are faring may not be totally honest. That's why you should correct papers until you identify the checker, and the checker should correct papers after that.

■ Don't allow students to correct any errors the checker discovers. Students who get more than one wrong are expected to complete the regular assignment, starting with the easier

problems. In the first few days, some kids may come to you to protest, "I was working too fast. I made a careless mistake. I really know how to do it!" Your reaction is always the same: "Then that means you need more practice time. You can try again tomorrow." Once students realize that your rules are firm, they will accept the checker's decision.

■ No student should be the checker more than once a week. Some students will want to be the checker all the time as a way to avoid doing the challenging extension activities.

■ If there are a lot of students who need a checker, appoint a second checker for that day.

As you can see, this strategy doesn't create additional work for you, nor do you spend any extra time entering grades. You can still enter all grades at the same time and be available to help your struggling students.

Most Difficult First can be used with students who return from pull-out classes, to document their mastery of the content you have been teaching in their absence, without requiring them to make up all the work they missed. You get the evidence you need that the kids are competent with the material, and they learn that participating in a pull-out class will not lead to more work for them. Everybody wins!

> **NOTE** A few teachers in our workshops have reported that this method becomes a privacy issue for their school. If this is true for you, make an answer key available for students who need it. Remember, the checker sees only the papers of students who volunteered for that to happen.

⭐ STRATEGY

Compacting One Week at a Time: Pretest for Volunteers

For curriculum that takes about a week to cover, such as spelling or vocabulary work, the pretest for volunteers is the best compacting method to use. With this method, the assessment you plan to use at the end of the week's work should be available for volunteers to take at the beginning, as a mode of formative assessment. At the start of the class period, give all students a few moments to look over the upcoming content. Then invite volunteer students who think they can demonstrate they are already at a mastery level to take the pretest. Tell them that the scores they get on the pretest will *only* be entered into your grade book if they represent mastery. Be sure that they understand that the reason for the pretest is to find out how much they know about the content so you can decide together if compacting the week's work is a good option for them.

Here's an example of what you might tell your students at the start of a new week:

> "We're about to start working on _____. I will give you 30 seconds to survey the word list to see if you think you are familiar enough with the words to take the end-of-unit test right now. If you score 90 percent or higher on the pretest, you have demonstrated that you do not need the required practice to become proficient. Instead, you can spend your time each period working on extension activities. For each day you do extension work, your pretest grade of A will be entered in my records as an 'equivalent grade' for the unit work you are not required to do. Your extension work will *not* be formally graded, so feel free to choose challenging words to learn."

The acceptable score on a pretest for mastery is 90 percent or higher. Students may stop taking the pretest and return to the whole class activity at any point where they think they will not get the required amount of test items correct. They do not have to turn in their pretest in this case.

> **NOTE** Never do a quick review—not even of the specific rule being demonstrated—before students look at the unit's content to decide if they want to take the pretest. As the students peruse the content, it is their job to determine if they understand the rule being illustrated.

Pretests should *always* be optional. The practice of having all kids take a required pretest at the beginning of a unit of work in order to have data about students' competencies before they have been taught a chunk of content can be extremely frustrating and even embarrassing for students who aren't familiar with the content. Just try to remember the first time you rode a bike, sat at a computer, or tried to play a musical instrument, and you will realize how totally disheartening it would have been if you had been required to take a pretest before you had any instruction. The same is true for struggling students, who see their peers proceeding with some degree of competence at something that is totally unfamiliar to them. They may wonder, "What's the matter with me? Why do these other kids seem to know more about this than I do?"

However, if your school or district requires that all students take every pretest, you will have to comply. Students who score at or above the 90th percentile on a weekly pretest will still experience compacting and differentiation for the remainder of that week, and may even be excused from taking the post-test, if district policy allows.

Scenario: Elizabeth

Elizabeth was a twice-exceptional child with strong map skills, which she demonstrated by acing the voluntary end-of-unit test before the unit began (see pages 22–23). For the next six weeks, while the rest of the class learned basic map skills, she spent those 45 minutes a day working on a project that represented true learning for her. ***Note:*** This scenario illustrates a modification of Pretest for Volunteers, since the unit of study is longer than a week.

We discussed several options, and she chose to create an imaginary country. Because her learning disability prevented her from writing well, she made a papier-mâché model showing the population centers, natural resources, manufacturing centers, agricultural products, and other features the class was studying in the teacher directed map unit. Thankfully, her teacher realized that it was not appropriate to require Elizabeth to spend the map learning time remediating one of her low performing areas. The teacher realized that when compared to her classmates, Elizabeth was advanced in map skills. As an advanced student she had the same right to experience differentiation as others who would experience compacting in several curriculum areas.

During that time, how many students complained, "That's not fair! Elizabeth doesn't have to do the same work we're doing"? None, because everyone had been given the same opportunity to document mastery by taking the pretest. However, students did ask, "Can we do what Elizabeth's doing? It looks like fun!" In response to their interest, and after Elizabeth had shared her project with the class in an oral report with a multimedia component, a similar activity was offered to small groups as a culminating project for the map unit, during which time Elizabeth served as a "create-a-country consultant" to the groups. Her self-esteem soared as her image changed from a needy student with a learning disability to an expert others turned to for help and advice.

NOTE This strategy suggests paper-and-pencil pretests, but you should feel free to use other types of formative assessment that are compatible with your teaching philosophy and style. *Examples:* Before beginning a map unit, you might ask students to locate features on actual maps. Or ask the class to tell you what they already know about maps, and observe for students who seem extremely knowledgeable. Any method that helps you identify students who need compacting is fine. See chapter 8 for more information on formative assessment strategies.

Scenario: Liam

In Monica Wheeler's seventh-grade social studies classes, an extraordinarily gifted student named Liam demonstrated a very advanced grasp of geography content. When Ms. Wheeler contacted Liam's parents, they told her that Liam was a returning contestant in the state's geography bee. This information validated Ms. Wheeler's conclusion that Liam would need a lot of compacting in geography this year.

Each time Liam passed a pretest on an upcoming section of geography content, his formative assessment (pretest) grade became his summative assessment (recorded grade) for that particular chunk of content. Since the pretest was available to all students who wanted to take it, there was no resentment toward Liam or the teacher regarding the fact that Liam did not have

---

The Compactor
Joseph Renzulli and Linda Smith

Student's name: **Elizabeth**

Areas of Strength	How Mastery Was Documented	Alternate Activities
Map unit	Achieved an A on pretest	Will create a country from papier-mâché Will present report to class Will consult with other students to help them create their own countries

to do much of the grade-level practice which he already knew. Occasionally other students would pass the pretest and were encouraged to work on other extension activities while those students who needed direct instruction received it from Ms. Wheeler. That year, Liam placed first in the state geography bee and went on to place seventh in the national contest, bringing lots of pride to Liam, his school, and his friends and relatives.

Scenario: Ava Marie

Ava Marie had great spelling skills and consistently earned high grades on her spelling tests. Her spelling was amazingly accurate in her written work. It seemed clear to her teacher that she did not need as much instruction or practice in spelling as her classmates. After each successful spelling pretest, she was allowed to choose from the Extension Activities in Spelling and Vocabulary on page 52.

Extension Activities in Spelling and Vocabulary

If you are teaching spelling and vocabulary, you may find that many students will enjoy choosing one of the following activities:

* Working with a partner who also passed the pretest, to find 10 unfamiliar words.

* Keeping track of words they misspell in their own writing. This is called functional spelling,

since it helps students learn the words they need to function well in their writing. Some teachers use the Extension Activities in Spelling and Vocabulary with all students. Kids who test out on the pretest study the alternate words; kids who don't, study the regular words. All kids choose the way they will study their own list.

Technology-Assisted Extension Work in Spelling or Vocabulary

Here are a few ideas on how you can use technology to differentiate spelling and vocabulary lessons for ability levels, learning profiles, and student interests.

Word Lens from Apple is an app that allows students to hold a camera lens up to any text and it translates it into another language automatically. This is fun to use when studying other cultures or foreign countries. Download the app from the iTunes store on an iPad, iPhone, or iPod touch.

Rosetta Stone (rosettastone.com) is an ideal program to get kids started learning foreign languages in the primary grades. Students might choose to select a new language every year.

Bookworm, another free game from Yahoo! Games, encourages players to link letters together to make words. Just don't let the red tiles reach the bottom, or the library will catch fire!

The Compactor
Joseph Renzulli and Linda Smith

Student's name: **Ava Marie**

Areas of Strength	How Mastery Was Documented	Alternate Activities
Spelling	Passed pretest with an A	Will choose from list of extension activities OR write ongoing stories, poems, etc.

Word Games (wordgames.com) is a website that provides different puzzles and word games. The selection includes word searches, crossword puzzles, and more to boost vocabulary, critical thinking, and spelling skills.

My Vocabulary (myvocabulary.com) is a "vocabulary university" for students of all ages. The site includes extensive word work for all age groups.

Words with Friends (zynga.com) is a popular app that can be used on a smartphone, iPad, or Kindle, or on a computer via the Facebook website. Players exchange turns forming words horizontally or vertically on a board, trying to score as many points as possible for each word. For students age 13 or older.

For more suggestions, simply enter search terms such as "vocabulary activities" or "spelling games" into Google.

Note: Students may use the Daily Log of Extension Work on page 92 in chapter 3 to keep records of their differentiated spelling and vocabulary activities.

★ STRATEGY

Compacting One Chapter or Unit at a Time: The Learning Contract

While trying out the Most Difficult First strategy, described earlier in this chapter, you may have noticed its shortcomings. Gifted students still have to sit through the teaching of standards they may have already mastered. They are not allowed to demonstrate mastery until homework (practice) time begins. And some students may need more structure for the time they buy back.

The Learning Contract strategy has none of those shortcomings. It's the most effective strategy for compacting pretestable content and skills within units lasting longer than a week. This method incorporates *both* of the previous strategies: Most Difficult First and Pretest for

Volunteers, and presents a compacting option in which students complete extension activities, yet may still receive direct instruction in areas in the unit they have not yet mastered.

The Learning Contract strategy works best for students in second grade and higher. In the primary grades, you can use the same process described here, but you would keep a record of the standards for which direct instruction is required, rather than giving the students a paper copy of the contract. For days in which no direct instruction is needed, just list students' names on the board at the beginning of the period to indicate that they can spend the day's lesson time working on extension activities.

Scenario: Julie

When Julie was in fifth grade, she consistently got A's in her daily math work and assessments. She appeared to remember most of what she had learned in previous grades and seemed to catch on quickly to new concepts. However, she began to develop some distracting behaviors during math class. She stared out the window, occasionally hummed softly, and was frequently found writing notes to friends. It became obvious that part of her problem was boredom with the pace and depth of the fifth-grade math curriculum.

When the Learning Contract option was explained to Julie, it was very appealing to her. She volunteered to take the pretest for the next chapter, with an acceptable score, and received the contract shown on page 54. Pages that were not checked represented standards on which Julie had demonstrated mastery on the pretest. On the days those standards were taught, Julie worked on math extension activities for the entire math period.

Pages with checkmarks indicated standards for which Julie did not demonstrate mastery on the pretest. On days when those standards were taught, Julie would join the class for direct instruction. However, every day after the initial direct instruction and during the first practice period, the Most Difficult First strategy was offered to all the students. More often than not, Julie would remember the content as the lesson proceeded, so she could usually demonstrate mastery with

text continues on page 53

Extension Activities in Spelling and Vocabulary

If you pass a spelling or vocabulary pretest with a score of 90 percent or higher, you are excused from the week's grade-level activities and the final test at the end of the week. Choose something to do instead from the list of extension activities below.

Using New Words

1. Working with a partner who also passed the pretest, find 10 unfamiliar words from glossaries of books in our room. (You choose 5 and your partner chooses 5.) Learn their meanings and spellings. When the rest of the class is taking the final test for the week, you will test each other on your personal word list. Here's how:

   a. Partner A dictates words 1–5 to Partner B, one at a time. Partner B gives a meaning for each word before writing it down.

   b. Partner A dictates words 6–10 to Partner B, who writes them down (no meanings needed).

   c. Partner B dictates words 1–5 to Partner A, who writes them down (no meanings).

   d. Partner B dictates words 6–10 to Partner A, who gives a meaning for each word before writing it down. In other words, Partner A defines 5 of the words, Partner B defines the other 5, and both partners spell all 10. Words are counted wrong if either spelling or meaning is not correct.

2. Keep track of words you misspell in your own writing. When you have collected 5 words, use them on your next personal list.

Keep a list of any words you don't master in activities 1 and 2. Learn them the next time you get to choose your own spelling list.

Using Regular or Alternate Words

3. Use all the words to create as few sentences as possible.

4. Create a crossword or an acrostic puzzle on graph paper. Include an answer key.

5. Learn the words in a foreign language. Use the words in sentences.

6. Group the words into categories you create. Regroup them into new categories.

7. Create greeting card messages or rebus pictures.

8. Create an original spelling game.

9. Create riddles with the words as answers.

10. Create limericks using the words.

11. Write an advertisement using as many of the words as you can.

12. Use all of the words in an original story.

13. Create alliterative sentences or tongue-twisters using the words.

14. Using a thesaurus, find synonyms for the words and create Super Sentences. Ask your teacher for a model.

15. Use the words to create similes or metaphors.

16. Work on a Super Sentence or create one of your own. Ask your teacher for a model.

17. Using an unabridged dictionary, locate and describe the history of each word (its etymology). Create flow charts to show how the meaning of each word has changed over time.

18. Create a code using numbers for each letter of the alphabet. Compute the numerical value of each word. List the words from the highest to lowest value.

19. Take pairs of unrelated spelling words and put them together to create new words. Invent definitions.

20. Create your own activity. Get your teacher's permission to use it.

the most difficult portion of the assignment. This meant that after the first practice period, she could usually be done with direct instruction for that day and move on to working on her extension activities. Julie started spending much more time on math each day, alternating between the regular content and extension activities. Her attitude and productivity in math improved dramatically, as did her behavior during math time.

Introducing the Learning Contract

In keeping with the practice of offering compacting opportunities to everyone in the class, you will want to introduce and explain the Learning Contract to all of your students. They can then decide for themselves whether to take advantage of the pretest opportunity and possibly receive a contract. When the contract option is presented this way, the students who do not choose to take the pretest will not resent those students who pretest successfully and receive a Learning Contract for a particular chapter or unit. The vocabulary and vocal inflections we use are critical in guaranteeing that the options for advanced students are not perceived as special treatment. We avoid words like "qualify" or "eligible" or "deserve" because those are win-lose words. Better phrases are either, "You have shown you do not need more practice," or "You need more practice." We also avoid "celebrating" when students compact out of work. Instead, we handle it in a very matter of fact manner.

Before starting a new chapter or unit, give your students the opportunity to pretest out of the content if they wish (see pages 48–51 in the Pretest for Volunteers strategy for details). Again, be sure that they understand that the only reason for the pretest is to find out how much they know about the chapter so you can decide together if a Learning Contract is a good option for them. They will soon understand that Learning Contracts are not a good choice for many students, and that is just fine. Those students who would benefit from more direct instruction will get that as well. Neither option—Learning Contract or direct instruction—is "better" than the other. Every

student is different and will be matched to the learning method that is best for them.

An acceptable score on a pretest for a Learning Contract is whatever represents a B or higher, because that demonstrates the student already knows 80 percent or more of the upcoming chapter content. Clearly, if a student is already competent with at least 80 percent of a unit of work, he would be wasting his time if he was required to do the same amount of practice as students for whom a good deal of the material to be learned is new. As always with a pretest, students may stop taking it and return to the whole class activity at any point where they think they will not get the required amount of test items correct. They do not have to turn in their pretest in this case.

> **IMPORTANT** You'll notice that the cut-off score for a pretest in the Pretest for Volunteers strategy is 90 percent (see page 48), versus 80 percent for a pretest for a Learning Contract. The cut-off score for the Learning Contract is *lower* because the strategy does not require that students demonstrate mastery of all chapter content. Students who are on a contract will still get instruction when you are teaching standards for which they did not show mastery on the pretest.

Schedule a meeting for those students who scored at or above 80 percent on the pretest. Students who attend the meeting can then decide if they want to use the Learning Contract method for this particular chapter or unit. Inform them that with a contract, they will be able to work through the chapter more independently and have a lot more time to work on extension activities during the course of the chapter work.

You may be wondering, "While some students are taking the pretest, what will the others do?" Let them use this time to work with your guidance on similar extension activities as those the kids with Learning Contracts will be working on throughout the chapter. Or they might work on extensions related to standards learned in earlier chapters. This simple technique eliminates much of the potential resentment students might feel toward kids who receive contracts, because

Learning Contract

For: Math Chapter 4

Student's Name: Julie

✔	Page/Standard	✔	Page/Standard	✔	Page/Standard
___	60	✔	64	✔	68
✔	61	___	65	___	69
___	62	✔	66 – Word Problems	___	70 – Review (even only)
___	63	___	67	✔	Post-test

- -

Extension Options: _____

SPECIAL INSTRUCTIONS

Versa-Tiles _____ ____ ____ ____ ____

Write Story Problems _____ ____ ____ ____

Cross Number Puzzles _____ ____ ____ ____

Student-Selected Activity (needs teacher approval):

_____ ____ ____ ____ ____ ____

- -

Working Conditions

1. Use your group's question chip carefully. Refrain from asking the teacher a question someone in your group can answer.
2. If you need help and the teacher is busy, ask someone else, keep trying, or go on to another activity until the teacher is available.
3. Work on math for the entire math period.
4. Do your work without bothering anyone or calling attention to yourself in any way.
5. Keep track of your contract.

Teacher's Signature: _____

Student's Signature: _____

---

pretest day can be an enjoyable day for all. It shows your students that you believe all kids can benefit from extension activities now and then.

How to Use the Learning Contract

1. Collect extension materials (both hardcopy and online) for the chapter or unit you are about to begin and set up an extension center in your classroom. Remember that the activities must be in the same subject area as the one being compacted, but they do not always have to be precisely connected to the required standards. To create the extension center, use an empty desk or table, or a learning center format. For extension materials, look in your teacher manuals, in the manuals of discarded series, and in the place where your school or district keeps materials that have been purchased with gifted education funds. Search online for sites that contain interesting activities for enriching the subject area on which you are focusing.

Note: Sometimes the extension activities will be called "enrichment" in your sources. The words mean the same thing but we prefer to use the term "extension." All students deserve an enriched curriculum, but only advanced learners require us to "extend" the parameters of the grade-level standards.

If you don't have space for an extension center, think about where you want the contract students to work while you are teaching the rest of the class. Some teachers group those who are on contract in one area in the room near the place where the extension materials are stored. Some teachers have their contract students work in another room, under the direction of a resource person such as a media center specialist, a librarian, or an adult volunteer. Many teachers simply have the students work at their desks while the rest of the class is involved in direct instruction. It may be comforting for all concerned if they stay in the classroom, so they can at least be aware of your lessons and discussions while they are working on their extension activities.

Prepare a master Learning Contract for the chapter or unit. Use the reproducible form on page 56 or create your own. The Learning Contract should have three sections. In the top section, list the content for the chapter or unit, either by page numbers or standards to be mastered. The chapter tests in most teachers' editions indicate the page on which each standard is taught.

In the middle section, list and describe the available extension activities. *Tip:* To simplify contract management, offer one extension option for the first chapter plus a student choice option ("Your Idea"). Add a second option for the second chapter, and so on.

The lines to the right of each activity labeled "Special Instructions" may be used for students to record the date and other identification information about the day's extension activity near the end of each class period. Be sure to take a few moments near the end of the class period to remind students to do their record keeping.

In the bottom-third section of the Learning Contract, list the working conditions you expect students to follow. If your classes all take place in one room, you might create a chart labeled "Working Conditions for Independent Study" to display in your classroom. That way, you won't have to include conditions on every contract. You can get some ideas for the working conditions from the Working Conditions for Alternate Activities form on page 57. The Essential Rules on page 44 may also be perfectly adequate. Keep in mind that for young children, the expected behaviors must be taught, modeled, and monitored one at a time. Other behaviors are added cumulatively.

Another way to display the extension options is with a nine-square Extension Menu, several examples are given in chapter 4 on pages 111, 113, 114, and 138.

It will not be enough to just name certain extension activities. You will get better results if you create task statements that let students know exactly what they are expected to do with the designated materials. If you use an Extension Menu instead of listing the options on the contract, a different record keeping system will be needed. The Daily Log of Extension Work on page 92 could be used in this case.

2. Offer a pretest or other type of preassessment. Use the same tool you plan to use for a post-test at the end of the chapter or unit with all students. If the teaching materials you are using include both a chapter review and a chapter test, use whichever one is most comprehensive for the pretest.

If you want to add some items that are not included in the tests the publisher provides, also include them in the post-test you use to assess the other students later. It's unfair to make the pretest more comprehensive than the post-test only for those students who are trying to demonstrate they are ready for the Learning Contract.

3. Correct the pretests yourself or ask a student teacher to do it. Don't allow students to correct their own pretests. Many gifted kids are

text continues on page 58

Learning Contract

For: _____

Student's Name: _____

✔	Page/Standard	✔	Page/Standard	✔	Page/Standard
_____	_____	_____	_____	_____	_____
_____	_____	_____	_____	_____	_____
_____	_____	_____	_____	_____	_____
_____	_____	_____	_____	_____	_____

- -

Extension Options: _____

SPECIAL INSTRUCTIONS

_____ _____ _____ _____

_____ _____ _____ _____

_____ _____ _____ _____

Student-Selected Activity (needs teacher approval):

_____ _____ _____ _____

- -

Working Conditions

_____

_____

_____

_____

_____

Teacher's Signature: _____

Student's Signature: _____

Working Conditions for Alternate Activities

If you are working on alternate activities while others in the class are busy with teacher-directed activities, you are expected to follow these guidelines.

1. Stay on task at all times with the alternate activities you have chosen.

2. Don't talk to the teacher while he or she is teaching.

3. When you need help and the teacher is busy, ask someone else who is also working on the alternate activities.

4. If no one else can help you, keep trying the activity yourself until the teacher is available. Or move on to another activity until the teacher is free.

5. Use soft voices when talking to each other about the alternate activities.

6. Never brag about your opportunities to work on the alternate activities.

7. If you must go in and out of the room, do so as quietly as you can.

8. When you go to another location to work, stay on task there, and follow the directions of the adult in charge.

9. Don't bother anyone else.

10. Don't call attention to yourself.

I agree to these conditions. I understand that if I don't follow them, I may lose the opportunity to continue working on the alternate activities and may have to rejoin the class for teacher-directed instruction.

Teacher's Signature: _____

Student's Signature: _____

afraid of losing face if anyone finds out they are not always perfect, so the temptation to "appear perfect" might be great. Also, don't use student checkers when giving pretests. Sometimes checkers are influenced by friendship issues. Other students or adult volunteers shouldn't know how students scored on the pretest. Finally, parent volunteers are also not a good choice because they shouldn't have access to sensitive, personal information.

4. Prepare contracts for students who score 80 percent or higher on the pretest. You will have already listed the page numbers or standards for that chapter or unit on your master contract. For each student's contract, simply place a checkmark to the left of the page number or standard for which the student did *not* demonstrate mastery on the pretest. Those are the pages/standards for which the student will join the rest of the class for direct instruction. See Julie's contract on page 54 for an example.

   Tip: Before giving out the contracts, indicate in your grade book which pages/standards you've checked for each student. One way to do this is by highlighting the space or using a different color, font type, or icon for those standards or pages. As you begin each class, you'll be able to tell at a glance which students will be receiving direct instruction and which will be working on extension activities. If some students who should be attending direct instruction start moving toward the extension area, simply say, "Some contract students are going to the wrong place right now. Please check your contract to see if this is one of your direct instruction days."

5. If you use cooperative learning groups, create them now. Place contract students together in their own groups. Place all other students in heterogeneous groups in which kids who are capable in the subject are mixed with those who are average and below average. (For more on cooperative learning, see chapter 7.)

6. Invite contract students to an informational meeting with you during class time. See, "At the Contract Meeting" that follows for

suggestions about what to include at the meeting.

7. Offer Most Difficult First (see pages 42–47) daily so gifted kids can still do compacted work even on days when they are attending direct instruction with the larger group for the first part of the period. *Tip:* Most Difficult First is also an effective way to allow students returning from out-of-class experiences (such as pull-out programs) to document their mastery. If kids only have to make up five of the examples they missed, they won't feel so torn about leaving the homeroom class.

At the Contract Meeting

1. Greet the students and explain that everyone there scored 80 percent or higher on the pretest. *Tip:* Reassure students that their pretest grade was not recorded, but was used simply to discover which students might benefit from a contract. The perfectionists in the group might be upset if they think a lower than perfect score has been recorded!

2. Hand out the Learning Contracts. Draw students' attention to the first section that lists the pages and standards to be mastered. Explain that a checkmark indicates a standard they have *not* mastered. On the days those standards are taught, they will join the rest of the class for instruction. No checkmark indicates standards they have mastered. On the days those standards are being taught, they are not required to attend the direct instruction event, because they will be working on extension activities for the entire period.

3. Tell students they are not to work on any of the checked pages or standards independently. They must wait until the class learns that material under your direction.

4. Explain how to use the extension center. Demonstrate one extension activity. Call students' attention to the "Your Idea" option, which invites them to create their own alternate activity. Instruct them to bring their ideas to you. They will need your permission to proceed. *Note:* Some teachers are expected to direct their students to

[handwritten in margin: Logistics nightmare]

choose activities that reinforce the standards covered in the chapter. Others may allow students to choose any activity, as long as it relates to the subject area being taught. All activities should be self-correcting. Parents of gifted students may be willing to help create answer keys for extension activities.

Demonstrate how to keep daily records of extension work. Under "Special Instructions," each short line represents one day's extension activity. When all the lines for a particular activity are filled with dates and labels, students should select another activity, unless they are involved in a long-term activity that requires more time. It is also okay for them to vary the type of activities they do.

Students will need a place to store their "work in progress" when they leave the center and on days when they join the rest of the class for direct instruction. One simple solution is to give each student in the class a file folder and provide a plastic crate to contain them. In the folder they may keep unfinished work and a record sheet, such as a daily log. When parents return their comment sheet from the Extension Activities and Differentiated Homework Report on page 94, file those as well.

5. Students working on extension activities on regular instruction days may work on different activities and help each other when help is needed. Let them know that you want them to be there to support and motivate each other as they work on the challenging activities.

IMPORTANT Refrain from directing students to work on specific extension activities, and don't expect them to complete an entire activity during each period. If you do, students may feel the need to choose easy activities or rush through the activities and not benefit from their selected extensions. Your whole purpose for providing differentiated learning will be compromised. Your most important task with kids working on contracts is to encourage them to persevere even when they become frustrated, and to praise them for their willingness to work hard on challenging problems.

6. Reassure contract students that you will be working with them several times each week, and that you expect them to need help with the extension activities from time to time. This is important, since they will be experiencing unfamiliar topics. See the Question Chip Technique on page 61 for a way to deliver on your promise. If gifted students perceive that students on contract rarely get the chance to work with you, they may stop taking the pretests. They have a right to your attention as they engage in challenging work.

Reassure contract students that you will be working with them several times each week, and that you expect them to need help with the extension activities from time to time.

---

7. Review the working conditions thoroughly and answer all questions.

8. Tell students how their grade for the chapter or unit will be determined. (See chapter 8.) Make sure your contract students understand that working on contract will not lower their recorded grade.

9. Sign the contracts and get students to sign their own contract. This creates formal agreements with obligations and responsibilities for all. In most cases, it is not necessary to have parents sign the contracts. These are agreements between you and the students, not you and the parents. You want to avoid creating a situation in which parents become over-invested in having their children remain constantly "on contract." Since most of the work will be done in school, just like any other schoolwork your students are completing, there really is no need for the parents to sign. They will see the results at the end of the chapter when you send home the extension work, Learning Contract, and Daily Log, along with the Extension Activities and Differentiated Homework Report (page 94).

Some teachers choose to send a letter home at the start of the chapter or unit introducing and explaining the contract method. Then, at the end of the chapter or unit, they send the contracts home along with any extension activities or student logs they want the parents to see. Some find it helpful to coach students in how to tell their parents about the contract work they are working on. Parents are asked to invite their child to explain the contract and the extension work. Parents then complete and return only the Extension Activities and Differentiated Homework Report to be filed at school in the students' extension folders.

10. Caution the students not to brag about being "on contract." Explain how this situation doesn't mean they are better than other students, only that they need a different type of learning plan.

> **IMPORTANT** If you require a contract student to rejoin the direct instruction group for the rest of the chapter because he had trouble following the working conditions, avoid making it sound like a punishment. You wouldn't want those students who are always working in the direct instruction mode to feel there is anything unsatisfactory about that arrangement.

Day-by-Day Plan for Using the Learning Contract

Day One

MATH
- Have all students survey the content to decide if they want to take the pretest. Tell them precisely the number of problems they will have to do correctly to demonstrate that a learning contract is the best option for them (80 percent or higher).

- Demonstrate the enticing extension activity available that day for the students who choose *not* to take the pretest. Reassure all students that the activity will be available for those taking the pretest to work on later in the unit.

- Stop scoring the pretest as soon as the student's incorrect answers bring his or her score below the required limit. In this case, do *not* enter the pretest grades into your records. If students ask what their pretest grade was, tell them you did not record it. We are trying to diminish their addiction to grades and transfer their attention to moving forward in their learning.

- Prepare contracts for students as needed.

Day Two

- Assign all students to learning groups for the chapter. Students who are contract will be grouped together. All other students will be in heterogeneous learning groups with stronger and weaker students working together.

- Give the contract students an extension activity to do while you teach the other students the content for the day. Explain to students that their learning groups have been arranged so there is help available for all group members as needed. Explain the Question Chip method described on page 61. Begin the day's lesson and try to keep your direct teaching time to 15 minutes or less.

- Allow noncontract students to practice what you just taught in their learning groups while you hold the contract meeting with the contract students so they can begin their independent work. Explain all the contract procedures, the working conditions, and the record keeping expectations, and answer any questions. This meeting should be limited to 15 minutes so you can get back to the other students and move on with direct instruction.

Day Three and Beyond

- Each day, tell contract students to check to see if they need to attend the direct instruction group today. Those who do not need to attend can go quietly to the extension center.

- Direct students to their learning groups and conduct the direct instruction of the lesson. If it goes a little longer than 15 minutes, don't worry, since your advanced students are working on extension activities you have provided.

- Always offer the Most Difficult First option to all students attending direct instruction.

Sometimes, students on contract will still be able to compact out of the lesson at this point and proceed to the extension center.

- After the direct instruction lesson, provide a guided practice time for all students, whether or not they are on contract, and allow students to get needed help from their learning group members. *Tip:* If you are lucky enough to have another adult in the room, you might designate them to work at times with the students on contract, rather than always working with struggling students.

IMPORTANT Every day, the first group you should visit during this guided practice time is the students who are on contract. Those students appreciate knowing they will not lose contact with you just because they are working more independently. During your brief meeting with this group, help them understand the contract requirements for record keeping and show appreciation for their willingness to work hard on difficult tasks. Answer any questions regarding how to do the extension activities, but do not give answers or indicate that some answer they already have is correct or not.

The Question Chip Technique

Naturally, all this sounds a little overwhelming. You are wondering how you are supposed to get around to all of your students during a particular class or period, especially if different students are working on different tasks. Here's a method that will help you offer these options without losing your mind!

First, consider that students' brains can only take so much direct instruction at a time before it must be processed or lost. Translating this into classroom practice means that you should never teach for more than 10 to 15 minutes at a time (depending on the grade level) before giving students some time for guided practice. Of course, it's not reasonable to teach the entire standard in that time, but presenting information in meaningful "chunks" makes good teaching sense. This "chunking" allows you to be more available to the kids on contract, since you can spend some time

with them while the other students are practicing the lesson portion you just taught.

At the start of each period, give each group or pair of discussion buddies one Question Chip (poker chip or other plastic token). Ask students to raise their hands if they sometimes feel annoyed when their conversation with you is interrupted by another student. Explain that it is important to respect the needs of every group to have your undivided attention when you are with them. Explain that you've set up the learning groups so there is ample help available from group mates. However, you're aware that a group might get stuck and need your help sometime during the period. Hence, you'll be able to take only *one* question from each group during the guided practice part of each instructional period. If nobody in their group can answer a question, they may send someone to find you. That student must bring the chip, because when you answer the question, you will keep it.

The most amazing thing usually happens: Almost no one will come to ask questions! They want to keep their chip at all costs, so usually they work within their group until they find an answer. If kids ask what they will get for their saved chips, you might suggest that the accumulation of a certain number of chips will lead to homework passes, head-of-the-line passes, five minutes at the end of the class period for students to "groom and chat," or other equally desirable perks.

Remind students that during direct instruction time, they may ask all necessary questions. Suggest that if they have more questions after their chip is gone, they write it down to ask at a later opportunity.

Especially for Primary Teachers

Many teachers in the primary grades believe that their gifted students don't yet have the necessary skills to work independently. In fact, there is ample evidence that these skills can be taught to gifted kids of all ages. Several primary teachers we know have been successful in managing differentiation for their students. After all, if primary students' mental capacity significantly exceeds their chronological age, they should be able, with guidance, to learn the skills of working independently in your classroom.

Many young gifted kids start out each year with a desire not to miss anything the teacher is doing with the rest of the class. They may not be able to handle the paper Learning Contract. You can differentiate for them by preparing guided practice work at two levels of difficulty: entry and advanced. When your direct instruction has ended say, "When I call your name, please go to a table that has a red block on it." That would be the advanced-level task. Then, with the same level of excitement, say: "When I call *your* name, please go to a table with a blue block," which would have the entry-level task for the day. Of course, you don't tell the students which block represents what level task, since tomorrow, you will swap the colors. When the students complain that they are doing different tasks, say, "I know—isn't that wonderful! Since we are so different in so many ways, it's perfectly okay to be different in the type of learning task we need." The younger students are when they learn this truth, the more respect they will have for all kinds of individual differences.

When your primary kids get ready for contracts, you could keep the information in your grade book, so you will know which students should participate in direct instruction, and which will work on extension activities. Use highlights or different colored fonts to indicate the standards for which each student needs direct instruction. Each day, when you write the instructions for a particular lesson on the board, list the names of contract kids who do not have to attend the direct instruction. Tell the class, "If your name is on the board today, you may work on extension activities during the entire period. Start new work, or continue your work from yesterday, and I will come to see you about 15 minutes after the start of the period." In this way, children can begin to start before you get to them. It's a routine they can learn, just like any other routine.

Whatever method you use, call the contract group together for a few minutes on the first day of a new unit or chapter before you teach the large-group lesson. Explain the task that awaits them, and coach them on how to go to the designated spot and start the work while you get the rest of the class going. Reassure them that you will visit their group often, so they know they won't lose contact with you.

Other Learning Contract Options

Following are three unique methods for customizing Learning Contracts: for accelerated learning, for problem-solving focus, and for specialized math programs. Because the basic concept of the Learning Contract is so widely applicable, and because Learning Contracts are so easy to use, it's fairly simple to customize this strategy to meet the needs of individual students.

The Contract for Accelerated Learning

Once in a great while, you may encounter students who are so precocious that they may be able to teach themselves much of what they need to learn. Such students may be given more independent working time than others. Keep in mind, however, that some adult must keep checking with these students to make sure they are making adequate forward progress and keeping accurate records.

Scenarios: Lucas and Martina

Consider the situation with Lucas, a fifth grader, who is very talented in mathematics. When he took the grade-level yearly benchmark assessment at the beginning of the school year (prior to having been taught the material), he didn't miss a single problem. Lucas then took the benchmark assessment for one grade level above and he still didn't miss a single problem. It wasn't until we went two grade levels beyond his actual grade that we could find material that he had not yet fully mastered. If we had not done this out-of-level benchmark testing, we would have wasted valuable learning time for Lucas, and he would have wasted the entire year in his math class.

However, caution may be required, too. With Martina, an eighth grader who was also exceptional with math, we encountered a surprise. Based on the testing, we found that Martina had a huge gap in the area of data analysis because she had previously skipped over some material. So we went back, filled in that gap, retested, and then she too was ready to accelerate. Going back to address that one area did not slow her down; to the contrary, it allowed her to be more successful as she moved forward. We need this documentation to prove that students will not be missing information when we accelerate their math program.

The Contract for Accelerated Learning (see below) helps you document mastery of 95 percent or higher on an entire chapter, in which case students will not be required to complete any pages in that chapter. Receiving full credit for that chapter, they continue to pretest until their instructional level is found. In some cases, these kids could be placed in higher grades for math and return to their own class for their other subjects. When this

is done, it must become part of a written multi-year plan that involves the parents, administrators, and anyone else who would be affected by such acceleration. For seriously advanced students, especially in math, it's not appropriate to have them spend an entire year only on extension. Some acceleration is needed as well.

How to Use the Contract for Accelerated Learning

1. Give very precocious students the end-of-chapter tests for as many chapters as they can demonstrate mastery with a score above

---

Contract for Accelerated Learning

Student's Name: Lucas

_____ Chapter One	_____ Chapter Four	_____ Chapter Seven
_____ Chapter Two	_____ Chapter Five	_____ Chapter Eight
_____ Chapter Three	_____ Chapter Six	_____ Chapter Nine

Extension Options:

Chapter # and Standard	Extension	Acceleration

Teacher's Signature: _____

Student's Signature: _____

95 percent. These tests may be taken out of sequence, since some students will have mastered standards here and there throughout the text.

2. On the top part of the contract, record the dates when mastery was documented. Date all tests and keep them in the student's compacting folder or in an electronic database.

3. On the bottom part of the contract, keep track of the activities or program changes you choose for the student. If acceleration is not an option in your school, describe the extension activities in which the student will be engaged.

4. Explain the Essential Rules for Independent Work (page 44) students must follow to be allowed to work at this advanced level of learning.

CAUTION Accelerated students who stay in their own classroom for instruction should not use the actual subsequent grade-level materials to avoid the possibility of textbook repetition in the future. There are a couple exceptions to this rule. First, a separate class may be formed for students accelerated in math and a scope-and-sequence developed that guarantees these students will not repeat the use of texts, even if they fail to remain in the accelerated class. Second, if your school creates cluster groups of gifted students, more than one student may be working at any given time on the advanced-level curriculum. Never make acceleration arrangements without informing the other interested parties, such as parents, other teachers, and administrators. Any acceleration of content requires careful planning beyond the current school year.

The Contract with Problem-Solving Focus

In some situations, such as those involving specialized math programs, the traditional Learning Contract approach is not appropriate and must be adjusted to focus more on problem solving.

Scenario: Elena

Elena's class was using a math curriculum that stressed critical thinking and problem solving. It didn't lend itself to the more traditional Learning Contract approach. Elena's teacher had been told to teach the entire class as one group, and she was having trouble keeping the gifted students interested while the rest of the class went over the same standard several times. Because Elena wanted to please her teacher, she never complained. However, her parents were hinting that they didn't think their daughter was being adequately challenged.

Elena's teacher planned activities to extend the basic problem-solving experiences for her highly capable math students. Then she created a Contract with Problem-Solving Focus, as shown on page 65. This contract made it easy to meet the differentiated learning needs of students like Elena. Even when all students are working on similar problem-solving strategies, the problems themselves can be different, reflecting the degree of difficulty each student is capable of handling.

How to Use the Contract with Problem-Solving Focus

1. Find or design an assessment tool or pretest for each problem-solving strategy. Offer the pretest before you teach each strategy, or when you observe that certain students have mastered a particular strategy.

2. On the top part of the contract, record the dates when the student masters specific strategies.

3. Create extension options and list them on the contract. Explain how students should keep track of the extension activities they do. (See "At the Contract Meeting" on page 58.)

CAUTION Students' grades should come from the top part of the contract, which represents grade-level work. You may choose to give credit for time spent on the extension activities. However, this should never be "extra" credit in addition to completed regular work. It should replace credit that was not earned due to the student compacting out of the easier, grade-level work.

Using Contracts with Specialized Math Programs

Contrary to some beliefs, it is entirely possible and practical to use Learning Contracts with standards-based math programs or those that focus on problem solving.

For teacher-directed programs that focus on hands-on learning, such as Everyday Mathematics, we suggest a slightly different compacting approach. As long as a student is performing in the range of 90 percent or higher, he or she may be excused from the direct instruction and classwork two or more days a week to work on extension activities. Since these programs are spiral, and standards are always revisited, this arrangement works well for advanced math students.

For highly structured programs that rely on large amounts of practice and homework, such as the Saxon Math Program, advanced students should be required to complete only one problem of each type on any classroom or homework assignment. Some teachers require only one or two compacted homework assignments per week as long as students maintain an average of 90 percent or higher.

Contract with Problem-Solving Focus

Student's Name: Elena

___Make tables or graphs

___Estimate first, check later

___Use objects; use manipulatives

___Make pictures

___Create an organized list

___Use logical thinking

___Make diagrams

___Work backward

___Simplify the problem

___Find a pattern

___Act it out

___Write an equation

Extension Options:

Create story problems for the class to do

Choose a method from the top of the contract; create 4 to 6 problems at different levels of difficulty

Study a math textbook from a higher grade level that is different from the adopted text; find and record problems that require specific problem-solving methods; name the methods

Select a problem that our school is experiencing; apply several of the methods listed above to solve it

Apply several of the methods to solve a personal problem

Create an activity related to problem solving

Teacher's Signature: _____

Student's Signature: _____

Using the Learning Contract in Other Subject Areas

The contract method may be used for skill work in any unit of study. Several examples of how to use this method for the skill areas of reading and writing are described in detail on pages 104–142 in chapter 4. You are invited to use contracts in any subject area when the method seems to meet some teaching and/or learning needs.

Here are some tips to try:

1. Always offer Most Difficult First, selecting problems from each category.

2. Pretest by categories of content and arrange the contract so students know which categories they can skip.

3. Allow students who maintain an average of at least 90 percent to skip every other day of direct instruction and work on extension activities instead.

4. Assign only odd- or even-numbered problems as daily practice.

Helpful Tips to Make Learning Contracts Work Well

- Do not grade the extension activities and average those grades into the students' overall grades for the chapter or unit. If you do, gifted kids may resist working on extension activities, especially challenging ones. Why should they risk getting a lower grade than they're accustomed to? Instead, for each day they work on extension activities, record the A they earned on that standard on the pretest as long as they were following the Essential Rules for Independent Work that day. Always remember that if you were not compacting and differentiating for these kids, the only work you would have to assess would be the grade-level work.

- If students were not following the Essential Rules, have a quick, private conference to explain that the next time they are not able to follow those rules, it will be showing you that they are not comfortable with or ready for the independent work plan and they will be expected to return to the direct instruction group for the rest of the chapter or unit.

- At regular intervals, offer the whole class a day to work on extension activities. When all students have opportunities to engage in learning tasks that are interesting, meaningful, and fun, there will be little or no resentment toward the students who spend a lot of time on extension activities.

- Once a month, have all students, including those on contract, work on activities that provide practice in already mastered skills and standards. This will reassure you, your principal or supervisor, and the parents that these students are keeping up with the required standards. Strive to make sure these activities are highly interesting. Check the internet for some possible options.

- Give mini-assessments at regular intervals to make sure the groups are on track. At the appropriate time, give all students the formal end-of-the-unit assessment—the same assessment that you gave at the start of the unit.

A Word About Homework

When you differentiate any skill-based lesson, you must also differentiate the homework. Since most school districts that require homework use the language of "how many minutes per grade level," you can capitalize on this policy in the following ways:

- Allow advanced students to skip some practice and some homework as long as they maintain a designated grade average. If their average falls lower than what is expected, the students leave their contract and join the direct instruction group for the remainder of the work. The same happens if they fail to follow the expected working conditions.

- If you'd like to use a method that does not require an actual contract, you might allow students advanced in some skill area to skip the daily activities and the homework for a few days each week, as long as they maintain a designated competence in all assessments. While they maintain their expertise, they work daily in class only on the extension activities. Some activities can be reserved for homework only, and students will keep a log of the time they spend at home on those activities instead of on the regular homework tasks.

- Using a "Lunch and Chocolate" approach from page 147, invite colleagues to create Extension Menus for Homework Only. Include activities that you used to enjoy teaching but that are no longer available to you because they are not connected to your assigned standards. Explain in each square of the menu what you want students to learn or do regarding a certain task. Students will keep a separate Daily Log (page 92) for recording their home-based activities. Parents will be asked to monitor that the log entries are correct in terms of time actually spent on the work. Even if kids don't have adult supervision during homework time, they are often highly motivated to do the extension activities. Parents and students must both understand that the goal is not to complete a large number of suggested tasks, but to spend time exploring one or two topics in depth.

Assessing: Learning Contract Work

Here's one way to grade contract students that is nonthreatening for them and easy for you. Each day that you record the work done by the class, the students working on extension activities will not have a paper to turn in for a grade. This is because the pretest and their contract indicate they had previously mastered that standard. At the same time as you are recording grades for the class, record for the contract students the mastery grade (A) they earned for that particular standard on the pretest. This grade represents both their demonstration of standard mastery as well as their demonstration that they followed the Essential Rules for Independent Work during that instructional period. On days when contract students receive direct instruction with the rest of the class, record the grades they actually earn for that particular lesson.

Tips:

- As you prepare each contract, do not record A's for the lessons already mastered. In your grade book leave those spaces blank and wait to record those A's until you record everyone else's grades for that standard. When contract students are aware there are blank spaces in your grade book, it reminds them that anytime they cannot follow the working conditions, you might invite them back to the direct instruction group for the rest of the chapter's work.

- Some students may not be satisfied with "just an A." They want their grade point average to be "a very high A," and they want the grade book to reflect this. If that situation arises, you might offer to enter the student's actual average from the previous chapter or chapters.

- At the end of the chapter or unit, simply average all of the recorded grades earned during the days students attended direct instruction with the A's they earned from the pretest to get their grade for that chapter or unit of work.

See chapter 8 for more information on assessment strategies.

QUESTIONS ★ ANSWERS

Compacting and Extension Activities

"Why not require 100 percent accuracy for a student to receive compacting?"

We can't convince gifted kids to take risks and try challenging new learning opportunities if we also communicate the expectation that they must perform perfectly. It's important for them to know that making mistakes is part of the learning process. When a student accurately solves four out of five most difficult math problems or correctly spells 90 percent of the spelling or vocabulary words, that's surely enough to indicate mastery.

"Shouldn't I be concerned if some students just vegetate and waste their choice time?"

When you create a lesson plan, you have estimated the time it will take for average students to master the material. When some kids demonstrate that they don't need all the time you have planned, any remaining time should become their own for working on choice activities.

There is a phrase that is magical in its effectiveness regarding your need to impose expectations from outside sources. If a student wants to spend extension time working on assignments from another teacher or class, you might say, "I'm sorry, *I'm not allowed to* let you do that, so please select an available extension activity or suggest an idea of your own in this subject area." Once the student has recovered from the shock that you (the teacher!) are not allowed to do something, he or she will most likely get busy with an extension task in the targeted subject area.

NOTE Answer keys should be available for activities that require specific answers. However, appropriately challenging extension activities probably won't lend themselves to the use of simplistic answer keys. When students are working on these kinds of activities, their grade for that day might instead reflect how well they were following the Essential Rules for Independent Work or how well they were using available rubrics. However, if you need answer keys, try asking some parents of gifted students to create some keys with their child at home. In many classes, parents will have the discretionary time for this task, and they will be happy to help because they know their gifted child will benefit from your efforts.

"How should kids keep track of the extension work they do?"

Prepare an extension folder for each student in the classroom for storing work in progress and keep them in a hanging file folder box. Give students copies of a student log (see the Daily Log of Extension Work on page 92) and explain how they should use it. Show the logs to parents at conferences, since they document that you've been differentiating the curriculum for their children. Use the Extension Activities and Differentiated Homework Report on page 94 to send home completed extension activities, and use Daily Logs at the end of each unit to communicate your compacting and differentiation efforts to parents and other caregivers. Ask that an adult at home complete and sign the report and return it to you so it can be filed in the student's extension folder. Also include compacting contracts and dated assessments.

"What if some students need my help to choose and do alternate activities?"

Gifted students who need help from the teacher are still gifted, but they may lack the skills to work independently. Just because they are working on alternate activities doesn't mean they automatically know how to manage their time well, stay on task, use extension materials, ask for help when they get stuck, keep track of their work, put things away, and so on.

Meet with your students often to teach these skills—and to prove that they won't lose contact with you when they choose to work more independently. Some students have been known to avoid extension options because they fear losing contact with the teacher. Your plans should include spending regular time with students who work with alternate activities. See the Question Chip technique on page 61 for one way to manage all these irons in the fire without losing your sanity.

Remind students often that the purpose of doing extension activities is to learn that it's okay to work on challenging material and still be considered smart.

"Won't students who never experience compacting have self-esteem problems or feel resentment?"

When you find yourself considering this question, you will have two choices: You can either deprive your exceptionally capable students of what they need, or you can learn what's causing the self-esteem and/or resentment problems and do something about them.

When you carefully explain that you expect most students will have to do the grade-level work in order to master a standard, students will realize that nothing is wrong with those who don't need compacting. (Naturally, those who do experience compacting shouldn't brag about it or tease the others.)

Make sure that the activities available to gifted students are also available at other times to all students. When class members perceive that only the most capable get to do the work that looks like more fun on a regular basis, they are likely to resent it. All kids deserve an enriching curriculum—what author and educator Carol Tomlinson calls "respectful work," but only gifted students regularly need extension activities beyond the regular curriculum.

As teachers, we meet with few objections when we make modifications that benefit struggling students. We need to offer the same consideration to students at the top end, whose learning needs are just as different from the grade-level norm. Justice Felix Frankfurter said it best when he observed, "There is nothing so unequal as the equal treatment of unequals." Equality in education has never meant that all students should be treated the same. Rather, it means that all students should enjoy equal opportunities to actualize their learning potential.

"Is it necessary to keep a Compactor for every student who works on differentiated activities during time bought from the regular curriculum?"

It's always a good idea to keep a brief record of changes you make from the regular curriculum for any student, gifted or otherwise, who needs differentiation. Accountability is a critical concern in education today. If we choose to deviate from accepted practices, we are responsible for maintaining records to document that we are following a specific plan and we are never losing sight of the need for all students to document mastery of all grade-level standards.

"Some students seem unwilling to work without close direction from me. How can I give them the time they need without taking time away from the other students?"

When gifted students ask a teacher for help with extension activities, the last thing they want to hear is, "You're pretty smart, you should be able to figure that out yourself!" The unspoken message is that bright people should never have to ask for help.

Be sure they have opportunities to work with another advanced student on the extension activities. Getting the right answer isn't nearly as important as experiencing the problem solving needed to reach a solution. Gifted students also need and want time with the teacher. When you've gone to so much trouble to provide your students with truly challenging activities, they will need and welcome your assistance. When you make time to consistently visit their extension group, even briefly, over time they will feel less of a need to ask questions directly of you. Finally, the Question Chip technique (see page 61) can help you create time to work with groups of contract kids on a regular basis.

"Shouldn't my gifted students spend some of their time tutoring students who are having trouble learning?"

All your students have the right to learn something new in every subject every day. There may be some benefits for all students when gifted students interact in a teaching capacity with those who need help, but consistently having gifted students teach struggling students robs gifted students of their own right to struggle and learn. Your capable students might conclude, "Everyone else comes to school to learn math. Not me; I come to teach it!" Or, "Once I've finished the material in the book, there must not be any other math material for me to learn, since the teacher never provides other math activities for me."

It's possible that your highly capable (though not gifted) students will gain a better understanding of what they are learning by tutoring other kids on a sometimes basis. We know they will be more patient teachers than many gifted kids can be. Gifted students can become very frustrated at always being asked to tutor, and the students they are tutoring may say they understand a standard long before they really do, just to escape from an uncomfortable situation.

"Where can I find the extension materials my students need, and how can I afford them?"

Many of the extension activities can come directly from your current curriculum. Select only the truly challenging activities provided by the publisher in your textbook teachers' editions. Students can also provide ideas for the extension activities. One strategy that works well is to replicate the Topic Development Sheet on page 78 onto a large wall chart for each subject area you are teaching. Write in the standard or topic you are addressing. Then when your precocious students have an idea about something they'd like to do differently from how you are teaching it, have them write their idea on the wall chart. Formally incorporate those ideas into your extension menus, tiered assignments, or independent project work. The students will have total buy-in into completing that activity because it was their idea! They will also be excited to point out to their parents that you used their idea for an extension lesson.

You might also check the curriculum publisher's website, various teacher resource sites (see page 211 in chapter 8), or simply by doing a Google search for materials in the topic area. See the references and resources for this chapter on page 235 for more suggestions.

Most Difficult First

"What will students do with the time they have left after successfully completing the Most Difficult First problems?"

At the start of each unit, collect materials that represent extension activities for the standards taught in the chapter or the subject area in general. Create an informal extension center in your classroom, using part of a shelf, an empty desk or table, or a learning center format. Students who successfully complete Most Difficult First problems can spend the remaining practice time there.

For the first extension experience for a standard, some schools expect teachers to provide an extension activity that is closely related to the standard being taught. That task should require the student to explore the same topic with more depth and complexity. (See chapter 5.) For example, if your math program begins each year with review of whole number addition, subtraction, multiplication, and division, the extension activity could be to use those same algorithms with decimals or much larger numbers. This practice seems to help high-ability students move from *meeting* to *exceeding* the standards, a goal of all teachers and administrators.

After the first extension activity, however, you should feel free to provide experience with other topics in the same subject area but *not* confined to the required standard. Students working on extension activities should be able to branch out to consider some topics in math that might not even be taught that year. They should have choices with activities that *extend* their knowledge about math in general. Standards-based learning often dramatically limits the topics that must be learned in a certain grade or subject. The last thing we want students gifted in math to think is that when they have finished the grade-level content, they are "done" with math! This is the perfect time for them to encounter noticeably different topics in math or whatever the subject area happens to be. Parents appreciate that their children are not just waiting for the others to catch up and the teacher has thoughtfully extended the learning activity for their children.

Spend some time with kids as they work on extension activities. You might have a weekly meeting for them to describe their favorite activities and for you to monitor that they are keeping accurate records according to the method you have indicated they should use.

"Is it okay for Most Difficult First to be the only differentiation method available to gifted students in my classroom?"

No, because the students are still required to stay with the class during the entire lesson, and you may be spending many days teaching standards they have already mastered. Most Difficult First is designed to be used as your first attempt at compacting, so you can see that compacting doesn't create that much extra work for you, and that most gifted students can be trusted to fill their choice time with activities that are challenging for them.

"Does Most Difficult First work as well for other areas of the curriculum as it does for math?"

Yes. Feel free to try it with grammar, language mechanics, reading vocabulary, or other skill work that students may have previously mastered. It's also a good strategy to suggest to colleagues who want to try something for their gifted students but are worried that this might create too much extra work for them. Most Difficult First will relieve this concern and free teachers to move on to other differentiation strategies.

Pretest for Volunteers

"If kids are allowed to get one out of five wrong on the pretest, what grade should I enter in my grade book? Four out of five is 80 percent, and that's a B in our school."

Count that score as 80 percent, then add bonus points for demonstrating mastery. The issue is mastery, not having jumped through the hoops of completing unnecessary practice work. The letter grade for mastery is "A," regardless of how many problems or examples the student completed.

However, older students may have become jaded with the attitude that if there is no grade, there is no reason to do the work. You can entice them to work on extension activities to receive alternative credit for the week's work. In other words, they still get daily grades recorded, but the grades are always A, since they have already demonstrated their A-level competence on the pre-assessment option. As long as they follow the Essential Rules for Independent Work, their credit is recorded. The students get the high grades they desire by working on related material that has more depth and complexity. You get the joy of seeing them become involved in advanced learning activities. Their parents see that they are being held accountable for their grades through advanced learning opportunities. Everybody wins.

If you want your gifted students to choose more challenging activities and to work on difficult problems for long periods of time, you must provide an environment where it's safe to risk being wrong. If you grade gifted students' extension activities and average those grades into their formal grades

for that subject, they will resist challenging work, telling you that they would rather do "what all the other kids are doing."

"What can I do when students who might benefit from compacting choose not to take the pretest and indicate they would rather work with the class?"

Many gifted students equate being gifted with getting their work done quickly and easily. In their minds, someone who struggles must be less intelligent than someone who breezes through assignments. Make it clear that their alternative work will not be averaged in with the grade-level work, and that the grade they earn for this chapter or unit will be no lower than what they would have earned had they stayed with the class for direct instruction.

Sometimes this avoidance behavior reflects a bid for social acceptance. Sometimes it's a way of playing it safe. If they take a risk, if they choose to struggle, they might fail. And if they fail, they fear this will "prove" that they aren't really that smart after all. If quite a few students resist taking the pretest, this probably means that they don't understand that this option is risk-free.

Consistently communicate your firm belief that it takes more intelligence to hang in there when the going gets tough than it does to excel at easy work. Emphasize daily the importance of honoring individual differences.

The Learning Contract

"What happens when students on contract forget to join the group for instruction on the days they're supposed to?"

Just because students are gifted doesn't mean they are well-organized or totally responsible. They may need to be taught those skills. Whatever code you use in your grading system to indicate which students are on a contract, you should be able to see at a glance which contract students should join you for direct instruction on any given day. When you announce which page the class will be working on that day, remind the contract students to check their contracts to see where they should be. For a few weeks, you may want to write their names on the board to help them form the habit of checking when they should attend the class. When you notice that someone who should be with the instructional group is absent from it, gently remind all of the contract students to check their contracts.

"What should I do if students on contract waste time or disturb the class on the days they are working on extension activities?"

You can avoid potential problems if you plan to meet with contract students several times during the first few days of the unit. This helps them feel in touch, gets them focused, and starts them off on the right track. Then, speak to the students you are concerned about once or twice, referring them to the working conditions on their contract. Make sure they understand how to do the extension activities and find out if the activities are proving to be unrealistically difficult. Try to spend at least five minutes a day with kids on a learning contract, cheering their efforts and willingness to take risks with challenging content.

Even after all of this support, there may be some kids who simply can't or won't do what is expected of them. At that point, advise them to rejoin the direct instruction group for the rest of the chapter. Be sure they understand that this is not a bad thing, and reassure them that they will have a chance to show they are ready for a contract when the next chapter begins.

Do not lower the grade earned on any assessment because of behavior problems. Record the actual earned grade, but reserve the right to have the student rejoin the direct instruction group at any time during the length of the contract. Once they rejoin the teacher directed group, they remain there for the remainder of that chapter; they do not move in and out of Learning Contract status. However, you might encourage them to notice what other contract students are doing to meet the behavioral expectations, and suggest they take the next pretest when it is offered.

"Will correcting work for students on contract create a lot of paperwork for me?"

Extension work is rarely corrected, since much of this work is open-ended to invite consideration of various possibilities. If the extension work *does* require specific answers, you can ask a classroom volunteer, student teacher, or even parents of gifted students to review it and prepare the materials you need to continue offering extension opportunities for children in your class.

Chapter Summary

For skill-based content that some students have likely learned and mastered at an earlier time, compacting means:

1. Finding the students' areas of strength.

2. Allowing students to complete the most difficult problems in a lesson first and skip over the easier ones.

3. Offering voluntary pretests to students to determine which of the standards you are about to teach they already know.

4. Giving students full credit for the content they have already mastered without requiring them to do all the grade-level work.

5. Providing them with more challenging activities to work on when those activities will move them forward in their learning.

Success on pretests and difficult problems provides the evidence you need that some students don't require as much practice as others. Compacting frees them to use that time for work that is more challenging to them. Students with high ability should have frequent and consistent opportunities to demonstrate prior knowledge or skill mastery and use their school time for work that represents true learning for them.

Compacting is remarkably successful with students who have become behavior problems and who may be refusing to do their work. Many behavior problems of gifted students are caused by boredom and frustration. When we are in power struggles with such students and worry that they are not doing *their* work, we are actually insisting that they do *our* work. Use the methods described in this chapter with your students and watch the amazing results. You'll need to do some preparation, but once a system is in place, it will practically run itself. Your reward will come as you watch your students perk up and willingly engage in challenging work.

CHAPTER 3
Compacting and Differentiating for New Content

★ STRATEGIES

■ The Study Guide, page 73

As you read the previous chapter, you probably noticed that the strategies described would not be very useful in certain subject areas where the standards are more likely to be unfamiliar to the students, including literature, science, social studies, health, and other subjects that are more content-based rather than skill-based. Most Difficult First, Pretest for Volunteers, and Learning Contract options are applicable *only* if students have had opportunities previously to learn the curriculum. Other compacting and differentiating methods are needed for situations in which the curriculum may be new, but gifted students can learn it much more quickly than their age peers.

In content areas where the material is new for them, gifted students should be allowed to move through it at a faster pace than the rest of the class. These students are easy to spot. They are the ones who tend to ace quizzes and tests, sometimes dominate class discussions, but hand in little or none of the daily work or homework. They may also lack enthusiasm for going above and beyond the expectations of the regular classroom. They are trying to tell you that they can learn the material without doing the actual activities.

How can you let them work at a pace commensurate with their ability, while avoiding a power struggle over the work they may not need to do? The two methods described in this chapter for using the Study Guide strategy will help you capitalize on your gifted students' exceptional learning abilities by inviting them to move through the required content at a faster pace than their classmates, while sometimes becoming "resident experts" on related topics.

★ STRATEGY
The Study Guide

The Study Guide method, with all its accompanying components, enables you to compact new content in any subject area by reducing the amount of time gifted students must spend learning grade-level standards. At the start of a unit, students may choose to follow a prepared Study Guide of the material and agree to meet the required assessment checkpoints by pursuing their own independent study. In this way the method increases the amount of time students have for working on extension activities and exploring related topics of their choosing in greater depth. The most significant difference between the skill-based compacting strategies in chapter 2 and the Study Guide method is that we *do* pretest when the content is skill based and we generally do *not* pretest when the content is new, because it makes no sense for students to have to take a test on material about which they know nothing. Of course, if you are required by an administrator to give a mandatory pretest, go ahead. However, advanced learners, whether or not they take a pretest, still need compacting and differentiation opportunities.

We *do* pretest when the content is skill based and we generally do *not* pretest when the content is new.

The idea of exempting some students from regularly assigned work may make you uncomfortable. You may worry that they will develop poor work habits, or that other students will resent what they perceive as "special privileges" for only a few. Remember that you never excuse students from the regular work until they have demonstrated that 1) they have already mastered the required standards or 2) they can learn them in a much shorter time than their age peers. With the Study Guide method, you will have documentation that students have learned the required standards, because they are held accountable for demonstrating that mastery *at the same time as their classmates*. We do not want to offer assessments "on demand," but we do want to increase available time for working on extension activities. The faster pacing, along with student choice about the extension work, makes gifted students (and their parents) happy.

Scenario: Cleon

Cleon, an eighth-grade student, was "gifted across the board." His ability was exceptional in every subject area, as well as in art and physical

education. However, his actual classroom performance left a lot to be desired. His social studies teacher, Mrs. Hernandez, found it frustrating that he seemed to spend much of his class time daydreaming, and he seldom completed his homework assignments, but he had an annoying habit of always acing the tests!

Furthermore, Cleon behaved rudely during class discussions. He blurted out answers when he wasn't called on, and he delighted in making remarks under his breath that were designed to amuse and distract the other students. His teacher slowly realized that Cleon's negative behavior was related to his superior learning ability. Rather than disciplining him, she sought a management system that would allow Cleon to learn social studies in a manner more commensurate with his ability. Naturally, she also hoped that the added challenge would have a positive effect on his behavior.

When this situation was discussed with Cleon's parents, they wanted to take away his hockey lessons until he "shaped up in school." Mrs. Hernandez asked them not to do that. Cleon was a champion player, and his teacher believed there was nothing positive to be gained by taking away a student's source of joy and satisfaction until his or her schoolwork improves. Cleon's predictable reaction would be to become even more negative toward school. Since his performance on assessments indicated that he could learn the material without actually doing the required activities, it seemed reasonable that the solution should be found at school rather than at home.

At the time, the class was studying the Civil War. Mrs. Hernandez explained the Study Guide method and asked Cleon if he might want to try it. Cleon was interested in trains, so he said he would like to draw the trains and locomotives of the Civil War period. However, simply drawing the trains would not have provided an adequate challenge to his superior learning ability. So a product was negotiated that allowed Cleon to draw his trains on a huge piece of tagboard on which he also drew a map and located the major Civil War battlefields and manufacturing centers. A related task was to determine the extent to which the proximity of the manufacturing centers to the battlefields affected the outcome of the war. This forced Cleon to become more original with his thinking and to synthesize information from many sources to create and defend a hypothesis, making this a highly challenging activity for a gifted student. Of course, with access to the internet, there is no limit to the options at a student's fingertips.

Identifying Students for the Study Guide Method

One way to help students decide if the Study Guide method is right for them is by describing the characteristics and abilities they need to be successful with the method. It's best to do this during the unit before the one targeted for the Study Guide approach, but you can also do it at the start of a current unit. A sample script follows.

> "In this subject area, we need to work together for the first unit so we can determine which students might need faster pacing and more time to extend their learning with extension activities. At the beginning of the next unit, a method called the Study Guide will be available that will require more independent work, and it will include optional choice activities as well. For some of you this method will be a good match and will allow you to work at your own pace and develop your interest in a topic you would enjoy learning more about. However, this method is not a good choice for all students. Many of you will prefer to continue working with a larger group in a more teacher-directed manner.
>
> "The Study Guide method is a good choice for students who, during this first unit, can demonstrate that they:
>
> - Enjoy independent reading and understand what they read
> - Are very curious about topics we may not have time to include in our classwork
> - Find and bring to class information about topics from sources outside of

class, which shows their interest in learning about a topic in a deeper way
> - Maintain a B average or higher on formal assessments during the current unit
> - Show interest in becoming a resident expert on a topic related to the unit
> - Want to learn a lot about the topic and share their expertise with the class."

> **NOTE** You'll see that "Turn in all their homework" is not listed here. The Study Guide method is designed for students who can demonstrate mastery on assessments without doing the actual daily work. They don't need to complete the same assignments as students for whom a more teacher-directed approach is desirable and necessary.

The Study Guide method is a perfect match for students who can demonstrate the previously described behaviors, and for those students who suffer from what is called "The Empty Grade Book Syndrome." These students often don't turn in any work during a unit of study, complete no homework assignments, and then have the "nerve" to ace the assessment! This creates huge frustration for some teachers, and for the students and their parents, too. Teachers may feel that it is not right or fair to give the student the grade earned on the assessment as the actual grade for the entire unit. A more accurate question might be, "Why should a student who can learn all the standards without drawing the map or creating the flow chart or writing out all the necessary definitions be penalized for that?"

If we want to serve gifted students well, there should be no punishment for learning the required standards by means different than other students. No zeroes or Fs should be in the grade book. There should be no missing recess or special events, and no threats of not passing a grade level or subject. Gifted students should simply receive the same credit earned by students who *do* need to complete the assignments in order to learn the material.

IMPORTANT Students who are using the Study Guide method do *not* have to do the actual work described on the guide. They are only responsible for learning the described standards and achieving the agreed upon competence on the assessments.

Occasionally a student declares after looking at the Study Guide that they already know most of the required standards. In that case, you may decide to let him or her take the end-of-the-unit assessment immediately. If the test grade is in the A range, that student works during the entire unit on extension work, such as a related independent study project, following the working conditions on an Independent Study Agreement (see page 90). Then, you might use an Evaluation Contract (see page 96) to assess the student's extension work, and the final unit grade would come from a combination of actual grades earned at Study Guide checkpoint times, along with a single letter grade for the extension project.

Now, you are probably thinking, "Didn't chapter 2 say very clearly that we *shouldn't* grade the extension work?" Yes, it did! That chapter described the correct methods for differentiating skill-based work. The mastery result on the pretest actually provides the summative assessment, which tells us that these kids already know the required content. You do end up with grades in all the necessary spaces in your grade book because the average of one A for the pretest equals the average of any number of A's, so you can just fill in the blank spaces with A's. However, when we are teaching content that is *new* to the students, we cannot do the same thing for many reasons. Mostly because gifted students have great short-term memories. They can "cram" material quickly and store it long enough to ace a pretest. By the time the final assessment rolls around, some of these kids have forgotten a great deal of what they "knew" before.

Two Ways to Use the Study Guide

You may use the Study Guide alone or in combination with an Extension Menu. In both cases, students are expected to master the same material as the rest of the class, and they are held accountable with regular assessments. But they can learn at a faster pace and spend the balance of their time on activities that are more challenging and rewarding for them.

Using the Study Guide Alone

This option is the simplest. Some students become a resident expert on a different topic within the same general category. For example, let's say the upcoming unit is about the Civil War. Some students may already know a great deal about the Civil War and could easily ace the summative assessment for this topic by independently reviewing the concepts on the generic American Wars Study Guide (page 80). These students can instead do an independent study about a different war in which the United States participated, such as the Vietnam War. There would be no formal assessments on the Vietnam War, but students would be responsible for participating in all class checkpoint assessments for the Civil War unit. However, instead of doing the required work for the Civil War unit, they will share some of the information they have learned about the Vietnam War. This way everyone wins! Teachers get mastery data from all students about the Civil War. Students who already know those details spend their class time becoming experts on their chosen war. The American wars experience for the entire class is enhanced. Challenging behaviors from frustrated gifted students often disappear. And parents are delighted that their children are fully engaged.

Using the Study Guide with Extension Menu

This option invites students to become resident experts on a topic related to what the whole class is learning. They choose a topic from the Extension Menu (or come up with one of their own), pursue it in depth, and later report on what they learned to the class or other appropriate audience. This expands the unit and makes it more interesting and enjoyable for everyone.

A reproducible Study Guide and an Extension Menu are shown on pages 82 and 83. The next section explains how to create your own guides and menus. Use of all the Study Guide components will significantly improve the student's success. However, it is imperative to introduce the components in small doses, and we must give students ample time to understand what is required and expected of them. The effort you put into these explanations the first time students use this method will greatly pay off, because by the second time, the students you have already coached will be able to coach other students and eventually leave you out of the explanations altogether!

Preparing the Topic Development Sheet

Before you prepare a Study Guide with Extension Menu, you must first create your Topic Development Sheet (see page 78).

1. Choose the topic for differentiating and make it generic, which cuts down on your preparation time and allows the Study Guide itself to serve as the differentiation tool for several related units over time.

Instead of this:	Use this:
Civil War	American Wars
Ancient Rome	Ancient Civilizations
Digestive System	Systems in the Human Body
Ramona the Pest	Beverly Cleary Books
Sarah, Plain and Tall	Life on the Frontier
Tyrannosaurus Rex	Dinosaurs

2. Next, choose 8 to 10 standards to include in this unit and record them in the left column of the Topic Development Sheet, labeled Required Standards. You may combine standards, but your final list should not exceed 10 statements. List them in the order in which you plan to teach them. These topics will be transferred from this chart to the Study Guide you will prepare later.

3. Next, choose 8 to 10 topics related to the main topic and list them in the right column of the chart under Related Topics. Eight of these topics will become the Extension Menu. It is not necessary to create a related topic for each of the listed standards. Actually, it is preferable to list 8 to 10 different ideas that are related to the unit, but not confined to the required standards. Gifted students love learning all they can about an interesting topic, and they are frustrated when the curriculum is limited only to the required standards. The Related Topics list provides an opportunity for you to bring in topics related to the larger unit that you know students would enjoy studying.

A scary question may be running through your mind about now: What will these students be doing if they do not have to do the assignments? The answer is always the same: They should be working on extension activities or conducting independent research on topics related to the designated content, and they should share what they have learned with their classmates in order to enrich everyone's experience with the unit. The rest of this chapter explains, step by step, how to do just that.

Preparing the Study Guide

1. Choose 10 required standards statements from the unit. (***Note:*** If you are using the Study Guide with Extension Menu, these are the same 10 standards on the Topic Development Sheet.) Create a task description for each that tells students what they must learn about it. Write the statements on the Study Guide in the order in which you will teach them.

2. Include as much information about what students are supposed to learn as possible. Gifted students will use the Study Guide to learn the standards at their own pace while you are teaching the unit directly to the rest of the class, so task descriptions that are thorough result in fewer kids waiting in line for your attention! Examine the Study

text continues on page 79

Topic Development Sheet

Topic or unit to be learned: _____

Required Standards	Related Topics

Guides on page 80 and in chapter 4 to get an idea of how to word these tasks.

3. Insert the first checkpoint, along with the date at which it will occur, after standards statement number two. Schedule it to occur no more than three days after the unit begins. At that point, students who find they cannot demonstrate that they are keeping up with the required standards will return to the teacher-directed group for the remainder of the unit. This situation should be treated very matter-of-factly, and the students should feel comfortable knowing they will now be working with a format that is the best choice for them. They may return to the extension activity they started when the whole class does extension work at points during the unit or as a culminating activity at the unit's end.

4. Insert the second checkpoint, along with the date at which it will occur, after standards statement number five. This checkpoint will be cumulative for standards statements 1–5 for students who had to leave their independent work after the first checkpoint results. Those students are not required to "make up" the activities related to standards 1 and 2, because they were trying out the Study Guide Method at the time. Since the second checkpoint is cumulative, those same students will be assessed on all five standards at that point. Remember that all students, whether teacher-directed or working independently, will be experiencing all checkpoints together at the same time.

5. Insert the third and final checkpoint, along with the date it will occur, at the end of the Study Guide and make it cumulative for all the included standards.

Note: It is okay for the second and third checkpoints to actually happen later than the announced date if your teacher-directed students need more time, but they should never happen sooner. This is so students who are using the Study Guide method will know exactly what standards are being assessed on what day, which increases the likelihood they will be successful on those assessments.

Preparing the Extension Menu

1. Choose 8 of the related topics on the Topic Development Chart to create extension activities.

2. Write the extension activities. Use any or a combination of the thinking models described in chapter 5 on pages 145–163 to create activities that provide structure to your standards statement language on the Study Guide. Whichever model you choose, take the time to teach its components to the students, either to the whole class or to the students working on Study Guides.

3. In the extension activities, describe exactly what you expect the students to learn about the topics, but do not specify the precise ways students should share what they learn. We want to avoid situations in which a student is interested in the topic, but is not comfortable with the suggested product. Let students choose product ideas from the Product Choices Chart on page 87. Named products should always be negotiable. In subsequent units, add or subtract product options as the need arises.

Note: Younger students might feel more comfortable if you make specific product suggestions. However, they should always have the right to ask to create a different product to learn about a selected topic.

4. Record your 8 extension activities on the Extension Menu, leaving the center space free for Student Choice. Examine the Extension Menus in this book on pages 81, 111, 113, 114, 138, and 153. You'll find a reproducible blank Extension Menu form on page 83 and in the digital content.

text continues on page 84

American Wars Study Guide

Be prepared to:

1. Discuss the political, social, and economic causes of the war.

2. Explain the basis of the economy for both sides before the war began.

   *   **CHECKPOINT:**_____: **Assessment for 1–2**   *

DATE

3. Give the meanings of all designated vocabulary words.

4. Show on a map the disputed territory before the war began, at its midpoint, and at its end.

5. Recite from memory an important speech from this particular war period on a war-related topic. Be able to explain its background and significance.

   *   **CHECKPOINT:**_____: **Assessment for 1–5**   *

DATE

6. Describe typical battle conditions experienced by soldiers and commanders. Include information about commonly used battle tactics.

7. Narrate a first-person biographical sketch of a person connected to the war effort.

8. Write an account of a non-battle event related to the war and post it on an appropriate website.

9. Describe the peace plan—its location, components, and effects.

10. Summarize the implications of this war in today's time period. Hypothesize how history would have turned out differently if the other side had won. Make predictions for the decade following the war as well as for the present time.

   *   **CHECKPOINT:**_____: **Final Assessment for 1–10**   *

DATE

Present a detailed biography of an important person during the time of this conflict. Include evidence of this person's influence during the war period.	Research the patriotic music used by both sides in the war. Point out similarities and differences. Describe how music influences patriotism in civilians and soldiers. Compare the patriotic music of this war to that of other wars.	Locate information about the medical practices used on the battlefield and in field hospitals during this war. Include biographical information about famous medical people of that time.
Discover how military people communicated with each other and with their commander-in-chief during this war. Focus on events in which poorly understood or poorly delivered communications influenced the outcome of a military effort.	**Student Choice**	Investigate battles in which creative or uncommonly used tactics were employed. OR design strategies that you think would have led to more victories and fewer casualties. Be sure to use only the technology available during that time period.
Discover words or phrases that were "coined" during this war period and remain part of our English usage today.	Investigate other types of wars: between families, clans, children in school, mythical creatures, etc. Share information about them and include a comparison of elements found in a traditional war between countries.	Investigate and describe ways in which this conflict or wars in general could be avoided.

Study Guide

Be prepared to:

1. _____

2. _____

    *   CHECKPOINT:_____: Assessment for 1–2   *
                                 DATE

3. _____

4. _____

5. _____

    *   CHECKPOINT:_____: Assessment for 1–5   *
                                 DATE

6. _____

7. _____

8. _____

9. _____

10. _____

    *   CHECKPOINT:_____: Final Assessment for 1–10   *
                                 DATE

	Student Choice	

How to Use the Study Guide Method

The Study Guide with Extension Menu may be used for all grade levels, making appropriate adjustments as needed. For some students, it is preferable that they work only with the Study Guide *or* with the Study Guide with Extension Menu. The following sections will describe how to match each student with the best use of the Study Guide.

At the First Study Guide Meeting

1. Hold a Study Guide meeting to explain the method to *all* interested students. They can decide at the end of the meeting if they wish to try this method. Reassure them they will not miss required standards.

2. Distribute the Study Guide you have prepared for the target content. Explain all the standards and explain how the checkpoints will be used.

3. Explain that each student must choose which method they want to use by the next scheduled meeting (within three days): the *Study Guide Only* or the *Study Guide with Extension Menu.*

4. Tell students how their Study Guide work will be graded: "As the Study Guide shows, you will have to learn standards 1 and 2 before the first checkpoint when the whole class will have to demonstrate competence with those standards. If you can demonstrate that you have mastered those standards, you may keep working on your alternate topic or resident expert project until the next checkpoint. As long as you keep demonstrating mastery of the designated standards, and as long as you follow the working conditions described on your Independent Study Agreement (see page 90), you may continue doing your alternate work. If it becomes clear that you are not keeping up with what you need to learn, or you cannot meet the terms of the Independent Study Agreement, you will be expected to rejoin the teacher-directed group and do the assigned activities

from that day on. You may finish your project at home or when the rest of the class works on projects in class."

5. Explain that students will be tested only on the assigned topic on the checkpoint dates. For example, in a Tall Tale unit, they will be assessed only on the stories studied by the rest of the class, such as Paul Bunyan and Pecos Bill. There will be no formal assessments of the tall tales they are learning independently, or the alternate novels they are reading. However, they will be invited to share what they have learned with the class at certain times during the unit.

6. Describe the alternate choices for the Study Guide Only method. For example, if the class novel is *Sarah, Plain and Tall,* the Study Guide might be on Stories About Frontier Living. Make available a list of other novels with the same theme. Allow students to add more topics or books to your suggested list.

7. Take the time to describe and explain the topics on the Extension Menu, so that students who prefer this method know they have to choose only one topic to start with. You might say, "There's a lot more to this unit than is included in our required standards. I have also prepared an Extension Menu that you can use to become a resident expert on a topic related to our study of (name the generic topic). You will be expected to share some information with the class about your topic."

8. Explain the details about how they will share what they have learned with the class at certain times during the unit.

9. Allow students some time to study the Extension Menu and ask questions about it.

10. Announce the date of the second Study Guide meetings, and explain that by then students are expected to make their choice about which format to use and which extension activity they have chosen, if applicable.

11. Hold separate second meetings for students based on their chosen method. This prevents information overload and will probably lead

to better understanding of what is expected. You might color code the forms that belong to each option.

12. If students ask if they can work on their project at home, designate a section of the work to be done only at home, but make it clear that the work done at home will not be included in any formal grading.

Note: This Study Guide method is *not* designed only for differentiating homework after students have all participated in direct instruction on a particular day. It is designed to *replace* their school time with more independent study. Even though students may work on aspects of the topic at home, most of their Study Guide work, with or without the Extension Menu option, is to be done at school.

At the Second Meeting for Students Choosing the Study Guide Only

1. Examine the forms needed for this method. Students will use the same Study Guide and Daily Log of Extension Work as all others use, and a separate Independent Study Agreement on page 90.

2. Distribute the appropriate Independent Study Agreement (page 90) and go over each of its components slowly and carefully until students seem to understand the requirements for working independently. Once they understand and agree to each item, have them write their initials on the line to the left of the item. This represents their agreement to follow the requirement and their understanding that if they are not able to do so, they will join the teacher-directed group until the end of the unit.

3. Discuss grading with the students. Be sure they understand that their grade for the unit will come from a combination of their assessment results from all the checkpoints and their compliance with all the expected working conditions. Explain that the alternate work replaces the assigned work for the topic described on the Study Guide.

4. Remind students they will be expected to complete the assessments described at the checkpoints at the same time as the other students.

5. Describe how to use the Daily Log of Extension Work on page 92. The same log will be used for both groups.

At the Second Meeting for Students Choosing the Study Guide with Extension Menu

1. Examine the forms needed for this method. Students will use the same Study Guide and Daily Log of Extension Work as the students who are using the Study Guide only. However, they will use a separate Independent Study Agreement on page 91 as well as the Evaluation Contract on page 96.

2. Give students time to choose their preferred extension activity. Provide advice and approval for anyone who wants to suggest their own activity. Ask them to write out what they will do as a task statement, similar to the other task statements on the Extension Menu.

3. Remind students about the checkpoints and all the working conditions, and ask students to write their initials on the line to the left of each statement to indicate their intent to comply with it.

Note: All students who are working independently will use the *same* Study Guide and the same Daily Log of Extension Work.

IMPORTANT Be sure to reassure both Study Guide groups about the difference between "more" and "different" work. Tell them: "Please understand that this does not mean more work for you, since you do not have to actually do the activities described on the Study Guide. You just have to learn the described content, take the same assessments as others do, and spend lots of time learning about your selected topic for independent study."

The Product Choices Chart

After students choose a topic from the Extension Menu, they can use the Product Choices Chart to choose a way to represent the information they find. You might choose four or five from each column for each topic so that students are not overwhelmed by the huge list. The chart describes four types of products, three of which are linked to the learning modalities: auditory, visual, and tactile-kinesthetic. A fourth column suggests digital products that might be posted on your school's website or Intranet where grandparents, friends, and even students and teachers from other schools can view them to share the enjoyment of your students' work!

Auditory learners like typical school tasks that allow them to think logically, sequentially, and analytically. They like to read, write, make oral presentations, argue, and debate.

Visual learners like to make posters, dioramas, collages, pictures, video clips, iMovies, and other digital presentations, or other visual products.

Tactile-kinesthetic learners prefer demonstrations, Reader's Theater, skits, plays, role plays, or working with hands-on materials.

Don't be concerned if a student always chooses products from the same list. Your obligation is to demonstrate that students have mastered the content. How they show their mastery is of secondary importance. A reproducible Product Choices Chart is found on page 87. Further discussion of learning modalities can be found in chapter 5, page 143.

Tools to Use with the Study Guide

Like any form of compacting and differentiation, the Study Guide method should be carefully documented. This helps you know that your students are learning the required material, it holds students accountable for their learning, and it gives you a way to show parents and administrators that even though your gifted kids aren't doing the regular work, they're still learning what they're supposed to know. It also gives you proof in writing that you're providing numerous differentiation opportunities for each unit.

Like any form of compacting and differentiation, the Study Guide method should be carefully documented.

The Independent Study Agreement

The Independent Study Agreement is designed to guard against misunderstandings, disagreements, and claims such as, "You never told me I had to learn some content on my own!" All students who choose to use the Study Guide, with or without the Extension Menu, must enter into an agreement with you that describes the conditions of their independent study, including both learning conditions and working conditions. If students fail to meet the conditions, the logical consequence is that they will have to return to the teacher-directed group for the remainder of the unit.

There are two versions of the agreement: The Independent Study Agreement for Study Guide Only and the Independent Study Agreement for Study Guide with Extension Menu. Reproducible agreements are found on pages 90 and 91. Feel free to change any of the conditions or add new ones of your own. Those that are included describe things many teachers fear might go wrong with this method. Once all these issues have been openly resolved, you can relax knowing you have covered all the necessary bases.

Hand out copies of the Independent Study Agreement you decide to use. Go over the agreement with the students and make sure they understand all of the conditions.

You might say: "This agreement explains my expectations for you while you are working independently. As you agree to each condition, please write your initials on the line to the left. Then sign your agreement, and I'll sign it, too. Keep your agreement with your Study Guide at all times, and always keep both at school. They should *not* go

text continues on page 88

The Product Choices Chart

Auditory	Visual	Tactile-Kinesthetic	Technology
Audio recording	Advertisement	Acting things out	Animation
Autobiography	Art gallery	Activity plan for trip	App
Book	Brochure	Collection	Blog
Classifying	Coat of arms	Composing music	Broadcast over TV, radio, or the internet
Commentary	Collage	Dance	
Crossword puzzle	Coloring page	Demonstration	Competition
Debate or panel talk	Comic book or strip	Diorama	Cyberhunt
Dialogue	Costume	Dramatization	Digital game
Documentary	Decoration	Exhibit	Forum
Editorial	Design	Experiment	iMovie
Essay	Diagram	Field experience	Multidimensional video (e.g., 3D)
Experiment	Diorama	Flip book or chart	
Family tree	Drawing or painting	Game	Online quiz
Finding patterns	Flow chart	Game show	Podcast
Glossary	Graphic organizer	How-to book	Presentation
Interview	Greeting card	Invention	Research
Journal or diary	Hidden pictures	Jigsaw puzzle	Song or jingle
Learning Center task	Multimedia presentation program	Learning Center— hands-on tasks	Virtual site visit
Letter to editor/author		Manipulatives	Webquest
Limerick or riddle	Illustrated manual	Mobile	
Mystery	Illustrations	Model	
Newspaper	Learning Center visuals	Museum exhibit	
Oral report	Magazine	Patter creation/ demonstration	
Pattern and instructions	Map	Papier-mâché	
Petition	Mural	Photograph	
Position paper	Pamphlet with pictures or icons	Play or skit	
Press conference		Pop-up book	
Reading	Photo album	Project cube	
Scavenger hunt	Photo essay	Puppet show	
Simulation game	Picture dictionary	Rap or rhyme	
Song lyrics	Political cartoon	Reader's theater	
Speech	Portfolio	Rhythmic pattern	
Story or poem	Poster	Role-play	
Survey	Rebus story	Scale drawing	
Teaching a lesson	Scrapbook	Sculpture	
Trip itinerary	Slide show	Simulation game	
Written report (Auditory because people write thoughts they "hear" in their minds)	Travelogue	Survey	
	TV program		
	Video		
	Website		

home until your project is completed. If you work on your project outside the classroom at another location in school, bring your Study Guide and Independent Study Agreement with you."

When students take these documents with them outside the classroom, the librarian, media center specialist, or other adult has concrete evidence that students are expected to behave appropriately and stay on task while they are away from the classroom. He or she also has been told by you that it is okay to send these students back to your room if they are not following the agreement's expectations.

A few conditions described in the agreement might need additional explanation. Share as much of this with your students as you think will be helpful.

"I will participate in designated whole-class activities as the teacher indicates without protesting."

You most likely involve your students in many other interesting and stimulating activities, some of which everyone should be present to experience. Reserve the option of calling in your Study Guide students for these "special events," which might include field trips, speakers, video or film events, simulations, or other activities all students will enjoy. Since it may be difficult to pinpoint at the beginning of a unit the exact dates on which such events will occur, reserve the right to announce that today (or tomorrow) will be a whole-class activity. When the special event ends, the Study Guide students are free to return to their independent work.

"I will share a progress report about my independent project with the class or other audience by (date). It will not exceed five minutes and will include a helpful visual aid. I will prepare a question about my report to ask the class."

Resident experts should prepare a high-level question to ask the class. (See Build Blocks to Think on page 162.) This question should be recorded where everyone can see it before the progress report begins. An additional "mystery question" is allowed but not required. This sets up ideal conditions for listeners. If resident experts are given your Name Cards (see page 14) to use to call on students, listening will be magically accurate!

Resident experts (students working on Extension Menu projects) are not required to complete an entire project by the end of the unit. That's why their reports are called "progress reports." In real life, researchers may spend a lifetime on one research project. If they never finish, some other researcher will take up the same topic and continue the work.

The more often you bring the resident experts back for "special events," the less time they have to work on their project. Gifted kids have a unique capacity for wanting to learn all there is to know about a topic of interest. If they think their learning will be limited by a timeline, they might not volunteer for the Study Guide option again. In the real world, the goal of long-term research is accuracy and being able to make a contribution to a certain field, not to simply "finish" the work by a designated time.

Why would you want them finishing their projects quickly, since that would mean you have to help them find and plan another? The best thing that could happen is for a student to become so engrossed in a project that he or she wants to work on it for many weeks or extend it to subsequent units. As long as the learning and working conditions are being met, there is no reason to insist that students stop working on a project that clearly interests them just because the class is moving on to another topic. As an example, Cleon did not want to give up his train project when the Civil War unit was finished. Mrs. Hernandez was fine with that since he would receive the Study Guide for the next unit on Westward Expansion and he would be responsible for demonstrating he was learning that material at each checkpoint. So Cleon was allowed to extend his Civil War train project to a Westward Expansion train project. This allowed for him to compare and contrast the railway systems when he completed both aspects of the project.

Of course, it's also okay if resident experts want to switch topics at the end of the unit. Remember, they are still being held accountable for the required standards. They will be given a new Study Guide for the next unit for which they will also be held accountable for learning what the other students learn during the same time frame. If this bothers you or the child's parents, you might consider asking students to complete one of every three projects they begin.

Note: The report does not have to be written. Writing slows down the mental processing for many gifted kids. The purpose of the report is to demonstrate that kids are learning alternate material. The format should be decided by the student, with your approval.

The Daily Log of Extension Work

The Daily Log of Extension Work is useful as a portfolio record sheet and helpful in conferences with parents and administrators. It also helps gifted underachievers and perfectionists who have trouble completing long-term projects. A reproducible Daily Log is found on page 92.

Hand out copies of the Daily Log of Extension Work and tell students how to use it:

> "At the start of any class period during which you are planning or working on your project, fill in the left column with the date and the center column with a brief description of what you plan to accomplish during that one class period. Five minutes before the end of the period, complete the right column by recording information about the work you successfully accomplished. I will remind you to do this for the first week or so."

Tips for Using the Daily Log of Extension Work

■ Never take a student off a project just because he isn't keeping good records. This is a skill many gifted kids have to learn; it doesn't automatically come with high intelligence. Offer frequent reminders and modeling as long as needed.

■ By giving kids permission to accomplish less than they planned, you are teaching them an important survival skill: The world won't end if you don't finish everything today. State, "If you discover that you accomplished less than you planned, drop down to the next line in the center column and write a note about where to start again the next time you return to the project. Don't write a date because you may not know when you will have more time to work on

it. During your next working period, the note you wrote to yourself on your Daily Log will tell you where to pick up your work in progress."

■ Remind your students, "Remember that your Daily Log is *never* to leave the classroom until the class moves on to another unit. You may not take it home or to another room in the school, and do not put it in your backpack. It must stay in this room so that you have it handy whenever you need it to record progress on your project." The one exception to this rule is when you choose to send the Daily Log home with students to show their parents, along with extension work, a Learning Contract, and the Extension Activities and Differentiated Homework Report (page 94).

■ Show students the place where their Daily Logs will be stored. If you have several classes during the day, use color-coded folders to distinguish between classes. At the same time, demonstrate the method you want students to use to keep track of their papers related to this method. Pocket or manila file folders kept in a crate for hanging file folders works well. Provide a folder for each student in the class, since other students will have opportunities for project work every so often.

■ If your students are working at a location outside the classroom, ask the adult or older student who is monitoring them to tell the students to return to class before the end of the period. This will give them time to complete their Daily Logs and hear any announcements or discussion of plans for the following day.

> **NOTE** Have regular checkup meetings with your Study Guide students. Some students will reject this option if they observe that you rarely spend time with students who are working independently. Provide technical assistance with their projects and give them their fair share of your time and attention. Coach them on improving their research and record-keeping skills. Make sure their Daily Logs are up-to-date and they are keeping up with the learning goals listed on the Study Guide.

text continues on page 93

Independent Study Agreement
for Study Guide Only

Read each condition as your teacher reads it aloud. Write your initials beside it to show that you understand it and agree to abide by it.

Learning Conditions

_____ I will learn independently all the required standards described on the Study Guide. I will not have to complete the actual assigned activities as long as I am doing work related to what the class is learning.

_____ I will demonstrate competency with the assessments for the Study Guide content at the same time as the rest of the class.

_____ I will participate in designated whole-class activities as the teacher indicates them—without arguing.

_____ I will keep a Daily Log of my progress.

_____ I will share what I have learned about my independent study with the class in an interesting way. My report will not exceed five minutes and will include a visual aid. I will prepare a question about my report to ask the class when my report ends.

Working Conditions

_____ I will be present in the classroom at the beginning and end of each class period.

_____ I will not bother anyone or call attention to the fact that I am doing different work than others in the class.

_____ I will work on my chosen topic for the entire class period on designated days.

_____ I will carry this paper with me to any room in which I am working on my chosen topic, and I will return it to my classroom at the end of each session.

Student's Signature: _____

Teacher's Signature: _____

Date: _____

Independent Study Agreement for Study Guide with Extension Menu

Read each condition as your teacher reads it aloud. Write your initials beside it to show that you understand it and agree to abide by it.

Learning Conditions

_____ I will learn independently all the required standards described on the Study Guide. I will not have to complete the actual assigned activities as long as I am working on an independent project.

_____ I will demonstrate competency with the assessments for the Study Guide content at the same time as the rest of the class.

_____ I will participate in designated whole-class activities as the teacher indicates them—without arguing.

_____ I will keep a Daily Log of my progress.

_____ I will work on an independent project and complete an Evaluation Contract to describe the grade I will choose to earn.

_____ I will share a progress report about my independent project with the class or other audience by _____ (date). My report will not exceed five minutes and will include a visual aid. I will prepare a question about my report to ask the class when my report ends.

Working Conditions

_____ I will be present in the classroom at the beginning and end of each class period.

_____ I will not bother anyone or call attention to the fact that I am doing different work than others in the class.

_____ I will work on my project for the entire class period on designated days.

_____ I will carry this paper with me to any room in which I am working on my project, and I will return it to my classroom at the end of each session.

Student's Signature: _____

Teacher's Signature: _____

Date: _____

Daily Log of Extension Work

Student's Name: _____

Project Topic: _____

Today's Date	What I Plan to Do During Today's Work Period	What I Actually Accomplished Today

Extension Activities and Differentiated Homework Report

Your students' parents will greatly appreciate knowing the steps you are taking to differentiate their gifted students' learning experiences. The form on page 94 might be used at the end of each unit in which students experienced differentiation. The part of the form that is returned to you should be kept in the student's compacting folder.

The Teacher's Role in Independent Study

As a teacher, your role with gifted students is to be the "guide on the side" rather than the "sage on the stage." Since these students' abilities to quickly learn something and then take off and run with it on their own make them welcome opportunities to work independently, they appreciate a teacher who can smoothly facilitate that process and directly teach only when students need instruction. However, it is important to be aware that in all grades, kids appreciate knowing that you are willing to support their independent learning preferences and that you will not ignore them in the process. Remember that when they encounter challenging advanced learning material, they still need a teacher's guidance.

When students encounter challenging advanced learning material, they still need a teacher's guidance.

Following are several ways to make this happen:

- When other students are working alone or in groups, spend time with the kids using the Study Guide method.

- When your class is reading independently for 10–15 minutes, meet with your Study Guide kids.

- Invite your Study Guide kids to eat lunch with you in the classroom once a week.

- Invite an interested parent to come into your classroom to help kids locate resources, to supervise time spent on the internet, or to provide any other helpful services.

- Require students to keep all documents related to the Study Guide method at school at all times. Provide special folders for that purpose, and keep the folders in a central location.

- If students are having significant trouble completing tasks, show them how to use the Check-Off Sheet for Resident Expert Project (see page 182).

If parents wish to assist with the project at home, identify a separate part of the project as the "home project." Evaluate it separately from the school part of the project. We don't want to average it in with the work done in school if it gives an unfair advantage to some students with an extremely helpful and available parent. Suggest that the student keep a separate Daily Log at home to document the differentiated homework. See chapter 6 for more information on independent study as it relates to self-selected topics.

Assessing Study Guide Work: The Evaluation Contract
(for use with the Study Guide with Extension Menu)

If you, the student, and the student's parents are comfortable with the actual grade for the content area units coming from only the assessments at the checkpoints, then no other grade is required for Study Guide work. But by the time students are old enough to benefit from the Study Guide approach, they may have developed a resistance to doing any work that is not accompanied by a grade; the Evaluation Contract addresses that issue.

Once students choose a project from the Extension Menu, they indicate their choice on the Evaluation Contract (page 96) and specify the grade they want to earn for their work, based on the level of work they will do. When you hand out copies of the contract, say something like this:

"I will record your checkpoint assessment grades as you earn them. All other blank spots in the grade book will be filled in with your contracted grade for your resident

text continues on page 95

Extension Activities and Differentiated Homework Report

Student's name _____

Teacher's name _____

Date _____

Subject area represented _____

Time period covered _____

Dear Parent/Caregiver:

Your child will share with you some of the differentiated learning activities he or she worked on during the unit we just completed. Please take some time to allow your child to explain what was done. Then place a checkmark in the boxes if you agree with the statements.

☐ YES—My student showed me the extension activities and differentiated homework from this unit and explained some of those activities she or he liked the best. We also talked about the ones that were very challenging and I congratulated my student on her or his willingness to work hard!

☐ YES—I understand that this work represents the differentiated and more challenging learning activities that are being provided for my student in your classroom.

Please sign and date below. Write any comments and have your child return this form and the Daily Log of Extension Work to me within a week. Thank you for your assistance.

Parent's or Caregiver's signature _____ Date _____

Comments _____

_____

_____

_____

_____

expert project. That grade will replace the grade you would have earned from doing the regular daily work with the rest of the class, from which you have been excused."

The Evaluation Contract has a space where students describe the project they plan to do. They can use words or draw a diagram. This is your chance to check the appropriateness of each project. A resident expert project should be:

- Broad enough to be relevant to the unit.

- Complex enough to hold the student's interest for an extended period of time.

- Sophisticated enough to provide a valid showcase for the student's talents.

- Manageable enough for the student to work independently.

- Reflective of the student's ability to think in abstract and complex ways.

> **IMPORTANT** Because Extension Menus describe learning on different levels of thinking models such as the Taxonomy of Thinking (see page 145), you will want to make sure your students understand what this means. It is productive to teach each section as a critical thinking lesson so students are familiar with the concepts of various levels and kinds of thinking. So instead of saying, "Choose a high-level task," they will know, from their learning experience, exactly how a Recall activity is different from one that requires analysis. In other words, don't just tell them about levels and give them the verbs to describe them—create an activity so they can actually have an experience with each type of thinking task.

The Evaluation Contract also includes a generic rubric that may be used to evaluate any project. The rubrics exist to help students produce high-quality work on their projects. Rubrics can eliminate the frustration we face when students work on a project for a long time and produce disappointing products.

The grade earned by a resident expert should reflect the complexity and sophistication of the content and thought process used, rather than the appearance of the product or the number of activities done by the student. A grade below B is not possible, since the student would have to revise the work until the basic conditions for an acceptable grade had been met. After all, if a student could get a recorded grade lower than a B, why should she or he volunteer for the Study Guide options? See chapter 8 for more information on assessment.

The Study Guide Method Summarized

- Students who choose the Study Guide, with or without the Extension Menu, are allowed to work in this more independent path through the required standards as long as their assessment results for this content are at an acceptable level. If at any assessment point they are not able to demonstrate competency at the required levels, they must return to the teacher-directed format for the remainder of the unit. If that happens, the independent study on which they were working may be completed outside of class for alternate credit or during the time the entire class is working on Extension Menus.

- Students are excused from doing the daily work assigned to the class as long as they meet the learning and working conditions set forth in the Independent Study Agreement.

- Students who work on these independent study options are expected to share what they have learned with their classmates, thus enriching the unit for all students in the class.

- When time permits, all students can work on activities from the Extension Menu for a shorter time period, perhaps in groups, as a culminating experience at the end of the unit.

- Students who choose this method must complete an Independent Study Agreement, an Evaluation Contract, if applicable, and a Daily Log of their progress.

- Select some time each week to meet with students working more independently to

text continues on page 97

Evaluation Contract

I am choosing a grade for my project based on these criteria:

For a grade of B:

1. I will use secondary sources of information that have been gathered and recorded by other people, including some from several reliable websites.

2. I will prepare a traditional product. I will present it using a traditional reporting format.

3. I will be learning on the lower levels of Bloom's Taxonomy: Recall, Understand, and Apply. This means that I will find information and be able to describe what I've learned.

For a grade of A:

1. I will use primary sources that were created by me or people who lived during the time about which I am learning. These include interviews, diaries, speeches, letters, official records, creative products, virtual tours, and other sources.

2. I will produce an original type of product. I will present it to an appropriate audience using a unique format.

3. I will be learning on the higher levels of Bloom's Taxonomy: Analyze, Evaluate, and Create.

This is the project I will do: _____

_____

_____

_____

_____

This is the grade I intend to earn: _____

Student's signature: _____

Teacher's signature: _____

Date: _____

assess their progress and assist them in their research.

■ Expect students to keep a folder of their independent work in your classroom so they always have it to work on. Anything that goes home would represent the "home part" of the project, and although it would be included in the project report, it is not considered as part of the grade.

QUESTIONS ★ ANSWERS

"What happens if the resident experts don't finish their projects?"

Ask yourself why you want them to finish their projects. Once they're through, you'll have to help them find and start another! Remind yourself that people who make their living in research sometimes spend a lifetime working on one project. Often, the only deadlines they have to meet are related to getting their grant applications in on time. So they hire logical-sequential thinkers with a penchant for meeting deadlines who are very successful at keeping the project on track.

Besides, your resident experts have to be ready for the checkpoint assessments, so they *are* meeting deadlines. If it weren't for the Study Guide option, that's all the content they would be learning. We need to lighten up about deadlines for independent study projects.

If you require your resident experts to participate in many whole-class activities and special events, this further limits the time they have available to work on their projects.

Some kids may not want to carry their current project into the next unit of work. Others will want to work on only one project for the semester or year. Always remember that the Study Guide holds students accountable for the required content. Make your decisions about their project preferences on an individual basis. It's absolutely justified to hold students accountable for the progress reports as described on the Independent Study Agreement.

Keeping all this in mind, there may be times when you and a student decide it's in his or her best interests to return to the direct instruction group for the daily work. If you create resident expert opportunities for the entire class as a culminating activity, the student could finish his or her project at that time.

"What happens if students purposefully sabotage their results on an assessment because they really want to stop working on their project?"

During your initial meetings with the students, be sure they understand they should talk to you about any frustrations they encounter as they work through this method. During your checkup meetings as the unit progresses, ask students directly about their comfort level with the Study Guide method. If they are feeling overwhelmed, help them select smaller chunks to work on one at a time, rather than worrying about the entire project all at once. Show them how the Daily Log of Extension Work can help them break overwhelming tasks into more manageable short-term goals. If you want to make the goal-setting focus even more obvious, use the Goal-Setting Log (see page 21).

"How can I make sure that a student's parents don't become overly involved in trying to influence the content or quality of the resident expert project?"

Interested parents can assist their resident experts by helping them locate information, either by taking them to museums or finding other sources of information. Or a certain portion of the project may be designated as the "home part." It is not included in the formal evaluation but may be included in the progress report. The student keeps a Daily Log at home to record progress there. In this way, even homework can be differentiated.

Remember that the project doesn't go home until it is completed. It is designed to be done in school so more capable students have meaningful work to do while the rest of the class is learning the basics with the teacher. The project represents the student's "real work" in school, and it must be available in school whenever it is needed. This includes work on any visual aid.

"How can I guarantee that students' independent work will be of high quality?"

Keep in mind that quality is measured not so much by the product's physical appearance, but by its substance. However, the Evaluation Contract (page 96) is designed to let students know certain conditions must be met for the project. You can also use John Samara's Product Guides and Bertie Kingore's Portfolio Assessment tools for this purpose. See the references and resources section on page 237.

"Are identified gifted kids or kids who have been placed in a gifted cluster automatically able to use the Study Guide method?"

No, they are not. Always remember that gifted kids who have been identified for a cluster in your classroom must demonstrate they are ready for and would benefit from any compacting or differentiation option in the same way other students are asked to demonstrate it. Likewise, any student who has not been identified as gifted, but who can meet the criteria for eligibility for differentiation, should be allowed to participate in the compacting plan. For more about cluster grouping, see chapter 7.

"What if a resident expert is extremely uncomfortable presenting a progress report to the class, or just refuses to do it?"

You might provide an alternate audience— another class, a community group interested in the topic, or even a private conference with you.

Chapter Summary

If you have ever been in a situation in which you felt you were trapped by the need to be polite to a teacher or lecturer, even though the content was extremely boring, you can understand how gifted students feel when, for the sake of struggling students, we slow down the pace of learning to a point at which it becomes completely ineffective for advanced learners. This chapter has demonstrated two ways in which to compact and differentiate the curriculum in subject areas that are completely new to students.

The Study Guide Only option allows gifted students to study other examples of the specific unit being learned by the class. The Study Guide with Extension Menu invites students to become resident experts on topics related to the regular curriculum learning new material from a more challenging perspective.

You have learned specific, classroom-tested ways to compact and differentiate instruction for students in subject areas that may or may not lend themselves to pretesting. Some teachers still provide pretesting opportunities in these subjects and use the Learning Contract approach described in chapter 3 to manage the alternate activities for students who pass the pretest. Some teachers pretest and use the Independent Study Agreement to manage the students' alternate activities. The choice is yours!

Assumptions — teach elem. or English
Agree — Vocab. activities w/
Argue to Vocab etymology
builders; Vocab
builders
Aspire to / Act upon
Etymology

Spelling
in school,
spelling,
grammar,
mechanics

CHAPTER 4
Extending Reading and Writing Instruction

How well are your reading and writing programs meeting the needs of students who are gifted in those areas? How can you accommodate the passion for reading shared by so many gifted students? How can you provide appropriate challenges in all of the language arts for students who need it? This chapter answers these and other questions. It also describes a host of reading and language arts strategies that challenge gifted students and may be used as extension activities.

Characteristics of Readers Who Are Gifted

When trying to identify the advanced readers in your classroom, look for students who:

- Comprehend reading materials that are two or more years above grade level.

- Understand abstract ideas quickly and easily; have very little to learn from being required to participate in grade-level reading instruction.

- Know, understand, appreciate, and use advanced vocabulary.

- Love to read and do so with great concentration and enthusiasm.

- Retain what they read for a long time.

- Make connections between various reading selections and between what they are reading and other content areas.

- Understand authors' styles and the uses of various literary elements.

- Read earlier than age peers. Some are spontaneous preschool readers; some start school having already mastered basic reading skills. Most learn to read independently soon after classroom instruction begins.

- Need less drill to master reading skills and techniques, because they usually learn new content after one direct instruction lesson.

- Need opportunities to read at their own pace and demonstrate previous or early mastery of reading skills and vocabulary.

- Interact with what they read in creative ways. Gifted students don't simply read and absorb. They also question, examine, contemplate, argue, discuss, elaborate, and come up with new ideas based on what they read. They speak and write using complex sentences and vocabulary that are significantly more advanced than what is being produced by their age peers.

- Have interests in reading that set them apart from other readers. Their preferences may include science, history, science fiction, biography, travel, poetry, and informational texts, even sometimes those written for adults.

Scenario: Eric

Eric had failed fifth grade once, and he was now the tallest and biggest boy in his class. His former teachers described him as "lazy" because he never completed his homework in any subject. Some referred to his "poor attitude." Eric refused to read the stories from the required reader, never even opened his workbook, and had been overheard proclaiming, "I hate reading. It's dumb!" Over the years, he had spent many hours in the principal's office where he was often sent by frustrated teachers.

Eric's new teacher noticed that he always had a magazine about cars or trucks hidden in his desk. Eric delighted in challenging his classmates to a contest of wits over the engine capacity and speed potential of the latest cars, and he always seemed to have that information at his fingertips. It was obvious to his teacher that he was actually reading and understanding the material in his magazines. Yet he was still failing all of his classes, including reading.

One weekend, Eric's teacher attended a seminar on teaching gifted students. While listening to a description of characteristic behaviors of gifted kids, she realized that she had observed many of those behaviors in Eric. Upon returning to school, the teacher arranged to meet with other teachers and the school principal. She asked them to tell her which students came to mind as she read aloud a list of characteristic behaviors. Eric's name was mentioned over and over again. Could it be that his school problems were caused by boredom and frustration rather than laziness or a poor attitude?

The teacher decided to test her theory by offering Eric pretesting and compacting opportunities in several subjects, including reading skills and vocabulary. At first, Eric seemed unable to believe that a teacher would allow him to demonstrate mastery by doing less work than he had previously been asked to do. When he learned that he could spend class time reading his magazines, as well as novels and books about car racing and race drivers, he couldn't believe what he was hearing.

The results were nothing short of miraculous. Within days, Eric was on the right learning track, completing his compacted work quickly and demonstrating a more positive attitude about school than anyone on staff had ever observed. His mother commented to the teacher about the remarkable changes she was seeing in her son. After about two weeks, the principal dropped by the class to see if Eric had been out sick since he was no longer being sent to the office to be disciplined! Eric's story provides ample evidence that modifying the curriculum can help us see gifted kids we once perceived as lazy in a totally new light.

Teaching Reading to Gifted Learners

Most reading programs, whether traditional or literature-based, fail to meet the advanced learning needs of gifted students. Most high-ability students have already mastered the vocabulary and skills they will be expected to "learn" in any given year. They need opportunities to demonstrate those competencies and to work with advanced reading materials in order to maintain their natural enthusiasm for reading.

Most reading programs fail to meet the advanced learning needs of gifted students.

Gifted students who are exceptionally strong readers process and understand materials designed for older students. Therefore, their instruction in reading must be differentiated from the program that is suitable for grade-level learners. It should focus on interacting with more complex or higher-level reading and comprehension skills. The books these students read should be excellent examples of rigorous use of language, syntax, and challenging literary elements such as simile, metaphor, allegory, foreshadowing, and others. Content should demonstrate challenging examples of enriched language and multiple opportunities for readers to experience the interaction of text with critical and creative thinking.

Critical reading is more complex than the ability to simply comprehend the text. To be a critical reader, the student must be able to assess the selection's effectiveness and understand its use of highly challenging content. Appropriately challenging selections allow students to experience reading as a series of thinking processes. Readers are encouraged to project their own attitudes and experiences into the story. Advanced vocabulary study complements gifted learners' delight with etymologies, syntax variations, and the use of customized vocabularies for different reading and writing purposes.

When readers who are gifted are grouped together, their entire reading experience is greatly enhanced. They feel safe in articulating their thoughts, reactions, and emotions, and can feel confident that the other students in their group will understand, identify with, and react appropriately to all that happens in the group. They enjoy less-structured approaches to their reading instruction and activities. Opportunities for meaningful choices allow students to feel connected to the text and characters in unique and satisfying ways.

Scenario: McKensi

McKensi came to our school as a first grader. When she was tested for academic placement, she scored at the sixth-grade level in reading comprehension. All other scores were near her age level. She was placed in a third-grade reading program and worked with her age-mates in all other subject areas. In early December, her teacher asked for help from the gifted program coordinator.

The teacher explained that she was frustrated because McKensi would not complete her reading assignments, which consisted of completing first-grade phonics workbook pages. When asked why McKensi had to do that work, the teacher replied, "Just because McKensi is reading at an advanced level does not mean she knows the phonics rules." The coordinator explained that since the goal of phonics is to learn accurate decoding and word recognition, and since the child was using some method that worked well enough to allow her to pronounce words correctly and easily handle the third-grade reading program, it was unnecessary for her to complete the required first-grade phonics program. The teacher was relieved to hear this information and appreciated the "permission" to allow McKensi's decoding ability to speak for itself. The requirement for the phonics assignments—both classroom work and homework—was released, and everyone involved breathed a sigh of relief.

For all skill and vocabulary work, you can provide regular pretesting and compacting opportunities using the methods described in chapters 2 and 3. You'll find a blank reading contract on page 108 of this chapter and a sample writing contract on page 137. Contracts allow you to see which vocabulary words and specific reading and writing skills students have already mastered. Students who demonstrate mastery should be engaged in alternate activities at the same time as others in the class are working on the standard instruction. Ideas for alternate activities are presented throughout this chapter.

The reading program that is most appropriate for all students and essential for gifted students is one that allows them to read, discuss, analyze, and write about literature that challenges them, while excusing them from practicing skills they have already mastered. They should be able to do this either independently or while grouped with other advanced readers. The literature that advanced students read should:

- Include a variety of forms including prose, poetry, biographies, nonfiction, and outside sources including newspapers, magazines, and journals, both print and digital.

- Be open to other interpretations and various viewpoints.

- Contain rich, challenging, and varied language forms.

- Provide opportunities for them to learn personal problem-solving behaviors that are relevant to their lives and experiences.

CAUTION Be careful about having kids read books that offer challenging vocabulary and content but describe situations that are beyond the levels of their maturity and life experiences.

In some districts, teachers are expected to use whole-class instruction, keeping all students on the same reading level, even on the same page. Although there may be a good reason to prevent students from using basal texts assigned to different grade levels, their access to literature at all levels of reading should never be restricted. Some staffs or districts have decided to earmark a limited number of novels for each grade level, and they have asked their colleagues to refrain from using those books not assigned to their particular grade. When the number of restricted novels is limited, this practice is perfectly reasonable, since there is clearly an abundance of available materials from which students may choose their independent reading selections. However, trying to convince enthusiastic readers that they should postpone reading a book they are interested in just because they will read it later in class is probably an exercise in futility!

One of the most significant purposes of teaching reading is to generate a lifelong love of literature. Any classroom practices that accomplish

that goal should be preferable to those that cause students to avoid reading and writing whenever they can. Talk to parents about their kids' attitudes toward reading at home, and observe the extent to which your students choose to read when they have opportunities to make choices in the classroom. Incorporating highly motivating strategies such as those presented in this chapter will help you keep your gifted learners enthusiastic about reading.

The figure on page 103 shows, at a glance, how you might differentiate reading for your gifted students.

Reading for Gifted Children in the Primary Grades

Not all gifted kids come to kindergarten reading, and not all kids who come to kindergarten reading are gifted. But show us a youngster who taught herself to read without any apparent support from adults and we'll bet the child is gifted.

For decades, educators believed that most kids who were reading when they started school would "plateau out" or revert to the levels of more average readers by third grade. Many of those who did plateau were cited as proof that they were taught to read before they were truly ready. Recent studies have shown that advanced readers who were expected to do the *regular* reading program in kindergarten and first grade did become more average later, but advanced readers who were taught at their challenge level, regardless of their grade level, generally continued at advanced levels into the upper grades. Advanced readers need to be taught at their challenge level in reading, regardless of how soon (or late) they learn to read.

Dr. Bertie Kingore discusses this dilemma in her book *Reading Strategies for Advanced Primary Readers*:

> For decades, educators assumed that children who read early or at advanced levels had been pushed by a well-intending adult. The accompanying conventional wisdom has been that these students plateau and read at grade level by third or fourth grade. Indeed, advanced readers who are limited to a grade-level reading

Differentiating Reading

Whole-Group Instruction	Differentiation for Readers Who Are Gifted
All read the same book	All read different books on the same theme
Whole-class learning	Study Guide Only or with Extension Menu (see page 73)
Students read different books but do the same learning tasks	Students read self-selected books and do differentiated learning tasks
Skill work by direct instruction	Compacting and contracts for selective skill work and faster pacing
Theme-based literature circles; teacher-directed learning	Self-selected literature with Study Guide Only or with Extension Menu (see page 73)/ Reading Activities Menu (see page 109)
Standards and regular curriculum are taught directly to students	Students take direct instruction only on content they have not mastered
Great Friday Afternoon Event (see page 141)	Great Friday Afternoon Event (see page 141)

program can regress in their pace of progress. However, when advanced readers are taught with resources and instruction commensurate with their needs and abilities, regression need not take place. By eliminating work on skills already mastered and progressing through the language arts curriculum at an accelerated pace, students generally continued to extend their reading proficiency (Gentry, 1999; Kulik & Kulik, 1996).

The lack of challenging materials is one factor that discourages the continued reading development of advanced readers. However bright students may be, they are less likely to demonstrate advanced or gifted performance if learning experiences are limited to the regular, grade-level reading curriculum (p. 111).

You can use the pretest and contract methods described in chapters 2 and 3 with your precocious primary readers. The Contract for Reading Skills and Vocabulary in this chapter (page 108) can also be helpful. For litereature, use either the Study Guide Only as a genre or author guide, or with a related Extension Menu. Read the section, "Especially for Primary Teachers" in chapter 2 on page 61 for suggestions on how to manage differentiation for students in the primary grades.

Alternative Reading Approaches for Primary Students

Readers who are gifted should experience compacting opportunities in all work involving reading skills. You might use the Most Difficult First strategy or even weekly pretests. They should be allowed to read self-selected books while the class learns a skill or has a discussion in which they do not need to participate. You can provide weekly meetings for the independent reading group and center discussions on book or story recommendations, author styles, genre components, character development, interesting vocabulary, plot details, and unique qualities of particular books. Instruction on skills or literature aspects that require more directed teaching are included in this group time. Avoid round-robin reading, as it slows down the excited reading pace of advanced readers. Don't worry about errors in oral reading, advanced readers often skip words as their eyes dance far ahead on the page. The only accurate test of a reader's ability is comprehension.

Ask students to participate in some of the reading lessons, if you determine that their time would be well spent in that way. Your skills of diagnosing what students need to make continuous forward progress, combined with your skills of prescribing specific beneficial activities, can present a reading program that will keep gifted learners very interested and enthusiastic.

Students should not be required to finish a book before being allowed to share what they are reading at these small group meetings. Book reports in a formal way are never required. Instead, the group discusses alternative methods for sharing what they have learned with others. Students use their Books I Want to Read list on page 124 to record information for future reference. You might want to use the Teacher's Conference Record Sheet on page 122 to keep track of meeting details.

Acceleration of reading level is another way to accommodate the advanced learning needs of readers who are gifted. While the typical reader in the primary grades is unable to comprehend advanced texts, readers who are gifted can be guided to view reading as both a thinking and a language process. Combining reading skills with learning in the content areas is another way to accelerate the reading program for advanced readers.

Readers who are gifted can be guided to view reading as both a thinking and a language process.

See the references and resources on pages 236–237 for specific recommendations for readers who are gifted.

★ STRATEGY

The Contract for Permission to Read Ahead

This simple strategy will save you many headaches as you differentiate reading for your gifted students.

As you no doubt already know from experience, most advanced readers ask the same question at the beginning of any reading selection: "Can I please read ahead?" Perhaps you think that if you tell them you don't want them to read ahead, they will honor your request. In fact, they will probably read ahead anyway.

Would you ever let anyone tell you how much time you should take to read a story or book, or how quickly or slowly you should read it? Especially one in which you are intensely interested? It's not surprising that these passionate readers will finish the whole story or book before dawn tomorrow. What can you do to manage this situation?

Group these accelerated learners together and ask them each to sign a Contract for Permission to Read Ahead (page 105). Tell them it's okay to read ahead, but they need to understand how important it is to honor the terms of the contract. They shouldn't spoil the selection for others by giving away plot twists or endings. And when they hear other kids talking about a book or story and what might happen next, they should avoid joining in.

This contract is a simple way to help advanced readers understand the rules they should follow if they want to read ahead. Use the strategies and activities in this chapter to keep them challenged and motivated during reading class.

★ STRATEGY

The Reading Activities Menu

Use a Reading Activities Menu when you want to provide your more capable students with

text continues on page 106

Contract for Permission to Read Ahead

Check each statement to show that you agree with it. Then sign the contract.

❏ I will not tell anyone anything about the story until everyone in the group has finished reading it.

❏ I will not participate in prediction activities.

Student's Signature: _____

Contract for Permission to Read Ahead

Check each statement to show that you agree with it. Then sign the contract.

❏ I will not tell anyone anything about the story until everyone in the group has finished reading it.

❏ I will not participate in prediction activities.

Student's Signature: _____

Contract for Permission to Read Ahead

Check each statement to show that you agree with it. Then sign the contract.

❏ I will not tell anyone anything about the story until everyone in the group has finished reading it.

❏ I will not participate in prediction activities.

Student's Signature: _____

alternate activities that extend the regular reading unit. Students who compact out of the regular work in reading may choose from the list of options. The menu also allows for choice days, when students may create and work on their own activities or continue with listed activities.

If you prefer, you may present alternate activities in an Extension Menu format. See the Extension Menus on animal stories and on biographies on pages 111 and 113. Also examine the sections in chapter 3 on Preparing the Study Guide and Preparing the Extension Menu. Use the information and forms in that chapter and this one to design and use Study Guides and/or Extension Menus with your differentiated reading curriculum. Choose several products for each learning modality from the Product Choices Chart (page 87) for students to use for their extension activities.

How to Use the Reading Activities Menu

1. Prepare a list of activities that will provide your students with several options they can choose to complete. Or use the reproducible menu on page 109 that is designed for use with any literature selection.

2. Tell students they may choose an activity to work on during times you designate. They can continue working on their activity until it is completed; they do not have to start and finish an activity by a specified deadline. This will help encourage them to explore the topic in depth. They should record the dates they begin and end each activity on the date lines.

3. Invite students to come up with their own ideas for projects or activities. They should discuss their ideas with you before starting to work on them. After you give your permission for a specific project or activity, the student should record it on the menu in one of the blank spaces provided.

4. Have students record their work on a Daily Log of Extension Work (see page 92).

NOTE Literature responds extremely well to the Study Guide method. The Study Guides can be about specific books, but they work better when they are about the specific genre being considered at that time.

⭐ STRATEGY

The Contract for Reading Skills

Appropriate interventions with students working at advanced levels in reading and writing often require a combination of the compacting methods in chapter 2. The strategies described in that chapter—Most Difficult First, Pretest for Volunteers, and Learning Contracts—address effective reading skills, grammar, and vocabulary which these kids often have previously mastered.

Scenario: Leandra

Leandra was reading several years ahead of her age peers. Her writing was sophisticated and colorful. Her teacher recognized that it was not necessary for Leandra to complete all of the skill-and-practice assignments at grade level, and she created the contract shown on page 107 so Leandra could spend more time doing what she truly loved: reading and writing.

You'll notice that this contract doesn't list any specific activities as extension options since this option is designed for students who are already engaged in their own type of independent study based on a personal passion. Students may spend the time they buy back reading books they have chosen and/or writing and revising ongoing pieces. It's very important to realize that it isn't necessary to provide paper-and-pencil activities to replace those activities students have been excused from doing. Students should have much freedom of choice in how they spend time they buy back.

Contract for Reading Skills, Grammar & Language Mechanics

Student's Name: _Leandra_____

✔	Page/Standard	✔	Page/Standard	✔	Page/Standard
____	58 (plurals)	____	62 (compound words)	✔	65 (possessives)
✔	59 (subject/verb agreement)	____	63 (suffixes)	✔	66 (possessives)
____	60 (prefixes)	____	64 (suffixes)	____	67 (parts of speech)
____	61 (prefixes)	____	_____	____	_____

Alternate Activities

Record the way you spent your time while the rest of the class was working on standards you have mastered. The only expectation is that you spend your time reading and/or writing.

Date	Activity

Teacher's Signature: _____

Student's Signature: _____

To differentiate skill work in reading and vocabulary you can use the same general type of Learning Contract described in chapter 2.

A reproducible Contract for Reading Skills and Vocabulary is found on page 108. Directions on how to use it are contained in the directions for Learning Contracts in chapter 2, page 51. The vocabulary words from a reading selection may be pretested using the directions for voluntary pretests on page 48.

text continues on page 115

Contract for Reading Skills and Vocabulary

Student's Name: _____

✔	Page/Standard	✔	Page/Standard
_____	_____	_____	_____
_____	_____	_____	_____
_____	_____	_____	_____
_____	_____	_____	_____

- -

Vocabulary Words for Unit

_____	_____	_____
_____	_____	_____
_____	_____	_____
_____	_____	_____

- -

Working Conditions

_____

_____

Student's Signature: _____

Teacher's Signature: _____

Date: _____

Reading Activities Menu

Student's name: _____

Directions

During the next _____ days, create your own menu of activities from the list below to do in place of the regular assignments.

Date(s)   **Activity**

_____   Create and perform a puppet show of the story or book.

_____   Interview a person who read the book and share your conversation with others.

_____   Write a letter to the author.

_____   Write another chapter.

_____   Write a different ending.

_____   Using a thesaurus, find synonyms for your six favorite words.

_____   Create a dialogue between two characters and read it with a friend for an audience.

_____   Read other books by the same author. Compare/contrast.

_____   Read another book of the same type. Compare/contrast.

_____   Write a story or book of the same type, which contains similar elements.

Include three free days. Add on days to the activities listed or create your own activities:

_____   _____

_____   _____

_____   _____

Animal Story Study Guide

Be prepared to:

1. Identify and discuss all of the elements in our story map as they appeared in this story.

2. Discuss the meanings of the vocabulary words for this story.

3. Describe the animal(s) that are important characters in this story. Include information about physical appearance, behavior, likes and dislikes, wishes, and the problem the animal(s) need to solve.

   * **CHECKPOINT:**_____: **Assessment for 1–2** *
   DATE

4. Create a dialogue between a human and an animal in this story in which the animal describes what he or she really wants. Continue by inventing a plan they form to make the animal's wish come true.

5. Explain the evidence from the story that shows a bond between humans and one or more of the animals.

6. Use a visual to chart the similarities and differences between an animal in the story and a "real" animal of the same species.

   * **CHECKPOINT:**_____: **Assessment for 1–5** *
   DATE

7. Make a chart that describes the human qualities each animal in the story possesses. Write a story with anthropomorphic qualities. (Anthropomorphism is a technique in writing that makes animals appear to have human characteristics.)

8. Illustrate in some manner some differences between wild and domestic animals of a certain species.

9. Prepare a want ad in which a human in the story advertises his or her need for an animal to help with a problem, OR in which the animal advertises for help from a human.

10. Create a brochure describing how a child should care for an animal in this story, if the animal were the child's pet.

    * **CHECKPOINT:**_____: **Final Assessment for 1–10** *
    DATE

Write a first-person story in which the main character is an animal who tries to live with humans.	Do a research study about an organization that is working to save endangered animals from extinction. Plan a campaign to save an animal you admire.	Read 10 or more poems about animals. Write poetry about animals that interest you.
Read about people who have tamed and lived with wild animals. Describe the characteristics such people have in common.	**Student Choice**	Plan and present a debate about the merits of preserving a certain area for the use of its existing animals and plants. The other side of the debate would give reasons to develop the area into homes or shopping.
Pretend you're an archaeologist who has just discovered the remains of an extinct animal. Share information about how the animal lived, why it became extinct, and how it might have been saved from extinction.	Investigate a situation in which a government is in conflict with animal rights activists over which species are good to keep and which are not. Hypothesize some of the potential negative outcomes of the conflict.	Create a composite animal with elements of several animals. Convince someone else that it's the best animal in the world.

Biography Study Guide

Be prepared to:

1. Describe details from the subject's early years, including place and circumstances of birth, childhood, schooling, siblings, parents, and relatives who influenced him or her.

2. Describe details from the subject's adolescence, including hobbies, education, and memorable experiences.

   * **CHECKPOINT:**_____: **Assessment for 1–2**   *
   DATE

3. Describe the personal aspects of the subject's adult life, including relationships, commitments, and significant events.

4. Explain when and how the subject found his or her way to a chosen career. Include information about the people or events that influenced him or her.

5. Describe what qualities, circumstances, or events made this person important enough to have a biography written about him or her.

   * **CHECKPOINT:**_____: **Assessment for 1–5**   *
   DATE

6. Prepare a timeline of the subject's career, including both helpful events and setbacks.

7. Describe how the subject's life ended, as well as any awards or honors he or she received.

8. Understand the meanings of all assigned vocabulary words.

9. Describe how the biography helped you better understand the events of the times in which the subject lived and worked.

10. Find some events in the biography that you think might not have happened as they were portrayed. Find another source of information about the subject and decide how accurate the portrayal is in the biography.

   * **CHECKPOINT:**_____: **Final Assessment for 1–10**   *
   DATE

Create a bibliography of biographies in a specific category. Examples: women, astronauts, children, musicians, inventors, sports heroes, entertainers. Read those that look interesting to you. Find a way to get others interested in reading them.	Read three biographies in a specific category (see the box at the left). Illustrate the elements they have in common.	Illustrate the relationship between the subject's life and the time period in which he or she lived. Include information about specific events and how they influenced the person's life.
Describe gender or ethnic issues in biographies written for your age group during the past 10 years, and during the first 5 years of any previous decade.	**Student Choice**	Discover some things about which the subject would have been proud. Use these to create his or her obituary and epitaph.
Create an illustrated timeline showing major and minor events in the subject's life. Create a second timeline showing things the person might have wanted to do or accomplish.	Act out a biography of a person who was connected to a particular historical event your classmates are studying. Challenge your audience to guess the person's identity.	Use photography to illustrate the "snapshot method" of biography, in which you show common themes or elements found in three biographies.

Author Extension Menu

Read interviews with the author. Write a short biography of the author based on that information.	Discover other things the author has written that don't follow the same style of the book you are reading.	Write something of your own in the same style as the author.
Write a letter to the author. (Get contact information from the publisher.) Give your reactions to the book and ask the author some questions about himself or herself.	**Student Choice**	Find out if the author has worked with other writers and/or illustrators. Compare the author's "working alone" style with his or her "working with others" style. Is there a difference? If so, describe it.
Read other books of the same type by different authors. Compare and contrast the styles of the various authors.	Learn the steps a person has to take to become a published author. Illustrate at least three paths to publication, including hard copy and electronic materials.	Determine how e-books and other digital publications impact author and publisher income. Share what you have found with a group interested in publishing.

⭐ STRATEGY

Teaching Reading Skills in a Trade Book Reading Program

Another way to extend reading instruction for accelerated students is to let them read literature of their own choosing, then discuss what they have read with each other and with you. Students may be grouped for skill work by their assessed reading levels, but have more latitude in the books they select for their independent reading. This is generally the format advanced readers prefer for at least part of their reading time. They may all read the same novel, different books of the same genre or type, or books by the same author. You may decide to let each student read a completely different book. It is possible to find skill-building books for reading skills that are not tied to any specific reading series. (See pages 236–237 in the references and resources for ideas.) See Strategy: Individualized Reading starting on page 117.

Regardless of the approach you use, provide challenging reading and related writing activities for these students. Expect only one or two activities per selection; kids who love reading will balk if there is too much written work. The choices could also be used in meetings of students who are reading independently as discussion starters.

- Locate inferences, cause and effect, and other examples of critical thinking.
- Find foreshadowing, personification, metaphor, or other literary elements.
- Analyze the theme and its relationship to other books.
- Analyze the bias of characters and/or the author.
- Hypothesize and describe in writing what would happen if different characters had interacted or if the same characters had interacted in a different manner.

- Evaluate the quality of this particular book when compared to other books by the same author or other books of the same type.
- Discuss personal opinions with others in the reading group.
- Create pieces of writing related to the book's content or message.
- Rewrite certain events or create a new ending.
- Write a similar story.
- Write the same story, set in a different time period.
- Write a new ending.
- Write a new chapter to insert in the book or an epilogue.
- Write a letter to the book's author explaining your reaction to the book and asking questions about the author.
- Discuss the validity of the content and events described.
- Using an interesting format, create a dialogue between you and one of the characters in which you try to convince that person to behave differently.
- Create new possibilities for plot or character development.
- Share the story as a storyteller would. Deliver the story in that manner to an appropriate audience.
- Read biographies about real people in similar situations to the one(s) described in the novel.
- Research the life of a famous person and write an original biography.
- Compare and contrast books by the same author.
- Compare and contrast books of the same genre.
- Create a dramatic reading or short play about the story.
- Create illustrations for a story or book that doesn't have them.

- Understand and be able to describe point of view and characters' various perspectives on an issue.

- If your class is using Accelerated Reader, use any of the thinking models in chapter 5, including Build Blocks to Think on page 162, to create more challenging questions for the most popular books.

Using Internet Resources for Self-Selected Reading

- Create a "Fakebook" page for one of the characters (www.classtools.net/FB/home-page). Have the character's "friends" post comments that relate to what is occurring in the story.

- Start a blog with another group of advanced students in another school, state, or country who are reading the same story.

- Create a Wikipedia page for your book, or add facts to the book's existing Wikipedia page.

- Summarize information found on websites devoted to the book or its author.

- Develop an online project using Google Docs or Dropbox with advanced students from another school, state, or country who are reading the same story.

- Create an individual presentation on your book using Keynote or PowerPoint, or a shared presentation with advanced students in other schools using online programs like Prezi or SlideRocket.

- Select a theme in the book and create a digital movie to post to your class website to share information on your book.

- Use Storybird (storybird.com) with one or more other students to collaborate on a story in a round-robin fashion by writing your own text and inserting pictures.

- Use WordArt.com (wordart.com), a more advanced version of Wordle, to create a word cloud in which every word is linked to Google search results for that word.

- Use the Author Extension Menu on page 114 and record your progress on a Daily Log of Extension Work (page 92).

All Reading the Same Novel

1. Give the pretest on reading skills and vocabulary for the designated class novel to anyone who wants to take it.

2. Offer students who already know a predetermined percent of the required skill work a Contract for Reading Skills and Vocabulary (see page 108).

3. Help this group agree on a novel they would like to read together by describing several alternative novels that match the genre being read by the other students in the class. If the group chooses two different novels, that should also work well.

4. Relate the vocabulary, writing activities, and other skill work to their alternate novel. In some cases, you may be able to use selected pages from the same skill work the whole class is studying, instead of having to create new activities. Remember to provide voluntary pretests for the skill and vocabulary work. Notice also the many ideas for extension work contained in this chapter.

NOTE Many companies have produced inexpensive and comprehensive prepackaged units for teaching novels. Some have these supplemental materials online for little or no additional cost. Searches for online resources can yield dozens of related ideas you can use. Check them out before you use precious planning time to come up with your own activities.

5. Meet with this group in much the same way you would with a typical reading group. The main difference is that your discussions and activities will relate to their chosen novel instead of the selection the rest of the class is reading. If you wish, you may prepare a Study Guide to help students notice the most important elements. Students who finish the novel ahead of the others may use the remaining time to read other books by the same author or in the same genre.

Don't be surprised if the group studying the novel is much more enthusiastic than the group working with your anthology or required reader materials. If this happens in your classroom, you may decide to occasionally have *all* students study a novel related to a theme or genre.

You may decide to occasionally have *all* students study a novel related to a theme or genre.

Most skills can be taught in any context, and you can use games to teach the vocabulary words students would otherwise miss. Some teachers use this method as a transition to a literature-based program, setting aside one day of the week for literature study while staying with the designated material for the other four days, or replacing one entire unit with literature-based reading, making sure to include the skills and vocabulary assigned to the unit being skipped.

Some students who read quickly and love to read can't resist sharing, even if it means giving away the ending of a novel or important plot twists along the way. To discourage spoilers, have them sign a Contract for Permission to Read Ahead (page 105).

All Students Reading Different Novels by the Same Author

If you choose this option, you may want to use a flexible grouping or cooperative learning format. Put the advanced readers together in one group and provide them with more complex novels to choose from. Removing them from the other groups will encourage the rest of the students to work more actively. Also, when gifted students are allowed to work in their own cooperative learning group, they are more likely to participate in the group activities than when they are in a completely heterogeneous group that slows down their reading pace and limits their penchant for engaging in complex thought and discussion. For

more about gifted kids and cooperative learning, see chapter 7.

Meet with each group separately to discuss their particular novel. Discussions of the author's style, vocabulary, and use of literary elements may take place with the entire class, since everyone is reading books by one specific author. Use the Author Extension Menu on page 114 to invite students to specialize in one aspect of the author's life and work.

Students Reading Different Novels of the Same Genre

When you want all students to read different novels of the same type or genre, use a Study Guide and/or Extension Menu that describe the common elements of the specific genre. Please examine the Study Guides and Extension Menus in this chapter or in the accompanying digital content.

When you use the Study Guide method and allow kids to choose what to read, the Study Guide will help them know what to look for in their own selections. This is much more effective than telling kids to "go read other biographies of this person." For example, if your class is working on a unit on folk tales, your highly accomplished readers can finish the designated selection at their own pace, and then read other folk tales, such as those from different countries. Class discussions would center on the characteristics of the genre as described on the Genre Study Guide, and the students who had read more widely would contribute to the discussion now and then of the assigned book, adding information from their alternative reading.

⭐ STRATEGY

Individualized Reading

To meet the needs of gifted students and boost interest for all students, consider letting everyone read a different book. Perhaps you could start with this option one day each week, and let it grow from there. You will want to have a variety of titles, topics, and reading levels available in the classroom. Several publishing companies distribute collections for this purpose. See references and resources for this chapter at the end of this book.

Initially, students should be free to browse through any books that interest them. Advise them to use the "Rule of Three" to select any book they actually plan to read. Tell them to:

> "Open the book to some page in the middle, preferably a page without pictures, and start reading. Whenever you come across a word you don't know, hold up one finger. When your count exceeds three words on one page, the book is probably too difficult for you to read independently. Go to another book and try again."

If you are concerned that students will choose books that are too easy, suggest that they try to read three consecutive pages from the middle of the book. If they don't find any unfamiliar words in that section, they should probably look for another book.

Have students keep track of what they read. There are many ways to do this. Two of my favorites are the Circle of Books and the Reading Response Sheet. Both are easy to understand and use.

The Circle of Books (page 120). When students finish reading a book, they place a tally mark in the appropriate section of the wheel. The marks help them (and you) see if they are reading from a variety of categories or limiting themselves to one or two. They should bring their Circle form with them to any reading conferences they have with you. Naturally, you may use other categories than the ones shown on the reproducible form.

The Reading Response Sheet (page 121). Gifted students may balk at having to do too much writing connected to books they are reading for pleasure. However, it is alright to have students who are working independently spend a few minutes at the end of some reading period, jotting down their thoughts about and responses to their self-selected books.

These might include their reactions to events and characters, predictions about upcoming events, character studies, rewritten chapters or endings, and so on. Completed pages may be collected to form a Reading Response Journal, which might be kept in a dedicated spiral notebook or on a Word document. Students must keep their journal or log in school so it is available for your reading conference, until such time as you allow them to take it home to share their differentiated work with their parents. See the Extension Activities and Differentiated Homework Report on page 94.

Students are also invited to keep records of interesting words from their reading. You might suggest activities that will help them learn these words, or students might discuss their words when they meet with other students who are doing individualized reading. See the special section on Vocabulary Activities on pages 126–128 of this chapter.

CAUTION Low-level vocabulary activities and writing activities that are designed to help students with knowledge and comprehension can become very tiresome for prolific readers. If too much writing is required, gifted students might resist differentiated reading. Some students will appreciate not having to complete reading response sheets for every book they read.

Keeping Tabs on Individualized Readers

Schedule brief weekly conferences with students who are reading self-selected literature. Keep an ongoing Teacher's Conference Record Sheet (page 122), using one hardcopy or digital copy of the sheet for each student. Have one regularly scheduled conference per week for independent readers, and provide a sign-up sheet they can use to request other conferences. See page 122 for a form you can use. Tell students they must meet with you on their scheduled day, whether or not they have finished their book.

1. In the far left column, record the date of each conference.

2. In the second column, record the title of the book the student is reading.

3. In the third column, make notes about the conference discussion. Here are some questions and suggestions to spark and guide your discussion:

   ▪ What's the best part of the story? Why? The worst/most boring part? Why?

   ▪ What techniques does the author use to hook you and draw you into the story?

   ▪ What is the primary theme in the story?

   ▪ Find a good descriptive passage. As you read it to me, please point out your favorite phrases.

   ▪ Which characters do you like? Which do you dislike? Tell why.

   ▪ How does the author get you to feel close to the characters?

   ▪ Which character is the most thoroughly described? The least thoroughly described? Which type of character description do you prefer and why?

   ▪ Select and define some of the interesting vocabulary words you found.

   ▪ Describe any parts of the book that didn't seem to belong.

   ▪ What did you admire about the author's style that you might use in your own writing?

   ▪ Was there anything confusing about the author's style? Explain.

   ▪ How would you change the book? The ending?

   ▪ If you use the Recommended Books chart (see page 125) you might also ask, What will you write about this book on the Recommended Books chart?

4. In the far right column, note any tasks you ask the student to complete. These may be related to vocabulary development, story mapping, character study, or anything else you would normally use to teach a story.

5. Before the conference ends, write the date of the next conference in the far left column. This helps you keep track of when students are expected to return, and also makes it harder for students to "forget" to come to conferences for long periods of time.

If students need additional conferences, have them sign up at a specified location.

Book Sharing

Provide one or more ways for students to share their books with each other. They can share print books and/or e-books if they all have compatible e-readers (such as Kindles, Nooks, or iPads) or if there are e-readers available for them to borrow. Some e-book programs allow buyers to share their books with others for a limited time after purchase, which can save costs. Avoid requiring formal written book reports, since these generally have a negative effect on students' attitudes about reading. Advanced readers are about as excited as you would be if you were required to keep written records of all that you read. Keep in mind that avid adult readers rarely wait until they have finished a book before sharing something about it with other interested readers, usually in a conversational format. Instead of book reports, you and your students might prefer frequent book sharing times, during which students give brief verbal reports about a book they are currently reading or have recently completed.

Book Logos

Book logos are very easy for students of all ages to use to keep track of the books they have read. They can also generate excited discussions about books between the students. Here are instructions:

1. Gather as many colors of paper as you have students in your room. Add a few extra colors so you're ready for new students. You'll need several sheets of each color.

2. Cut 8.5" x 11" sheets in half. (A helper can easily do this part.)

3. Prepare two sample swatches of each color. Drop one of each into a container. All swatches should be the same size.

text continues on page 123

Circle of Books

Each time you finish a book, put a tally mark in the appropriate section. Check to see if you are reading from a variety of categories or limiting yourself to just one or two.

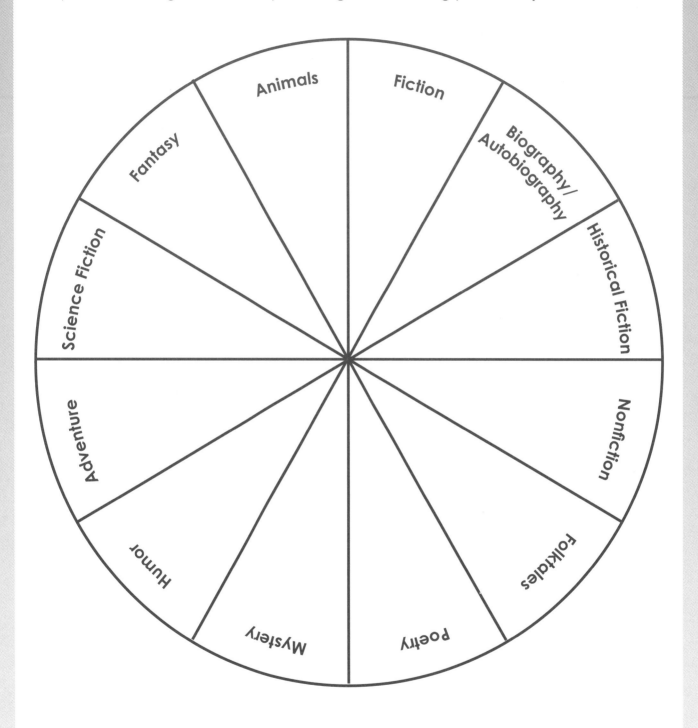

Reading Response Sheet

Student's name: _____

Title of Book: _____

Author's Name: _____

Today's Date: _____ Pages Read Today: _____

My reactions to today's reading: _____

_____

_____

_____

_____

_____

What's really great about this book so far: _____

_____

_____

_____

_____

What I would like to change in this book: _____

_____

_____

_____

_____

An interesting word from this book: _____

Teacher's Conference Record Sheet

Student's Name: _____

Date	Book	Conference Discussion	Assigned Tasks

4. Have students select their colors by drawing swatches from the container. Tell them to write their name on their color and give it back to you.

5. Attach the appropriate matching swatch beside each student's name on a Book Logos chart. If possible, laminate the chart before displaying it to prevent fading.

6. Give each student a folder filled with a supply of her or his color paper. Label each folder with the student's name and corresponding color swatch. Use a storage box to keep all the Book Logo folders together.

7. Direct the students to make a logo for each book they finish reading (or just for their favorite books, if they are highly prolific readers). You might explain it this way:

   "Cut out a shape from a piece of your paper that represents the essence of your book. This is your 'logo' for that book. Using dark colored marker, print the title of the book and the author's name on your logo."

   An alternative method is to have students create their logos digitally using graphics they find online or create themselves.

8. Display the logos around the room. They display particularly well along the border area at the top of walls. When you run out of space, display them in the hallways or other common areas. Students may decide whether or not to show their logos when they talk about their books to the class.

NOTE Be careful about holding or joining contests that give prizes for the most books read. Readers who are gifted are intrinsically motivated to read, and when we offer them extrinsic rewards for simply doing what they love, they might lose some of their intrinsic motivation. We have also seen some students obsess over the number of books read to the extent that they don't want to do anything *but* read!

One class of 27 fifth graders read 384 books in one year. The logos filled the available space in the room and eventually spilled out into the hall and wound its way around the entire floor. Imagine the lively conversations about books that were stimulated by the presence of these colorful logos. Furthermore, if students wanted to recommend certain books they had read to other students, they could easily locate the appropriate logo by its color, which would remind them of the books they wanted to share.

Imagine the lively conversations about books that were stimulated by the presence of these colorful logos.

This method of keeping track of the books your students read is certainly preferable to the traditional chart where each student's books are listed individually, representing a visual reminder of who the slower readers are. With the logos, an observer would have to work very hard to add up the number of books read by any particular student. Since the purpose of the logos is to provide a forum for discussing books, nobody really cares about the numbers anyway.

Books I Want to Read

You know how frustrating it is to try to remember titles of books people have told you about. The Books I Want to Read method eliminates this frustration for your students. See page 124 for a form you can use in your classroom. Whenever you find yourself with a few extra minutes with advanced readers, try this activity.

1. Give all students a copy of the Books I Want to Read chart. Tell them to keep it in their desk or reading folder at all times. It never goes home. If students in your school have access to a school Intranet where they each have their own account, they can keep their list posted there. This way, parents can have access to the list and encourage their children to read the books on it.

text continues on page 126

Books I Want to Read

This list belongs to: _____

Author's Name or Call Number	Title of Book	Notes

Recommended Books

My Name	Title of Book	Author's Name or Call Number	Why I'm Recommending It	People I Think Would Like This Book

2. Tell students how to use the form. You might say:

> "When I announce Book Sharing Time, take out your Books I Want to Read chart. Raise your hand if you want to volunteer to share a book today. It is not required that you have finished the book. The only requirement is you think others will want to read this book, too.
>
> "You will have two minutes to 'sell your book'—that is, make other students want to read it. First, please write the title and the author's name on the board. At the end of two minutes, please repeat the title and author of the book.
>
> "Listen carefully as the speakers share information about their books. If you think the book is one you would like to read, write the author's name and book title on your chart. You may also want to write down a few notes about the book in the right column of the chart.
>
> "When you go to the school library, please take your list with you so you will know exactly which section of the library your book is shelved in. If one book is checked out, you can look for other books on your list. When you finish reading a book, cross it off your list."

Recommended Books Chart

Using the example shown on page 125 as a model, create a large chart (at least 24" x 36") to post on a wall or bulletin board. Attach a few pencils. Watch the chart fill up with student recommendations! Post a sign reminding students to use soft voices at the chart, which is sure to become a center for engaging discussion about books and authors.

Vocabulary Activities

Many gifted kids love vocabulary activities, once they are introduced to the magic of words. All gifted students should have their own thesaurus, access to unabridged dictionaries for regular use, and also access to online dictionary and thesaurus sites, if possible.

To get your whole class hooked on words, bring in a copy of a baby names book. Students will become fascinated with the history of their own names. Once they've been enticed by that, they are likely to be excited about studying the history of other words as well. Working with the school media specialist, children's librarians, or internet resources, you can collect a variety of materials that help kids experience the delights of playing with words, understanding how words change through time, and learning how new words are added to our language. Use your internet browser to find sites that focus on word play or fun with words. (See the references and resources on page 236 for specific suggestions.)

The next step in this process would be a study of etymology. Word histories can be fascinating. It's fun to learn that "alligator" comes from the Spanish *el lagarto,* or lizard. Or that "fan" (as in sports fan) is short for fanatic. Or that "sideburns" were named after General Ambrose E. Burnside, a general in the United States Civil War.

Give students copies of Etymologies Activities (page 130) and the Etymologies Chart (page 131). Invite them to select an activity from the list. Then have them find 10 or more words or phrases that fit their chosen category (names, places, sports, etc.). Turn them loose with unabridged dictionaries, college-level dictionaries, and other print and online resources. Have students fill out an Etymologies Chart (page 131) for each category they investigate. Explain that to complete the chart, they should write:

- The original word or phrase in the far left column.

- The original language of the word or phrase in the next column (usually only available in unabridged dictionaries).

- The meaning of the word or phrase in the original language in the center column.

- Today's meaning of the word or phrase in the next column.

- An original sentence using the word or phrase in the far right column. (To make this more fun and interesting, students might write a rebus sentence.)

Vocabulary Builders

Look for books and websites that help you teach one or more of the topics listed on the Vocabulary Builders chart on page 129. Introduce one category at a time, giving several examples. Then challenge students to come up with at least 10 more examples in the same category. Since gifted kids are highly competitive, many will work very quietly on these so nobody else steals their ideas!

Any and all of the activities described on the Vocabulary Builders chart can be modified and expanded. For example, students can transmogrify mottoes, proverbs, movie names, game names, or book titles. They can even transmogrify stories or tales. Have them start by writing a one-page summary of their chosen story, and then consult a thesaurus to put it in more sophisticated words. This could be the basis of a class competition, with different groups working on different stories, folk tales, or fairy tales. When the groups are finished working, you may have to read their stories aloud to the class, since many of their words are too cumbersome for them to read themselves. The winning story is the one that takes the longest to "decode." Or, have your students read all of them as part of a blind review process (removing the author's name) and vote on their class favorite.

The Vocabulary Builders form provides many weeks of excellent work with words. Brooke, a sixth grader, once told her teacher after the class had been studying challenging vocabulary for several weeks, "Guess what, Mr. Guardino? They just started using some of our words in the political cartoons I look at every day online!" Of course you have guessed that Brooke just started *noticing* the challenging words that had always been there.

Super Sentences

These challenging vocabulary activities have enthralled gifted students in many classrooms and include all levels of the Taxonomy of Thinking on page 145. The two Super Sentences included here (see pages 132 and 133) are from *Super Sentences* by Susan Winebrenner, which include 22 examples (11 from Level One, 11 from Level Two). Here are instructions for use:

1. Group students in pairs. Pair the outstanding vocabulary champs with each other. Hand out copies of Super Sentence: Level One (page 132) for word mavens in grades 2–5, or Super Sentence: Level Two (page 133) for word mavens in grades 5–12. Some classes may need to use some sentences from both levels.

2. Read the sentence aloud several times, pronouncing all capitalized words in an exaggerated manner. Tell students to listen carefully and try to determine the parts of speech for the words in capital letters. They should write the part of speech above each word to make sure they select the correct dictionary entry when they go to look it up. As a group, check for accuracy before proceeding to the definitions.

3. Tell students to work with their partners using advanced or unabridged dictionaries—either hard copies or online—to complete the chart. Explain that they should list the "mystery words" (those in capital letters) in the far left column, write the pronunciation of each word in the center column (using the pronunciation key from a dictionary or from *Super Sentences*), then write the meaning of the word in the far right column using their own words rather than the dictionary definition.

4. Tell students that to complete this activity, they should be able to pronounce and define each mystery word, read the sentence as it appears—pronouncing all capitalized words correctly—and translate it into simpler words. This may take more than one class period for students to complete. Super Sentences may also be used individually as an Extension Menu choice when studying language or grammar.

5. When the students are ready, bring the pairs together in a circle, if space permits. If not, have partners sit together for this activity.

   ▪ The first student reads the sentence up to and including the first capitalized word.

- The next student starts where the first leaves off, and reads all words up to and including the next capitalized word.

- Students keep taking turns until someone asks to read the entire sentence aloud.

- When several students have read the sentence aloud, ask for volunteers to translate and reread it using simpler words.

Challenge students to make their own Super Sentences from vocabulary they are learning in independent reading of books, newspapers, magazines, the internet, or other sources. Be sure they prepare an answer key as well. This is another great Extension Menu idea.

See the references and resources section on page 236 for information about Susan's book *Super Sentences*.

Vocabulary Web

Educators at the College of William and Mary in Williamsburg, Virginia, have produced many self-contained units for gifted students in several subject areas. Their Vocabulary Web model is ideal for helping gifted kids study words in depth. The goal of the web goes beyond simply learning a particular word. See page 134 for a completed web and page 135 for a blank version you can copy and give to your students.

Students can work alone, but it's more fun to work in pairs. Assign words or have students choose their own words. Use one Vocabulary Web sheet for each word. Students write the word in the center circle, and then work out from there, defining the word, finding synonyms and antonyms, writing a sentence using the word, giving examples, and analyzing the word. By the time they are finished, they have a thorough understanding of the word.

Give students the option of sharing their findings with the class or other appropriate audience. Create a bonus system when students use their Super Sentence words in other forms of writing or speaking.

Bibliotherapy

Bibliotherapy is guided reading that helps readers cope with and solve problems, understand themselves and their environment, build self-esteem, and meet the developmental challenges of being a gifted kid. It can be especially powerful with gifted kids because of their love of reading, their ability to empathize, and their advanced grasp of literary devices including metaphor.

For gifted students, reading a story or novel about other gifted kids is a safe way to investigate, clarify, and validate their feelings. Confronting issues objectively through fictional characters gives them practice in dealing with their own real-life issues. Reading about characters who are like them, with similar abilities, emotions, and experiences, helps gifted kids know they're not alone.

For gifted students, reading a story about other gifted kids is a safe way to investigate, clarify, and validate their feelings.

Bibliotherapy involves more than handing books to your students and sending them off to read. Judith Wynn Halsted, author of *Some of My Best Friends Are Books: Guiding Gifted Readers from Preschool to High School*, notes that:[1]

Rather than merely recommending a book to a child, bibliotherapy includes three components: a reader, a book, and a leader who will read the same book and prepare for productive discussion of the issues the book raises. To be effective, the leader must be aware of the process of bibliotherapy: IDENTIFICATION, in which the reader identifies with a character in the book; CATHARSIS, the reader's experiencing of the emotions attributed to the character; and INSIGHT, the application of the character's experience to the reader's own life. The leader then frames questions that will confirm and expand on these elements.

[1] Halsted, 2009.

text continues on page 136

Vocabulary Builders

1. **ACRONYMS:** Words made from the first letters of a list of words you want to remember.

   Example: HOMES for the Great Lakes: Huron, Ontario, Michigan, Erie, Superior.

2. **COINED WORDS:** Words created to fill a need that no existing word serves. Many trademarks are coined words.

   Examples: Kleenex, Xerox.

3. **DAFFYNITIONS:** Crazy definitions that make some sense.

   Examples: Grapes grow on divine. A police uniform is a lawsuit.

4. **ETYMOLOGIES:** The histories of words, including their origins and changes through time and other languages.

5. **EUPHEMISMS:** More gentle ways of saying things that sound too harsh.

   Example: "He passed away" instead of "He died."

6. **FIGURES OF SPEECH:** Expressions that mean something different as a whole than if you take each word literally.

   Example: There are many skeletons in our family closet.

7. **MALAPROPISMS:** Words misused on purpose or by accident. They sound like the words you mean to say but have different, often contradictory meanings.

   Example: "Complete and under a bridge" instead of "Complete and unabridged."

8. **PALINDROMES:** Words and phrases spelled the same forward and backward.

   Examples: Otto, Madam, "Madam, I'm Adam."

9. **PORTMANTEAUS:** Words made by blending parts of other words.

   Example: "Brunch" from "breakfast" and "lunch."

10. **PUN STORIES:** Stories that include as many puns as possible. Puns are plays on words.

    Example: The pancakes were selling like hotcakes because they didn't cost a lot of dough.

11. **SLIDE WORDS:** Words slid together from abbreviations.

    Example: "Jeep" from "GP" (a general purpose vehicle during World War II).

12. **SUPER SENTENCES:** Sentences made from very difficult vocabulary words.

13. **TOM SWIFTIES:** Statements that combine a word with its related adverb.

    Example: "I just cut my finger!" cried Tom sharply.

14. **TRANSMOGRIFICATIONS:** Simple thoughts expressed in sophisticated or challenging words.

    Example: "Scintillate, scintillate, asteroid minific" for "Twinkle, twinkle, little star."

15. **ROOTS:** Study the Latin roots of 10 words. Find words in other sources that have those roots.

Etymologies Activities

1. First names, either gender.

2. Last names that describe occupations. Examples: Hooper, Smith, Taylor.

3. Places or things named after people. Examples: sideburns, Mansard roof, sandwich.

4. Native American words or names.

5. Foreign words in common English usage.

6. Words or phrases from sports. Examples: strike out, take a new tack.

7. Words or phrases from television and movies. Examples: commercial, Foley artist.

8. Words or phrases from art. Examples: Impressionism, fresco.

9. Words or phrases from architecture. Examples: flying buttress, Baroque.

10. Words or phrases from medicine. Examples: penicillin, anesthesia.

11. Words or phrases from music. Examples: concert, bebop.

12. Words or phrases from computers and the internet. Examples: email, cyberspace.

13. Words or phrases from any other specialty or field of interest.

14. Words or phrases from a new category you create.

Etymologies Chart

Category: _____

Word or Phrase	Original Language	Meaning in Original Language	Today's Meaning	Use in a Sentence

Super Sentences: Level One

Directions: Work with a partner to pronounce and define each "mystery word" (words in capital letters), read the sentence as it appears, and translate it into simpler words.

We live near a GROTESQUE, HIDEOUS, DETERIORATED old house filled with TORTUOUS, IMPENETRABLE hallways that give me EERIE, GHASTLY feelings of CLAUSTROPHOBIA and TREPIDATION, especially when I hear the FORMIDABLE CACOPHONY of BABBLING voices when no one else is there.

Word	Pronunciation	Meaning

Translation:

Super Sentences: Level Two

Directions: Work with a partner to pronounce and define each "mystery word" (words in capital letters), read the sentence as it appears, and translate it into simpler words.

The TRUCULENT, OPPIDAN LICKSPITTLE SEQUESTERED himself from the BROUHAHA caused by the PUSILLANIMOUS MOUNTEBANK, and MACHINATED a MACHIAVELLIAN PREVARICATION to METE to himself some of the mountebank's LUCRE.

Word	Pronunciation	Meaning

Translation:

Vocabulary Web Model

Synonyms:

malicious, vicious, spiteful, hostile

Sentence:

"A bad idea, Professor Lockhart," said Snape, gliding over like a large and malevolent bat.

Definition:

1: having or exhibiting ill will; wishing harm to others; malicious

2. having an evil or harmful influence

Word:

malevolent

Antonyms:

benevolent, charitable, gracious

Example:

malevolent is to villain as benevolent is to hero

Maleficent was a malevolent villain

Part of Speech:

adjective

Analysis

Word Families:

malice, malicious, malign, malady, malefactor, malaria, malignant, dismal, volition, volunteer, benevolent

Origin:

Latin

Stems:

mal-, male-; bad, badly volens (velle): to want, to wish

Source: Center for Gifted Education, College of William & Mary, Williamsburg, Virginia. Used with permission.

Vocabulary Web

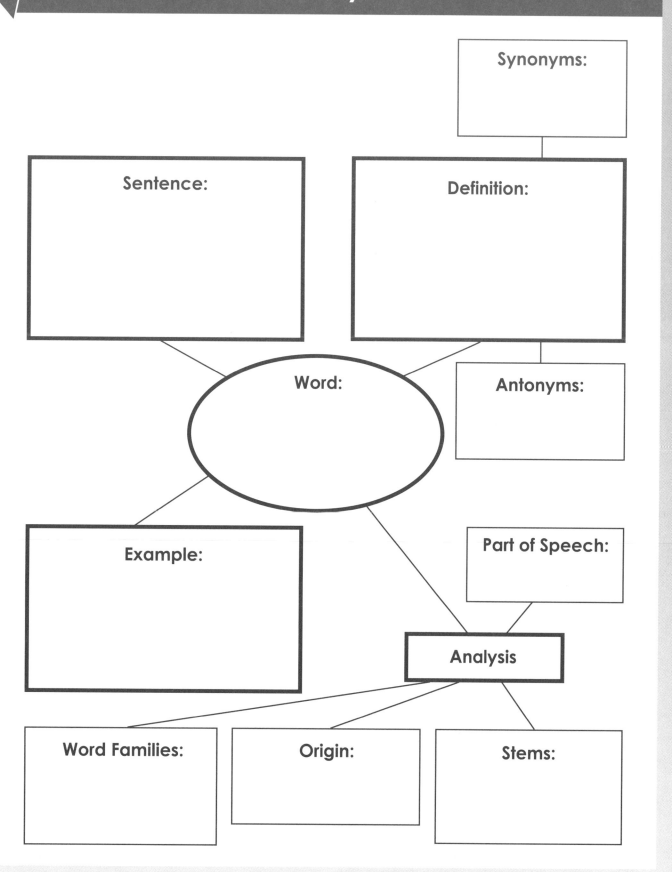

Synonyms:

Sentence:

Definition:

Word:

Antonyms:

Example:

Part of Speech:

Analysis

Word Families:

Origin:

Stems:

If you plan to use bibliotherapy with your gifted students, use the internet to find suitable books. The characters and stories don't have to match your students' lives exactly, but they should have some things in common. (See references and resources on page 237 for more information.)

Librarians or websites may also be able to help you locate other books to offer your students. You will want to become familiar with whatever your students read, either by reading the materials yourself, using internet resources for synopses and reviews, learning about them in reading conferences with the students, or by using pre-packaged units for individual novels. Then follow through with individual or group discussions.

Teaching Writing to Gifted Learners

Reading and writing are inextricably intertwined. In the activity lists in this chapter, both topics are included. Your outstanding writers, by the very nature of their sophisticated writing ability, need compacting and differentiation in their writing work. Many gifted students write stories, poems, and plays and keep them at home. Ask their parents about these writing projects, and invite the kids to keep an ongoing writing project in class and return to it whenever they buy back some choice time. Some talented writers do not want to do this, unless you promise you will not get overinvolved in the project. Sometimes, we can act as editors for students' writing efforts, but we should not write directly on their product. Sticky notes—both real and digital—can help with this effort.

Since much of the writing done in school is skill work (spelling, grammar, and mechanics), you can use Most Difficult First and Learning Contracts (see chapter 2) to make sure your advanced writers do not have to spend precious class time "learning" skills and formats they already know well. They need opportunities to do work that is meaningful for them.

The contracts allow talented writers to spend considerable class time on their individual writing projects. A sample Contract for Expository Writing is shown on page 137. For students who are using writing contracts but who need ideas for writing projects, the Expository Writing Extension Menu (page 138) offers several interesting choices. Using the interactive version of this form in the accompanying digital content, you can easily change the menu to fit other types of writing, such as descriptive or narrative.

Since writing is a skill-based activity and its elements can be pre-assessed, the Study Guide method is not as useful as the contract strategies described in chapter 3. Always have students record their progress on a Daily Log of Extension Work (see page 92) and keep it in their Compacting Folder.

Storyboards

Storyboards are a type of graphic organizer used to create digital stories. They are an exciting experience for many writers, and a downright miracle for some twice-exceptional students, who often find it very difficult to clearly understand a story's sequence—both in the stories they write and in those they read. They allow writers to plan the specific elements they want in a story, and then help them organize and reorganize the story components visually. There are no rewrites—multiple written revisions are not necessary. Imagine the allure of this to a twice-exceptional student who could always tell his or her story, but found writing it nearly impossible. With storyboards, it's not until all the essential components are in place that the actual story production begins.

A storyboard can help ease project development for your students. It gives them a plan and reduces frustration and the overwhelming feeling of not knowing how to proceed. When teaching storyboards, post written directions that walk students through the process. This is important because some students will be working on these projects independently or in small groups, while you are providing direct instruction to the full class. Students can then use the storyboards to make notes for their audience to follow while they are presenting their projects.

As students become more skilled with the technology, and if you have sufficient computers available to you, students can create their storyboards digitally. This planning takes time, but it

text continues on page 139

Contract for Expository Writing

Student's Name: _James_

Standard

____   The topic is narrow enough to manage.

____   The topic sentence (first in the paragraph) clearly expresses the
        idea to be developed.

____   There are at least three details to support the topic sentence.

____   Each detail is related to the topic sentence.

____   The sequence of the details makes sense.

____   Proofreading is evident for grammar, punctuation, spelling, and
        other mechanics.

Extension Activities:

Student-Selected Idea:

Work on *The Anatomy, Physiology, and Cetera of the Human Body* book

Working Conditions

I will not bother anyone.

I will not call attention to myself.

I will work on the extension activities during the entire writing period.

Teacher's Signature: _____

Student's Signature: _____

Expository Writing Extension Menu

Write an expository essay to submit to the editorial page of a local newspaper or news website.	Develop a lengthy piece of writing of your own choosing. Contract with the teacher regarding ongoing progress conferences and record keeping.	Prepare to speak at a government meeting to convince legislators to support your position on a topic of your choice.
Present a debate on a topic of your choosing with one or several other students to an appropriate audience.	**Student Choice**	Prepare to speak at a school board meeting to convince members to support your position on a school-related issue.
Evaluate the effectiveness of several expository paragraphs in a current nonfiction best seller.	Write an expository paragraph in another language.	Rewrite a paragraph or page from a textbook to make the expository language more effective.

helps kids create projects that are well thought-out and maximizes time and available technology.

See chapter 8 for more information on using technology to challenge gifted learners.

Writing Activities Gifted Learners Enjoy

Many of the great ideas for writing activities you've come across or used over the years will delight your gifted students. Some might be used as writing suggestions, others will serve as extension activities. Remember, gifted kids enjoy taking an idea and adapting it in some way to make it "their" idea. Here are several suggestions from which your students may choose:

- Rewrite a story from a different character's point of view.

- Write opposing viewpoints papers. Enlist a friend to help you present a two-sided argument that explores the two different sides of an issue.

- Write any kind of poetry you want. You can follow a form or not, use rhyme or not—whatever appeals to you. Find and explore internet poetry sites, and consider submitting an original poem for consideration in writing contests.

- Listen to a piece of instrumental music, classical, jazz, world music, relaxing music, or whatever you choose. Write about it. How does it make you feel? What does it make you think about? What images do you see in your mind when you listen?

- Write a description of a work of art, painting, sculpture, drawing, or photograph you admire or dislike. Include your interpretation of what you think it is supposed to mean or of what it means to you. Go online to access collections of many famous art museums all over the world.

- Explore the techniques of technical writing via online sites. After studying a technique, produce a sample on a topic that interests you. *Example:* Write a user's guide to playing a favorite game or using a new electronic gadget or toy.

- Contact a writer you admire. Interview him or her over email. Tell the author what you liked about a specific work, and ask questions about her or his writing process. Create a report about your interview.

- Choose a topic that interests you and write an essay about it at the start of the school year. Write an essay about the same topic in early May. Analyze your growth as a writer according to a rubric.

- Submit a favorite piece you have written to a writing contest. A quick search online will yield dozens of results for student writing competitions. Winning submissions are typically published.

- Analyze and assess your own writing using the same rubric provided by your teacher.

Another activity many students greatly enjoy involves U.S. towns and cities with unusual names.

1. Have students search an atlas, maps, or internet resources for unusual city or town names and list at least 10.

2. Working individually or in small groups, kids choose one city or town, and then write a story about how they think it got its name without consulting the internet.

3. Students write a letter or an email to the mayor or city council, enclosing their story and asking for information about how the town really got its name.

Some town names that are particularly intriguing are Embarrass, Minnesota; Bowlegs, Oklahoma; Bugscuffle, Tennessee; Boring, Maryland and Oregon; Horseheads, New York; Rough and Ready, California, New York, and Pennsylvania; Dime Box, Texas; Double Trouble, New Jersey; What Cheer, Iowa; Truth or Consequences, New Mexico; Zap, North Dakota; and Monkey's Eyebrow, Pippa Passes, and Mouthcard, Kentucky. Students will often receive replies to their letters and stories.

Getting Your Students' Writing Published

Students who enjoy writing and excel at it need opportunities to reach an audience beyond their classmates. School newsletters and newspapers are great, but when you find a writer who's truly exceptional, you'll want to go even further.

It's absolutely thrilling to become a published author, and several book and magazine publishers and internet sites welcome kids' writing. For a list of possibilities, see the references and resources on page 237. Students should contact publishers directly by writing formal letters of inquiry. (Your job is to coach them, not to do it for them.) Some publishers' websites provide information about how to submit work for publication.

⭐ STRATEGY

The Great Friday Afternoon Event

The Great Friday Afternoon Event is language arts fun for the whole class. It's a way to celebrate language as well as provide welcome relief from the required curriculum. See page 141 for a handout you can use with your students.

1. Divide the class into four heterogeneous teams.

   - If you have more than 28 students, form more teams and create more categories of events, such as Choral Reading, Commercials, and Storytelling.

   - On the handout, the teams are called A, B, C, and D, but it is fun for teams to choose their own names, slogans, etc.

   - Each week, each team is responsible for a different category. Each week, each team has a new captain who is in charge of making sure that all students contribute their part to the team's Friday presentation.

   - The teams stay together until all teams have presented all of the categories. Four teams stay together for four weeks, five

teams for five weeks, and so on. Each week a different student acts as captain of the team. After all teams have experience in all categories, you may want to change one or more of the categories. Or you may keep the same categories all year and have teams continue to rotate through them.

2. Make sure the teams understand their tasks as described on the handout.

3. Provide materials for students to use. Collect poems, plays, newspapers, news magazines, etc. Allow practice time during the week; help the captains help their team members rehearse. Create simple rubrics for good presentations. Invite parent volunteers to help collect the materials and come to the classroom to provide whatever assistance students need.

Although the teams are heterogeneous and all students contribute to the fun, gifted kids really enjoy this opportunity to showcase their talents. This event may be combined with Book Sharing Time, during which students add to their Books I Want to Read list (page 124). You might finish the Great Friday Afternoon Event with an academic competition in the style of a favorite TV show to review the week's learned standards in any or all subject areas.

QUESTIONS ⭐ ANSWERS

"How can I find the necessary time to provide alternate activities when I don't have enough time to finish the required reading program?"

Although some of the alternatives described in this chapter can be used as extension activities, they are not intended to be offered *in addition* to the regular program. They should be used *instead of* the regular program in many cases. The most common reason for using a prescribed program is because there's comfort in knowing you'll be teaching the required standards. When you pretest skill or vocabulary work, you can allow kids who achieve at the required level to work on extension activities instead of the regular curriculum. Even

text continues on page 142

The Great Friday Afternoon Event

How It Works:

1. The class is divided into four teams. Teams stay together for four weeks.
2. On Fridays, each team presents a different program to the class.
3. Teams rotate categories and captains every week.
4. After four weeks, all four teams will have presented all four types of programs.

	Poetry	Declamation	Play	Newscast
Week 1	A	B	C	D
Week 2	B	C	D	A
Week 3	C	D	A	B
Week 4	D	A	B	C

Poetry: Each team member reads or recites a poem. You can choose a poem by someone else or read a poem you have written.

Declamation: Each team member reads aloud or recites an excerpt or piece of prose writing. You can choose an essay, speech, book chapter, etc., by someone else or read something you have written.

Play: The team works together to read or act out a play or part of a play.

Newscast: The team works together to broadcast a 5–10 minute radio or cable news show about a current or historical event.

Other Possible Topics: Book or movie review, storytelling, speech, scientific discovery, humor, demonstration, persuasive message, PowerPoint presentation.

when the content is new and pretesting isn't possible, you can use Study Guides and Extension Menus. Chapter 4 describes the steps to successful implementation of these methods in great detail.

Invite grade-level colleagues to help you plan Extension Menus. Work during lunch or common planning times. Don't forget the chocolate! (See page 147.) Create the lessons using the templates in the digital content accompanying this book. Then email them to other colleagues. You can tweak the lessons you receive from others based on the needs of the students in your classroom and your curriculum. Most schools have an Intranet site where teachers can also share curriculum. Consider creating a repertoire of extension activities that teachers in your school or district can access and contribute to.

"How will parents feel if students aren't completing the required reading, or are skipping some skill work?"

Very few of the educational practices we use in today's classrooms resemble the way things were done in the schools today's parents attended. It's up to us to educate parents and keep them informed.

Whenever you implement a new strategy, send home a letter describing what you are doing. Bring parents up-to-date at open houses and parent-teacher conferences. Once parents see that their children are eager to go to school and learn, it's easy to convince them that your teaching methods are effective for their children.

"What about the truly precocious reader who is several years ahead of the others? Shouldn't that student have an accelerated program?"

Yes. For students who enter school reading several years ahead of their classmates, accelerated instruction may determine whether they keep their edge or slowly return to the level of their age peers. Remember never to accelerate students into out-of-level required reading materials without informing other people who might

be affected in subsequent years. Any decision to place students in higher-level materials in any subject must be made as a team. Your team might include other teachers, the principal, parents, and even some staff from the middle school or high school, since they will eventually be affected by your actions.

Even if you can't use some required reading materials, very few trade books should be off limits, giving kids almost unlimited choices with real literature. If you are at a school where acceleration is not allowed, keep to the grade-level basals and anthologies, but differentiate like crazy with self-selected materials. Pretest a lot! For more on the topic of acceleration, see chapter 9.

"Isn't it important for all kids to participate in the regular writing program, since writing is such an important skill in so many areas of learning and working?"

Never forget the difference between the words "teach" and "learn." Your state or province only requires you to document what kids have learned. You only have to teach your assigned content to students who have not yet mastered it. Keeping these principles foremost in your mind, you'll never have to worry whether extension activities in writing are appropriate for kids with advanced writing abilities.

Chapter Summary

Gifted students usually prefer a reading program that offers choices about what they read and the activities they do. If you are not presently using a literature-based program with your entire class, the strategies described in this chapter will help you offer independent learning options to better meet the reading needs of your gifted students. If you are currently using real literature for much of your reading program, these strategies may help you differentiate for your readers who are gifted. Advanced writers probably already know most of the writing skills you are planning to teach. They will benefit most from contracts and extensions.

CHAPTER 5
Planning Curriculum for All Students at the Same Time

Gifted students are expected to master the same standards, themes, and concepts as the rest of the class. The difference is that they require regular opportunities to become engaged with learning activities that require more depth and complexity, to accelerate through grade-level standards when needed, and to be able to make choices regarding their extended learning opportunities. At the same time that you're creating instructional activities for the entire class, you can also develop deep and complex activities for gifted students that provide more challenge.

This chapter describes several techniques that you may use either alone or in combination to increase the amount of experience your students have with appropriately challenging learning experiences. Each technique allows you to start the differentiation process with the required standards, and then move highly capable learners into unfamiliar content so they may experience authentic learning.

The term "higher level thinking" is generic. For many years, Benjamin Bloom's Taxonomy of Educational Objectives was widely used. More recently, other models have also emerged. The following sections describe these models for you, so you can apply your creativity in presenting them to your students. When educators limit their students' learning opportunities to simply knowing and understanding content enough to score well on related assessments, many students will leave high school having learned only a small portion of what was possible.

Learning Modalities

One way to create opportunities for differentiated learning is by offering learning tasks that appeal to various learning modalities. Students then choose the task that most appeals to them. You are not required to assign students to the "correct" task. This approach is predicated on the belief that all students can learn the required standards if the content is presented to them in ways their brains can easily process. Some teachers reject this notion, fearing that this level of accommodation will only pamper struggling students into lifelong helplessness. On the contrary, this approach empowers students to believe that if they are having trouble learning required standards, their goal should be to search for another method that will lead to success. A quote from Dr. Kenneth Dunn sums it up nicely: "If students are not learning the way we teach them, we must teach them the way they learn."

"If students are not learning the way we teach them, we must teach them the way they learn."

Students generally belong to one or more of three learning modality categories:

Auditory learners learn by listening, and the more their teachers talk, the better they like it. Auditory learners' favorite thinking styles are logical, analytic, and sequential. Most of the learning tasks in many classrooms favor auditory learners, because many teachers use learning tasks that require logical, analytic, and sequential thinking. Each time you ask students to listen carefully, learn and work in silence, take notes in outline form, follow directions exactly the way you gave them, or predict events, you are favoring auditory learners. Auditory learners do well on these tasks because they like information presented in logical, sequential lessons. They love to analyze the information, make predictions, and check out those predictions as the lessons proceed. They prefer learning from the parts to the whole. Unfortunately, auditory learners make up less than 25 percent of the students in most classes.

Visual learners learn by seeing, mostly through images and graphic organizers and other kinds of visual thinking tools. They do not enjoy learning in little bits and pieces and much prefer teachers who demonstrate the "whole" before teaching the parts. So in reading and literature, they like to know how the story turns out ahead of reading it. In science and social studies, they much prefer perusing the whole unit before being required to learn its individual parts. Because of the early ages at which our children now learn digitally, they expect school to be like those formats, and become impatient if they have to do too much reading before getting the "big picture." You might be shocked to know that in typical classes, visual learners comprise about 65 percent of all students. Therefore, teachers who are unwilling to use teaching strategies that make learning more accessible for visual learners actually become part of the problem, as a huge percentage of students who are in the bottom fourth of any grade level include visual (and tactile-kinesthetic) learners. Not because they are less intelligent than auditory learners, but because teaching methods have not been friendly to the way in which their brains process information.

Tactile-kinesthetic learners comprise about 80 percent of the group recognized as struggling students. They are unable to learn if they are forced to sit still for very long. There is nothing "wrong" with them—their brains just process better if they are allowed to move.

Once you identify your students' preferred learning modality, it becomes much easier to create learning activities that are highly likely to lead to success. For example, a kindergarten teacher discovered that her students' attention spans were dramatically improved when she took them for a run around the playground before starting the academic portion of their school day. A high school teacher discovered that his students learned significantly more about the literature they were reading if they could act out some key scenes in the story. Although these are simple interventions, the results are dramatically effective.

You don't have to worry about matching the right student with the right task. When you use the Curriculum Differentiation Chart (see page 152) it's impossible for students to choose the wrong task. And, since the tasks are designed to accommodate learning modality differences, you can rest assured that everyone will find things they can do with enjoyment and competence.

⭐ STRATEGY

Taxonomy of Thinking

One popular differentiation model is, of course, Bloom's Taxonomy of Educational Objectives[1]. It's an especially ideal model to use to create challenging activities for gifted students. It describes six levels of thinking, arranged sequentially from least to most complex. The original model placed Evaluate at the top of the figure. However, 20 years ago Susan began placing Create above Evaluate, maintaining that if the model is hierarchical, then the most challenging category should be on top. The 2001 revision of the taxonomy, led by Anderson and Krathwohl, reflected that change. As displayed in the Taxonomy of Thinking chart on page 146, the levels are as follows:

1. **Recall** is simply that. Students can say that they "know" something if they can recall it to recite it or write it down.

2. **Understand** means that students can say what they "know" in their own words. Retelling a story, stating the main idea, or translating from another language are several ways in which students can demonstrate that they understand what they have learned.

3. **Apply** means that students can apply what they have learned from one context to another. For example, they might use their knowledge of fractions to double a baking recipe, or they may be required to decide when to apply mathematical or social studies concepts to real-life situations.

4. **Analyze** means that a student can understand the attributes of something so that its component parts may be studied separately and in relation to one another. Asking students to compare and contrast, categorize, and/or recognize inferences, opinions, or motives would give them experience in analyzing.

5. **Evaluate** gives students opportunities to judge what they have analyzed. Susan's version of Bloom's model considers Evaluate after Analyze, since it's very natural to ask students to give their opinion or state a preference about something they are analyzing.

6. **Create** requires students to create a novel or original thought, idea, or product. All of the activities we call "creative thinking" give students experience with creation.

⭐ STRATEGY

Curriculum Differentiation Chart

The Curriculum Differentiation Chart (CDC) is a way to plan curriculum for all of your students at the same time, in the same place—literally on the same document. It includes your descriptions of different learning tasks for auditory, visual, and tactile-kinesthetic learners, plus your extension activities for gifted students.

Right now, you're probably thinking, "Where am I supposed to find time to design four different sets of learning tasks? Help!" We know it sounds daunting. The good news is, you don't have to do it alone.

When Susan gives teacher training workshops, she asks teachers to work in "job-alike" groups, sitting together by common grade level or subject area. As they work together to plan differentiation opportunities for their students, they are amazed at how much they can accomplish in 20 minutes or less.

Susan first discovered this during her classroom teaching years and learned how to

text continues on page 147

---

[1] Bloom, 1984; Anderson & Krathwohl, 2001. Note: The verb forms of the original category names (Recall, Understand, Apply, Analyze, Evaluate, Create) are used throughout this book.

Taxonomy of Thinking

Category	Definition	Trigger Words	Products
Create	Re-form individual parts to make a new whole.	Compose • Design • Invent • Create • Hypothesize • Construct • Forecast • Rearrange parts • Imagine	Song • Poem • Story • Advertisement • Invention • iMovie • Webquest • Cyberhunt • Other creative products
Evaluate	Judge value of something vis-à-vis criteria. Support judgment.	Judge • Evaluate • Give opinion • Give viewpoint • Prioritize • Recommend • Critique	Decision • Editorial • Debate • Critique • Defense • Verdict • Judgment • Roll-the-Die • Rubrics
Analyze	Understand how parts relate to a whole. Understand structure and motive. Note fallacies.	Investigate • Classify • Categorize • Compare • Contrast • Solve	Survey • Questionnaire • Prospectus • Plan • Solution to Problem • Report • Cyberhunt • Webquest
Apply	Transfer knowledge learned in one situation to another.	Demonstrate • Use guides, maps, charts, etc. • Build • Cook	Recipe • Model • Demonstration • Artwork • Craft • Playing a game by the rules
Understand	Demonstrate basic understanding of concepts and curriculum. Translate into other words.	Restate in own words • Give examples • Explain • Summarize • Translate • Show symbols • Edit	Drawing • Diagram • Graphic organizer • Response to question • Revision • Translation
Recall	Ability to remember something previously learned.	Tell • Recite • List • Memorize • Remember • Define • Locate	Quiz or test • Skill work • Vocabulary • Isolated facts

capitalize on it for everyone's benefit. When she wanted to plan an Extension Menu or Curriculum Differentiation Chart, she would post a note in a conspicuous place on the day she wanted to work. The note usually said something like this:

I need help with some curriculum planning today during my lunch time. From 12:15–12:45.

If you are available during this time, please come to my room and help with the brainstorming.

P.S. I'LL BRING CHOCOLATE!

The "lunch and chocolate" approach soon becomes a habit for teachers who appreciate that many heads are better than one for all types of planning experiences.

Scenario: José

José was a third grader who had always found schoolwork to be very easy. Recently he had developed some distracting behaviors. He had started turning in his work late, and much of it was sloppy and inaccurate. Even though José was capable of doing complex activities, his work always seemed to reflect his attitude of, "What is the least amount of work I can do and still stay out of trouble?" His favorite question was, "How many lines does this have to be?"

José's teacher recognized that he was bored by work that was too easy, and she decided to build some more challenging options into the upcoming unit on nutrition. She hoped that by offering José some choices with attractive incentives, he could function more like a gifted student should.

When she planned the next unit, she used the Curriculum Differentiation Chart shown on pages 150–151. All students could choose activities from the chart; the more capable kids could do fewer and more complex activities and skip the simpler tasks. José's eyes lit up when he heard the news, and his work in subsequent units was much more in line with his advanced ability.

Scenario: Shanaya

Shanaya had not had a very successful school record in terms of grades. However, she appeared to have a photographic memory for topics she really loved. She actually knew a lot about boxing, and claimed to have memorized many statistics on the topic, which she would often inject into conversations in the most unusual ways. She was always humming softly, and tended to use any available surface as a drum. Sitting in one place bothered her greatly, so she was constantly looking for excuses to leave her desk and move about the classroom.

When Shanaya saw the CDC on nutrition, she wanted to choose some of the extension activities, and work on designing a nutritional plan for—you guessed it—a female boxer in training! She chose a way to do it that complemented her tactile-kinesthetic learning modality. She actually prepared and tasted all the food she included, and even found a way to compute the nutritional content. Her teacher decided to allow her to do this as long as all the assessment expectations for the required standards were met. Shanaya attended all the direct instruction lessons but did all her actual work on her chosen extension activity. Shanaya got what she wanted and so did her teacher, as Shanaya's grades for her work in this unit were excellent.

Shanaya's experience demonstrates that once we have found the style of instruction that is most likely to lead to success for a given student, we should not hesitate to allow students to choose activities in that category, even exclusively. Some gifted students are equally comfortable with more than one learning modality approach. However, if a student is interested in a learning activity, but does not want to work on the suggested product, be flexible about letting the student choose another way to demonstrate what she or he has learned.

The CDC is designed to enable you to plan for all students' learning modalities simultaneously for an entire unit of work. A column labeled "Extension" is for critical thinking tasks that gifted students may be allowed to do instead of any of the other tasks on the same horizontal line.

How to Use the Curriculum Differentiation Chart

A reproducible Curriculum Differentiation Chart is on page 152 but you may wish to use the customizable file in the digital content instead, because it has expandable fields for more writing space. Or you may choose to make your own charts on larger sheets of paper.

1. Look back at Preparing the Study Guide and Extension Menu in chapter 3 (pages 77 and 79) for suggestions on determining standards and related topics.

2. Start each unit with an overview of the content. This is an essential step for some of your global thinkers, especially those with learning problems and gifted kids who are twice-exceptional (see chapter 1, pages 22–29). You might use graphic organizers or survey the content and have students ask questions about what they notice in the survey.

3. Write the standards as statements in the far left column of the Curriculum Differentiation Chart.

4. Working horizontally across the chart, plan the differentiated tasks.

   ■ The Product Choices Chart (see page 87) can help you design tasks that will appeal to auditory, visual, and tactile-kinesthetic learners. Feel free to add other products that support the standards and fit the learning modalities.

   ■ For ideas on how to phrase tasks, use the Trigger Words column in the Taxonomy of Thinking chart (page 146). Average and below-average students need considerable time with Recall and Understand tasks before they can move on to more complex tasks. We recommend that most of the tasks you design for your visual and tactile-kinesthetic learners fall into the Recall, Understand, and Apply categories. For the extension tasks, use the Apply,

Analyze, Evaluate, and Create categories. (Apply is a "swing" category, depending on the complexity of the task.)

   ■ All tasks on each horizontal line must teach the standard on that line. After you write each task, check back to make sure this is the case. Confirm that if a student completed only that task and none of the other tasks on that line, he or she would still be learning the standard.

IMPORTANT After entering all of the standards, you should always work horizontally across the chart until you have completed all four columns for each standard. This reinforces the idea that you're not finished planning until you've accommodated all types of learners. Once you've completed several charts, planning for differentiation with each new unit will become a habit.

5. If you need more than one extension task per standard, create an Extension Menu at the same time you're creating your Curriculum Differentiation Chart. See page 153 for a reproducible Nutrition Extension Menu.

   If you want to stretch this unit into other areas of the curriculum, create an Extension Menu that allows for this, with one subject per square. See page 154 for a reproducible example.

6. Let all students choose the task they want to work on. They can choose anything that appeals to them, as long as it's on the same horizontal line as the standard you're teaching. No matter what task they choose, they will learn the standard.

   Give students several days to work on their tasks. Then lead a discussion about what they have learned. Since students will have chosen different tasks and studied material from different sources, the discussion will be enhanced by variety.

7. To manage the students' extension activities, use the Independent Study Agreement (see page 91) or the Personal Interest Study Project Agreement (see page 183). Be sensitive to the fact that many gifted kids resist writing tasks. Writing slows down their thinking, and often it's not necessary for their mastery of a standard. Have students keep track of their progress using the Daily Log of Extension Work (see page 92).

NOTE Later in the unit, provide opportunities for all students to do higher-level tasks. They might select a culminating activity from the Extension column or a task from the Extension Menu, if you include one in your unit.

8. Decide how outcomes or grades will be determined. Use the Evaluation Contract (see page 96) or any other method of evaluating student projects. Be sure to tell students about the grading criteria you will use before they start working.

9. Plan the record-keeping procedures you will use. There are two parts to record-keeping. The first is making sure that students are working productively every day; the Daily Log of Extension Work takes care of this. The second is recording their grades.

Students who work on tasks from the learning modality columns (Auditory/Analytic, Visual/Global, Tactile-Kinesthetic/Global) earn daily grades for their work.

Students who work on extension activities may take several days to complete one task. In all available spaces in your grade book (or computerized grading program), enter the grade they earn for that task. This might require you to allow them to learn other standards on their own, without producing actual products related to each standard. As in the Study Guide method, these students would still be held accountable for assessments on all of the content at the same time the rest of the class is being assessed.

NOTE When teaching a thinking strategy to students, first use simple content so they can concentrate on the strategy. Then, use the same strategy with your required standards. Once students "get" the strategy, they can use it with greater understanding when the strategy is applied to actual content.

⭐ STRATEGY

Tiered Learning Experiences

Another method for differentiating for all students simultaneously is Tiered Learning Experiences, which uses the Taxonomy of Thinking or ThinkTrix (see page 157) to plan appropriately challenging learning activities for students at all thinking levels. The Tiered Lesson Planning Chart (blank form on page 156, example form on page 155) is created and used in much the same way as the Curriculum Differentiation Chart has been designed for using the Taxonomy of Thinking to plan lessons at several different levels of difficulty: entry level, advanced level, and extension level. The required standard is described in the left column. Working horizontally across the row, other activities should give all students practice in learning the described standard. Although the entry level task should be easier than the advanced level, the advanced level should *not* simply be more work than the entry level task. Rather, the advanced level task should connect to some of the trigger words on the three higher levels of the taxonomy: Analyze, Evaluate, and Create.

text continues on page 157

Curriculum Differentiation Chart

Unit: _Nutrition_

Required Standard	Auditory/Analytic	Visual/Global	Tactile-Kinesthetic/Global	Extension
#1: The government guidelines for nutrition are represented as a plate and illustration of the recommended portions for each meal. (See myplate.gov.) The five major food groups are vegetables, fruits, grains, proteins, and dairy.	Describe the foods you would eat to maintain a balanced diet for three days. Include three meals and two snacks per day. Compute calories, fat grams, and the percentage of food in each food group for each day.	Find or create pictures of foods from all five food groups. With these pictures create plans for three days of balanced, healthy eating for all meals and snacks.	Using the MyPlate form at myplate.gov, determine the percentage of food you eat that meets that plan's nutritional standards.	Investigate eating plans that don't take a balanced approach. Use your search engine to find "fad diets." Choose two of those diets and demonstrate, using the myplate.gov visual, which food categories are absent. Hypothesize the potential negative effects on the health of the person who has chosen to follow one of these diets.
#2: If you believe that you and your family are already making healthy food choices, explore the myplate.gov website to analyze how well your current eating plan follows the suggested standards for healthy eating.	Listen to and/or watch food commercials for one evening. Using the myplate.gov diagram, analyze how well the foods in the commercials follow the MyPlate guidelines.	Ask six students in your class to record everything they eat today and report the results to you in writing tomorrow. Using the diagram from myplate.gov, determine how many food groups each student's choices included. Create a visual to show the results along with your recommendations for change.	Make models of correct serving sizes of some foods from all food groups. Demonstrate to other students how to choose correct serving sizes.	Hypothesize what happens to a person's body if he or she eats too much or too little over a period of several months. Explain how overeating and undereating affect bodily systems and functions.

#3: People who don't eat a balanced diet may lack energy and may be more likely to have weight problems or get sick.	Use the internet to find several sources that explain how people's health is affected in countries where a balanced diet is difficult or impossible. Write a speech to convince people you know who don't eat a balanced diet to change their eating habits.	Draw a series of pictures illustrating how several months of unbalanced eating affect the body.	Use the internet to learn how people's health is affected in areas where people cannot find or afford healthy food. Search for ways in which this problem might be solved.	Hypothesize what would happen to a person's body if he or she omitted one entire food group from his or her diet for a period of several months. Be able to present evidence for your predictions.
#4: Junk food is high in calories and low in nutrients, so it doesn't fuel the body as well as nutritional foods. When people eat a balanced diet, they crave less junk food.	Keep a food diary for a week. Track the amount of junk food you eat versus the amount of nutritional food. Present your data to other students in a way that demonstrates your understanding of how to choose foods from all food groups.	Separate the groceries your family has at home into two categories: Junk Food and Nutritional Food. Draw pictures of the foods you find and place them in the appropriate categories. Highlight the category that has the most food items and the one that costs your family the most money each week.	Use the internet to learn how eating too much junk food affects the body. Choose a way to share your findings with the class.	Prepare a lesson on junk foods and present it to the class. Include information about why people crave junk foods, how junk foods affect the mind and body, and why they are a problem for many adults.
#5: Exercise has long-lasting, beneficial effects on the body, regardless of the degree to which one makes wise decisions about nutrition.	Locate at least two research studies on the benefits of exercise. Prepare a presentation tool that will communicate the recommended exercise program for children, young adults, adults, and seniors.	Prepare a multimedia presentation to illustrate several activities people can do to improve and maintain cardiovascular and muscular health.	Prepare a demonstration of aerobic and/or weight resistance programs that can help with weight control and overall good health.	Use the internet to locate statistics on this issue. Interview one person your age and one adult to get their input on this problem. Hypothesize reasons people use to avoid exercise. Come up with a plan to entice non-exercisers to start exercising.

Curriculum Differentiation Chart

Unit: _____

Required Standard	Auditory/Analytic	Visual/Global	Tactile-Kinesthetic/Global	Extension
#1				
#2				
#3				
#4				
#5				
#6				
#7				
#8				
#9				
#10				

Locate studies that have been done with babies who are allowed to choose their own foods from a high-chair tray. Discover the results and hypothesize the reasons for them. Should parents insist that their children eat balanced meals at all times?	Research the history of nutrition in the past 50 years. Notice how the attitudes toward what people eat have changed over time. Hypothesize the reasons for these changes.	Investigate eating disorders. Discover the similarities and differences in overeaters and undereaters. Find information about treatment programs and their rates of success. Which "cures" seem to last for five years or longer?
Dietary supplements (for general health, weight control, and muscle strength) are taken regularly by many people. Investigate supplements and hypothesize reasons for their popularity. Discover some negative effects of various supplements.	**Student Choice**	Invite a panel of professionals from local agencies that offer physical fitness programs to speak to your class. Help other students prepare questions to ask at the end of the panel's presentation. Moderate the panel.
Investigate the attitudes and behaviors of Americans and Europeans toward regular exercise and physical fitness from 1950 to the present day. Hypothesize reasons for the similarities and differences you find.	Design a menu of fitness activities that you think would appeal to people who are reluctant to exercise.	Investigate the problems faced by low income people in finding and buying wholesome food for their families. Find a new way to provide them with access to recommended food options on myplate.gov.

Nutrition Extension Menu for Other Subject Areas

Science

- Find images that represent the myplate.gov recommended food choices. Share this information with your classmates.
- Explain the concept of calories to the class.
- Predict how people's eating habits may change in the next 20 years.

Reading

- Read information on nutrition from several sources.
- Create several challenging questions about nutrition for the class.
- Read a novel or story about a person with an eating disorder. Give a talk about it to the class.

Writing

- Write a letter to your parent(s) describing good nutrition.
- Write a story about a food-related topic.
- Write about your need to eat in school during times other than lunch. Present your request to your teacher.

Talking

- Interview your parents about your family's shopping/eating habits. Chart your findings.
- Survey classmates about their eating habits. Chart your findings.
- Prepare and present a debate about school lunches.

Student Choice

Social Studies

- Collect articles about global or local food problems. Present a brief summary.
- Show how advertising affects food choices.
- Demonstrate how regional dishes rely upon regional agricultural products.

Mathematics

- Determine your average daily caloric intake. Count the calories you consume daily for a week and divide by seven.
- Compute the percentage of your family's weekly income spent on food.
- Create a more nutritious menu using the same budgeted amount.

Medicine

- Find information in medical journals or on the internet describing the annual costs of people losing work time due to illness. Create a tool to share this information with the class. Hypothesize which problems may be related to poor nutrition.

Politics

- Locate information about major candidates' positions regarding healthcare in this country. Hypothesize how their concerns may reflect nutritional issues.

Tiered Lesson Planning Chart Example

Unit: <u>Reading and writing standards through the study of the *Titanic*.</u>

Required Standard	Entry-Level Activities	Advanced Activities	Most Challenging Activities
Strand: Writing Concept: Publishing Objective: Prepare writing in a format appropriate to audience and purpose.	Read a newspaper account of the sinking of the *Titanic* and record six factual errors reported. Correct all errors. Cite sources.	Create a list of 10 changes that were put in place after the sinking of the *Titanic* to avoid similar future disasters. Explain the direct connection to mistakes made in the creation and operation of the *Titanic*.	Write a historical document detailing important events in the lives of three survivors from the *Titanic*. Include personal and professional information including obituary articles. Hypothesize how their survival impacted them regarding their lifetime contributions to the world.
Strand: Reading Concept: Comprehending Informational Text Objectives: ▪ Locate specific information by using organizational features ▪ Draw valid conclusions about expository text supported by text evidence	Write an imaginary interview conducted with an actual survivor about what he or she experienced during the voyage and after the *Titanic* hit the iceberg. Use a question and answer format, basing your questions and responses on facts. Identify the survivor by name. (Two students may also present this project in an interview format to the class.)	Create a large poster drawing of the *Titanic* detailing major components of the ship and labeling key parts of the ship. Include a history of any work-related incidents or other events that could be connected to the sinking.	Research and discuss in detail three examples of literary writings that foreshadowed disasters other than the *Titanic*. Discuss how accurate the fiction work was to the actual historical outcomes. Cite all title and authors.
Strand: Writing Concept: Literary Responses Objective: Write an informational report that includes: ▪ a focused topic ▪ applicable facts and relevant details ▪ logical sequence ▪ a concluding statement	Discuss at least six examples of the literary element of foreshadowing in the literary excerpt about the *Titanic* or from outside sources. Discuss how the foreshadowing actually played out in reality. Cite all sources.	Create a two-color bar graph showing survival and death rates for all classes of passengers and crew members on the *Titanic*. Or prepare a written report detailing the percentages of survival and death rates reporting which groups by gender and class level survived or perished. Cite all sources.	Research the life of Robert Ballard. Create a personal and professional history using a timeline showing his discoveries and contributions to shipwreck research on the *Titanic* and other ships.
Strand: Reading Concept: Reading Process Objective: Acquire and use new vocabulary in relevant contents	Find 10 challenging vocabulary words in the reading. Create a multiple choice vocabulary test for the words. Include an answer key for the correct choices.	Find 10 challenging vocabulary words in the assigned reading and learn their meanings as well as their etymologies. Use an unabridged dictionary or an internet source.	Pretend you are the ruling judge on one of the inquiries into the *Titanic* disaster. Create a written verdict of your findings detailing key events in the sinking, tactical mistakes, and possible solutions to avoid a similar disaster in the future. Use a thesaurus to transform simple words into more sophisticated synonyms.

Tiered Lesson Planning Chart

Unit: _____

Required Standard	Entry-Level Activities	Advanced Activities	Most Challenging Activities

NOTE The Curriculum Differentiation Chart and the Tiered Lesson Planning Chart both follow steps to ensure that all students learn the required standards. The difference between them is that the CDC relies on learning modality differentiation and the TLC on differentiating levels of thinking. On both charts, the actual learning task chosen by students will determine *how* that content will be learned. Assessments are experienced at the same time for all students, although you are free to use several different testing formats to give all types of learners an equal chance of success. Ultimately, all students feel empowered because they get to choose their specific work task and you feel empowered because you know all the standards are being taught with a goal of mastery.

⭐ **STRATEGY**

The ThinkTrix

A third model of creating differentiated learning tasks is the ThinkTrix, which is the creation of Dr. Frank Lyman, whose previous work included the Think-Pair-Share method. The ThinkTrix has been field-tested and researched thoroughly, and has proven useful at all performance levels, with all ages, and in all content areas.

The ThinkTrix, or thinking matrix, is a thinking taxonomy consisting of seven basic thinking types, or "mind actions." These are from simplest to most complex: Recall, Similarity, Difference, Cause and Effect, Idea to Example, Example to Idea, and Evaluation. Teachers and students, when fully comprehending and using the seven mind actions, are able to achieve a shared metacognition—that is, they know and understand *how* they know something. One way in which the the ThinkTrix is different from Bloom's Taxonomy is that the ThinkTrix is partially described by icons, is very friendly to all types of learners, and is especially friendly to visual and tactile-kinesthetic learners.

The ThinkTrix enables teachers to translate any thought process into one or more of these seven types of thinking. All writing and test questions can be categorized as to the precise thinking involved, and teachers and students can enjoy more clarity during oral communication. For instance, a hypothesis can be understood as a *cause or effect* hypothesis; a summary as an *idea or example* summary, and so on.

The ThinkTrix on page 158 demonstrates the model. Students, working cooperatively either in pairs or two pairs interacting with two other pairs, craft their own questions, identify the mind actions involved, and respond to the questions. This interaction can be done orally, in writing, using cognitive maps, or using a combination of all three. Gifted and high performing students appreciate the independence and ownership, the "enfranchising of their minds," that working with the ThinkTrix grid allows. The focal areas, or departure points, on the intersecting axis can be changed as the students and teacher determine what is the best fit for a unit or subject area.

Gifted students appreciate the independence and ownership that working with the ThinkTrix grid allows.

A sample ThinkTrix activity is shown on page 158 and a blank reproducible form on page 159. See the references and resources on page 237 for specific recommendations of materials that support the ThinkTrix model.

Using the ThinkTrix in Small Groups

A double version of the ThinkTrix can be used by two to four students working on independent studies. At several points during the research process, they could use this method to discuss what they are learning.

Two pairs of students (or two individual students) sit across from each other. The goal is for students to ask each other questions requiring response to class content or ongoing research projects. Questions may require critical thinking or they may be straight recall from readings or classwork. Each team must answer the questions

text continues on page 160

ThinkTrix on Global Warming

Objective: Help students understand global warming and its effects on human beings.

Required Standards:

a. Climate patterns are changing in our area and around the world.

b. Some scientists think a greenhouse effect is responsible for the changes.

c. Other scientists think the changes are simply a repeat of previous global patterns.

d. Some internet sites can be helpful and reliable sources of information.

Cause and Effect		What are some conditions that are suspected to cause global warming? What would be the effect, in your lifetime, of global warming on the environment, on growing things, on animals, and on humans?
Recall	R	What do you remember about global warming from our class discussion yesterday?
Similarity		In what similar ways do all power sources impact the earth?
Difference		How are the effects on the earth of coal and nuclear power different from each other?
Idea to Example	EX	Give several examples of how you and your family would be impacted by global warming.
Example to Idea	EX→	Given those examples, what is your hypothesis about people's responsibility to seriously address the issue now?
Evaluation		In what ways might it be dangerous to continue the debate without carrying out effective interventions?

Adapted by permission of Frank Lyman, ThinkTrix SmartCard, San Clemente, CA (800-933-2667).

ThinkTrix

Objective: _____

Required Standards: _____

_____

_____

_____

Cause and Effect	⟳	
Recall	**R**	
Similarity	◐◑	
Difference	◖◗	
Idea to Example	💡→EX	
Example to Idea	EX→💡	
Evaluation	⊤	

asked by the other team. In addition, the answering team must be able to identify the ThinkTrix category in which the question belongs. For this categorizing, partners may collaborate for 30 seconds or less to come up with a united answer or argument. Many questions could belong in several categories, and it is up to the asking team members to allow unusual category selection by the answering team members if there is a convincing argument in favor of the interpretation. Sometimes, another class member can serve as the judge to determine which category selections should or should not be accepted.

⭐ STRATEGY
The Kaplan Model

An alternate model of differentiating learning tasks by applying categories of thinking is to follow Dr. Sandra Kaplan's model of depth, complexity, and novelty. Dr. Kaplan has spent decades developing and refining the model and teaching educators how to use it to its best advantage. Her icon-driven program has been successful in raising expectations and the level of thinking and learning for all students. Many online resources can be downloaded and used with the Kaplan Model. See the references and resources on page 237 for recommendations.

The definitions that follow may be easily blended. Their characteristics often overlap and no effort should be made to assign specific categories to various learning tasks. [3]

Depth

Depth is a process of thought that seeks generalizations and universal principles. Students analyze details, patterns, trends, and ethical dilemmas.

Students practice how to:

- Learn as many details as possible, including traits, factors, variables, nuances, and elements that distinguish the topic being studied from other topics.

- Look for unanswered questions, including incomplete data, in the content being studied.

- Understand the ethics involved including discrepancies, inequities, injustices, biases, prejudices, and discriminations.

- Understand the specific language used by specialists in a particular discipline.

Curriculum based on depth moves quickly from the concrete to the abstract, from foundations to complexities, and away from isolated facts toward generalizations or universal themes. Students are encouraged to formulate questions instead of reciting facts.

Complexity

Complexity is the quality or process of thinking that combines many ideas or parts to develop complicated and interrelated wholes.

Students practice how to:

- Combine various ideas or parts to develop complicated and interrelated wholes to make interdisciplinary connections.

- Understand complex concepts, problems, and generalizations in order to create unique and effective solutions across many disciplines, over time, and from different perspectives.

- Examine elements from several perspectives that include viewpoints from technicians, historians, futurists, critics, philosophers, and people they know.

Novelty

Novelty is a unique perspective, interpretation, or solution through original insight.

Students practice how to:

- Work together to develop creative solutions to complex situations.

- Channel their talents into methods such as Future Problem Solving.

---

[3] Definitions have been adapted from various sources, including the website of the San Mateo/Foster City Schools (www.smfcsd.net).

⭐ STRATEGY

Learning Centers

If you're comfortable using Learning Centers, you can transfer the learning tasks you created for the Curriculum Differentiation Chart to color-coded, laminated task cards for use in a Learning Center format. In addition to the task cards (perhaps arranged by standard), a good Learning Center should contain:

- Clearly stated directions about how to use the center.

- Clearly stated objectives or purposes of the center.

- Interesting and inviting displays; enticing questions.

- Activities, resources, and materials that appeal to various learning modalities.

- Instructions about how to choose tasks.

- Copies of the Product Choices Chart (page 87).

- Examples of what completed tasks should look like.

- Answer keys, if needed.

- Tips about where to go for help.

- A description of the rubrics and other evaluation criteria used to grade students' work.

- Instructions on how to store work between visits.

- Guidelines for students' behavior.

- Ideas of what to do when students finish ahead of others. *Example:* They might prepare additional task cards on the same or related topics.

To reduce congestion at the Learning Center, try this variation. Set up four centers around the same unit: auditory, visual, tactile-kinesthetic, and extension. Let all students choose the task they prefer. They'll still be working on the same standards, and that's what really matters. The centers don't have to be elaborate. They can be located on bookshelves or small tables.

Regardless of the format you choose, pull the kids back for a large-group discussion after they have had a few days to gather information about a standard. Gifted students who have opted to learn standards more independently and are working on tasks from the Extension Menu may be excused from some of these discussions.

Students' grades should be a combination of the work they do on the tasks they choose and more formal assessments of what they have learned. Credit can be given for following behavior guidelines and working conditions.

⭐ STRATEGY

Socratic Seminars

Challenge your students' thinking with the Socratic Seminar, a time-honored question-and-discussion format. You might use it with your whole class or with small groups of high-ability learners as a differentiation tool. It's an outstanding way to move content from recall to true understanding, and all students benefit from it. Gifted kids love it because it gives them lots of opportunities to think and share their thoughts with others. You can use the Socratic Seminar to discuss literature, history, current events, school or community issues, or hypothetical situations. All students must have read or seen the same prompt in order for the discussion to lead to the best outcomes.

A Socratic Seminar is an outstanding way to move content from recall to true understanding.

---

1. After students have learned enough about a topic to think and speak intelligently about it, schedule a seminar. Plan about 30 minutes to start, then longer time periods as students become more comfortable with the process.

2. Have 12–15 students sit in a circle. The rest of the class forms a second circle, ideally with another facilitator. If this isn't possible,

text continues on page 163

Build Blocks to Think

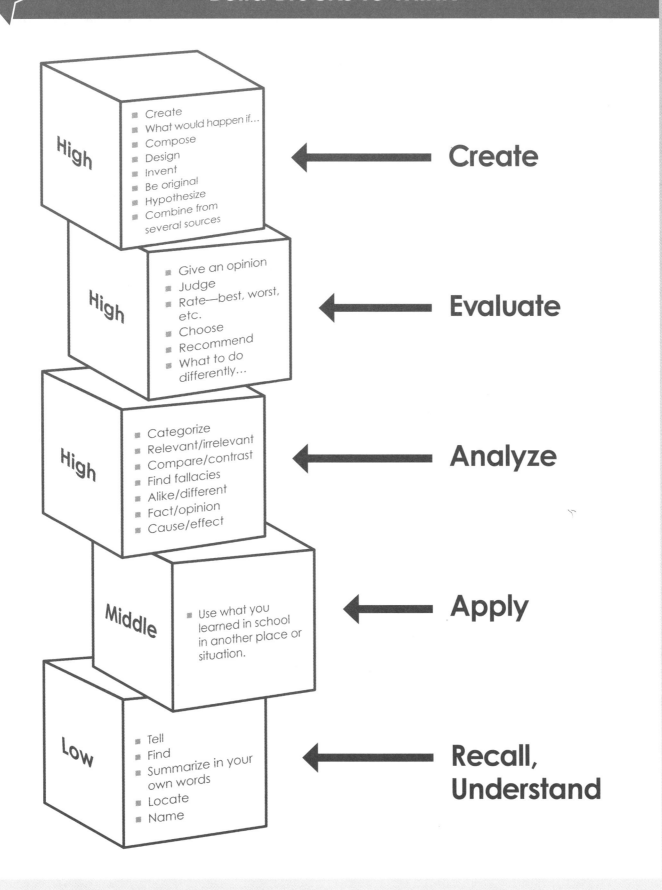

High
- Create
- What would happen if...
- Compose
- Design
- Invent
- Be original
- Hypothesize
- Combine from several sources

← **Create**

High
- Give an opinion
- Judge
- Rate—best, worst, etc.
- Choose
- Recommend
- What to do differently...

← **Evaluate**

High
- Categorize
- Relevant/irrelevant
- Compare/contrast
- Find fallacies
- Alike/different
- Fact/opinion
- Cause/effect

← **Analyze**

Middle
- Use what you learned in school in another place or situation.

← **Apply**

Low
- Tell
- Find
- Summarize in your own words
- Locate
- Name

← **Recall, Understand**

students take turns sitting in an "inner circle" as active participants and an "outer circle" as observers. Observers should be watching one specific student in the inner circle for the best de-briefing outcomes.

3. Explain the rules of discussion.

   - Students speak directly to each other, not to you.

   - They take turns contributing without necessarily raising their hands as long as they can handle the intricacies of talking to each other in this way. If not, raised hands may be in order.

   - When they give an answer or offer an idea, they should also give evidence from the reading to support it and announce its exact location in the text so everyone else can follow along. Evidence might come from what the student has read or learned, or from personal experience. Each bit of evidence should be clearly identified by its source.

   - When referring to something another person said previously, they should use the person's name. *Example:* "Jason, when you said _____, it made me think of _____." Students may challenge each other's statements in nonaggressive ways. Again, they should use names, not pronouns. *Example:* "I disagree with what Kari said, because the book says on page 32 that . . . "

     If it seems that students aren't listening well, try asking them to briefly summarize what the previous speaker said (using the speaker's name) before making their own contribution.

4. Ask an open-ended question—one for which there is no single or correct answer. Here are some examples, in no particular order:

   - Why do you think _____ happened? Could it have been prevented? Under what circumstances might the outcome have changed?

   - What feelings, emotions, or events might have caused the people to behave the way they did?

   - How do you think you would behave under similar circumstances?

   - Are you saying _____? (Restate or paraphrase what speaker has said.)

   - Tell us more about _____.

   - How is what we're discussing similar to _____ [another topic the group has discussed]? How is it different?

   - Would anyone like to speak to the other side of this point of view?

   From time to time, have students find something in the actual text that supports their statements or opinions.

5. Wait one to two minutes for someone to reply. Be patient and resist the urge to jump in. If no reply is forthcoming after two minutes, tell students that they may talk quietly to one other person to generate ideas.

   Your hardest task as teacher/facilitator is to stay out of the discussion. Your role is to ask questions that keep the discussion going, not to give your opinion or declaration of what is correct.

6. Allow 5–10 minutes for reflection on the Socratic Seminar process. Invite students' suggestions on how to make the next seminar more effective at demonstrating the best qualities for a seminar.

This process may take a long time to get comfortable and seem truly useful, but don't lose heart. The results are worth the wait. For more information about Socratic Seminars, see the references and resources for this chapter on page 237.

QUESTIONS ★ ANSWERS

"How can I create these alternate activities when I hardly have time for everything I already have to do?"

Differentiation is not about adding responsibilities to your already crowded schedule. Rather, it represents a holistic way of teaching that, in many classrooms, has replaced more traditional methods of treating subject areas separately. Time and again, strategies designed to benefit gifted students have found application with all students. If you try these methods with one unit, you'll probably discover that you enjoy teaching this way, since it allows you to be more creative while simultaneously guaranteeing that your students will still be mastering the standards for which you're responsible. Creating all your units to incorporate differentiation will soon become your natural, preferred way of planning.

See references and resources on page 237 for recommendations of differentiated units based on the revised Bloom's Taxonomy.

"What if some students complete the extension activities before the rest of the class is done with their work?"

Prepare and use an Extension Menu for the unit, similar to the ones found on pages 111 and 113 and in the digital content. Invite interested students to become resident experts on a topic they want to learn more about (see chapter 6). When you allow some students to become resident experts on topics related to the unit you're teaching, this enhances the experience for everyone.

Another strategy that works well is to teach the revised Bloom's Taxonomy directly to those early finishers, then have them create Learning Center tasks for other teachers. They should start by interviewing the teachers and getting a list of topics for which the teachers want tasks created.

You might also have the younger students use Build Blocks to Think (see page 162) to create questions based on the revised Bloom's Taxonomy for you to use for discussions or tests. Once students have learned the language of the taxonomy, they can be directed to create a certain number of questions by category.

"How can I translate these different activities into grades?"

You may already have rubrics students can use to decide the grade they want to work for before they begin any work. Much of the grade with these strategies comes from the student's willingness to

follow the rules and become invested in the strategy. If not, try the Evaluation Contract (see page 96). We also recommend John Samara's Product Guides (see references and resources on page 237) and Bertie Kingore's Observation Inventory tools (see chapter 8, page 203).

"Why should I offer alternate activities for my one or two gifted students, while my colleague next door is doing the same for her one or two gifted students? This doesn't seem very efficient."

There is a way to group gifted students without having to "track" everyone else. It's called cluster grouping. Only one teacher per grade level is primarily responsible for differentiating the curriculum for gifted students, and the gifted students are clustered in that teacher's class as part of a heterogeneous group. Cluster grouping allows gifted students to enjoy alternate activities together. They no longer have to choose between working with the class on less challenging activities or working alone. For more about cluster grouping, see chapter 7.

Chapter Summary

In this chapter, you have learned how to simultaneously plan curriculum units that reach and teach all of your students with appropriate levels of depth and complexity. You have learned to design learning tasks that are responsive to learning modalities and different levels of ability. You have learned how to manage a classroom in which students are working on different tasks simultaneously.

The first time you use the methods described here, the process may seem tedious and time-consuming. As you use these methods again and again, you'll actually spend less time on each unit plan. Your reward will be the positive response from students and their parents for the exciting learning opportunities available in your classroom. Rather than trying to find one way of teaching that meets all kids' needs, you'll be using one way of planning to challenge and excite all of your students.

CHAPTER 6

"I'm Done. Now What Should I Do?": Self-Selected Independent Study

As you have no doubt ruefully observed, gifted students often finish an activity before the rest of the group; sometimes, they finish an activity before others even get started! This may produce considerable anxiety for you, especially since you now know that extra credit work may not be the answer. You have learned that most gifted kids don't need to be spoon-fed activities to keep them busy. They just want time when they can spend school time learning things that are interesting to them without being required to account for their work following an arbitrarily imposed timeline.

If you have tried the compacting strategies described earlier in this book, you've already discovered how easy it is to allow some students to study what interests them when they compact out of the regular curriculum. Some kids like to read. Others may be in the middle of long-term writing projects and will eagerly return to them. Some may use their time to daydream and plan, which is essential to problem solving and creative thinking. Others may be curious about a topic, an idea, or a new technology they would love to spend some school time exploring. With the availability of online resources, the possibilities are endless.

Gifted students tend to get passionately interested in topics that may not be connected to the current school curriculum at the current time, which is one reason why school is often frustrating for them. They are seldom allowed opportunities to learn the things they really *want* to learn. Even when they are, those opportunities may not be very satisfying because they are not able to develop their ideas to the level they wish. The teacher says, "Write a report on (X topic)" with the underlying message, "Make sure it's done well, looks great, and that you use your time wisely." When we speak of using time wisely, we usually mean looking busy and producing an eye-pleasing product. We expect students to be reading something, writing something, or doing something else observable to indicate that they are staying on task.

The impression students get is that all learning done in school must be for a reason and must result in a formal product, such as a report. However, we (adults) frequently enter bookstores or other people's homes and browse through books, idly wondering if we would like to know more about a certain topic at a later time. We would be offended if a bookstore owner posted a sign proclaiming, "No browsing allowed!" Why not provide opportunities for students to browse in school?

Maybe you have been frustrated by gifted kids who lose interest in a topic shortly after they choose to investigate it. Many student researchers don't need coaching to learn how to get past traditional research methods into those that truly challenge and interest them. We want gifted students on independent study to experience how research can change the way they think and learn. We want them to discover how to synthesize information from many sources, to build on what they learn, to make connections between what they know and what they are learning, and to emulate adult researchers by using research methods that go way beyond simply looking up information.

In elementary gifted education programs, gifted students usually get lots of time to learn about topics that interest them. Frequently, our students would return to visit us when they were in the secondary grades, and they often complained that no one at that level seemed interested in even finding out what the students wanted to research. This chapter provides many tools to help you provide meaningful independent research opportunities at all grade levels that are exciting for your students and easy to manage for you.

⭐ STRATEGY

The Personal Interest Study Project

We can assume that many gifted kids have a desire to learn about some topic in great depth. We can give them a way to pursue their interest in school by undertaking a Personal Interest Study Project. This form of independent study differs from the independent study involved in the Study Guide method in chapter 3, because that approach is curriculum-related and this one is based purely on student interest.

> ## We can assume that many gifted kids have a desire to learn about some topic in great depth.

Allow time for students working on Personal Interest Study Projects to get together to chat, share resources, and brainstorm ways to solve problems in their research. Plan to spend some time with these kids as a group so they perceive you are interested in their projects and value the time they spend on them. If time is short, consider meeting in a convenient place as the rest of the class does sustained silent reading or works on reading activities. Kids on independent study are already avid and skilled readers; it won't hurt them to substitute these meetings for silent reading periods.

Personal Interest Projects for the Primary Grades

Even young gifted students relish opportunities to pursue topics of their choosing. For students in the primary grades, personal interest projects may be relatively unstructured.

Independent study with visual aids is a fairly unstructured and developmentally appropriate way for primary students to explore and share their areas of interest. Students enjoy it because they are allowed to investigate large amounts of information without immediately being expected to report on everything they learn. Most are willing to create more formal projects on specific subtopics later, when they have had the chance to satisfy their curiosity. The expectation that visual aids will be included in the presentation relieves them of the burden of doing too much writing.

Teachers enjoy it because kids learn how to work on the same project for several days or weeks, relieving them of the responsibility for providing numerous shorter activities for those students who are always "done" and don't know what to do next.

For additional suggestions, see Acceptable Student Projects on page 169. See page 185 for a project especially suited to primary students.

Personal Interest Survey

What if a student can't think of a topic? Here's where a personal interest survey can be very helpful. You'll find a reproducible survey on page 168. Interest surveys help you learn things about your students that may not typically come to your attention. You may wish to survey all of your students at the beginning of every school year. (For younger kids, you may want to send the survey home so parents can help fill it out.) Besides giving you insights into the kinds of things your gifted students may want to study in depth, the survey can also help you motivate reluctant learners. Raymond Wlodkowski, an educational psychologist and expert on motivation, has found that one of the quickest ways to motivate students is to discover what they are interested in outside of school, and then spend a short time each day talking with them about their interests. Watch for dramatic, positive changes in their attitudes.

Using an interest survey and conversations with parents and former teachers, help students identify topics of personal interest to them. Topics don't have to be related to any of the prescribed curriculum. Encourage students to select something they may be working on at home. Reassure them that you won't interfere with their ideas, creativity, or product choices. Sometimes gifted kids resist bringing their topics of passionate interest to school because they fear the teacher will take control.

Scenario: Rahul

By the end of the first day of school, Rahul was "done" with fourth grade. It was painfully clear to his teacher that there was little or nothing in the planned curriculum that represented new learning for him. Worse still, his class had more than its share of struggling students. No wonder his constant refrain was, "I'm done! Now what should I do?" Although Rahul was obviously precocious, his parents didn't want him promoted to a higher grade. Therefore, it was up to the teacher to find interesting and challenging work that would engage him in learning throughout the school year.

His teacher took Rahul aside one day and said, "I've noticed that you often finish your work very quickly and you have a lot of free time. Would you like to use some of that time to investigate a topic you are interested in?" Rahul's instant response was, "Yes! Antarctica." The teacher said, "That sounds like a very interesting topic. Let's start a Topic Browsing Planner on Antarctica and see what resources can be found."

The teacher and the media center specialist helped Rahul do a webquest to gather information from various sources. Rahul's parents agreed to help with the search, and that became a way to differentiate Rahul's homework. Soon Rahul had bookmarked an extensive listing of online resources. At the start of this experience, Rahul had asked the teacher, "Can I create my own project?" She had said, "Yes, but use the first week or so to explore your topic before you decide what you want your formal project to focus on." Relieved, Rahul became thoroughly engrossed in learning about Antarctica.

Rahul's Topic Browsing Planner, found on page 172, shows the results of several days of browsing. Whenever he discovered subtopics he found interesting, he recorded them. Eventually he became fascinated by the subtopic of how global warming affects icebergs and, by extension, other bodies of water. Rahul learned that an international committee had been formed to study the problem, and that a scientist from his own city was on the committee. He added this local expert to his list of possible interview subjects. To see how melting ice affects stationary objects, Rahul designed an experiment using melting ice cubes. This opportunity to present what he had learned using the visual aid of an actual experiment, which he demonstrated to the class, did wonders to rekindle the spark of learning in this young man.

text continues on page 170

Interest Survey

1. What kinds of books do you like to read?

2. How do you get the news? What parts of news reports do you look at regularly?

3. What are your favorite magazines or websites?

4. What types of TV programs do you prefer? Why?

5. What is your favorite activity or subject at school? Your least favorite? Why?

6. What is your first choice about what to do when you have free time at home?

7. What kinds of things have you collected? What do you do with the things you collect?

8. If you could talk to any person currently living, who would it be? Why? Think of three questions you would ask the person.

9. If you could talk to any person from history, who would it be? Why? Think of three questions you would ask the person.

10. What are your hobbies? How much time do you spend on your hobbies?

11. If you could have anything you want, regardless of money or natural ability, what would you choose? Why?

12. What career(s) do you think might be suitable for you when you are an adult?

13. If you could spend a week job-shadowing any adult in any career, which would you choose and why?

14. Describe your favorite games and why you like to play them.

15. What kinds of movies do you prefer to see? Why?

16. Imagine that someday you will write a book. What do you think it will be about?

17. Describe 10 things that would be present in a perfect world. Describe an invention you would create to make the world a better place.

18. What places in the world would you most like to visit? Why? Tell about your favorite vacation—one you've taken or wish you could take.

19. Imagine that you're going to take a trip to another planet or solar system. You'll be gone for 15 years. List 10 things you will take with you to do in your spare time.

20. What questions do you think should be on this survey that aren't already on it?

For primary students:

1. Create a digital presentation of a topic you want to investigate.

2. Survey others about a topic. Display and explain the results.

3. Create a game that others can play to learn required standards.

4. Create a digital dictionary of words in any category.

5. Learn vocabulary or spelling words in another language.

6. Create animated attribute webs.

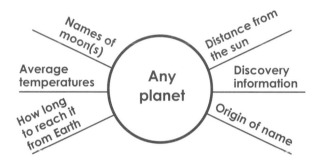

For students in all other grades:

1. Choose an idea from the primary section above.

2. Make a digital report on a topic of your choice.

3. Create and present a live or animated puppet show.

4. Create a radio or television broadcast, video production, or web page.

5. Hold a panel discussion, round-robin discussion, or debate.

6. Write a diary or journal of an important historical event or person. Write a speech a person might have made at that time.

7. Create a time line of events. They might be personal, historical, social, or anything else you choose.

8. Working with several other students, create a panel discussion about a historical topic.

Or play the roles of historical figures reacting to a current problem of today.

9. Create an invention to fill a personal or social need.

10. Study the life of a famous entrepreneur, such as Steve Jobs, Martha Stewart, etc. Create a manual: "How to Be a Successful Entrepreneur."

11. Write and perform a song, rap, poem, story, advertisement, or jingle.

12. Create a travel brochure for another country or planet.

13. Create an imaginary country. Locate and describe its features.

14. Make a model of an idea or invention. Describe its parts and the functions of each.

15. Create a product to represent a synthesis of information from several sources.

16. Write a script for a play or a mock trial.

17. Write a journal of time spent and activities completed with a mentor.

18. Collect materials from a lobbying or public service agency. Summarize the information. (Tip: Use the internet or the Encyclopedia of Associations found in the reference section of most public libraries.)

19. Write to people in other places about specific topics. Synthesize their responses.

20. Create a learning center for teachers to use in their classrooms.

21. Rewrite a story, setting it in another time period, after researching probable differences.

22. Gather political cartoons from several sources. Analyze the cartoonists' ideas.

23. Critique a film, book, TV show, play, concert, or other form of entertainment and post it on an appropriate website.

24. Write a how-to manual for people who need instruction on how to do or use something.

25. Contact publishers to find out how to get something you've written published.

⭐ STRATEGY

The Topic Browsing Planner

When we ask students to select a topic for a project, we usually insist that they do it quickly. Then we encourage them to narrow large topics down to smaller, more manageable subtopics. This leads to situations in which gifted kids start a project with great enthusiasm, but lose interest quickly and stop working on it. Sometimes the reason is that we have forced them to prematurely choose something they already know quite a lot about.

How can students decide on a subtopic before they have a chance to explore the larger topic? Given the speed with which information is growing and changing, we should be encouraging gifted students to explore a topic in depth before requiring formal feedback on a small part of it.

When kids are allowed extended time periods for browsing, they learn that really good ideas may come later in the process of searching for a topic. This relieves some pressure on perfectionists, who can relax about the need to find the perfect topic quickly.

The Topic Browsing Planner creates opportunities for students to pursue topics that interest them. It invites them to discover topics they never knew existed, any one of which may become the focus of in-depth research. The work is done in school, after they have completed their compacted work and instead of the work the rest of the class is doing. Students can buy back time for browsing by demonstrating mastery of certain standards on a pretest, by completing the Most Difficult First problems on an assignment (see pages 42–47), and/or by maintaining a grade average in the A range in any particular subject.

How to Use the Topic Browsing Planner

Every personal interest project (or potential project) should start with a Topic Browsing Planner. A reproducible form is on page 173. The Resources Record Sheet (page 174) may be copied on the back of the planner. A simpler version of the planner for primary students is on page 175.

1. Help students select topics to investigate. Make sure the students understand that the topics don't have to be related to the curriculum and have verified that enough resources are available for them to learn about the topic for an extended period of time.

   Explain that they will eventually choose a subtopic to focus on and a project to work on, but they shouldn't worry about that yet. For now, they should select something in which they are passionately interested.

> **NOTE** For students who are unable to think of a project, allow them to search on selected websites that you have bookmarked, such as Smithsonian, Discovery, National Geographic for Kids, or others. Another option is to have students browse through the books in the school or public library until they find a topic of interest.

2. Give students copies of the Topic Browsing Planner and Daily Log of Extension Work (see page 92) and explain how to fill them out.

3. Call students' attention to the Resources Record Sheet. Have them list possible resources they may investigate. Explain that you don't expect them to complete all of the sections or use all of the resources they list, and that you understand that additional resources will surface based on their searches. They can add those to the list as they proceed. The purpose of the form is to help students keep track of sources they may want to consult or return to as their project progresses.

4. Tell students that they are not required to take any formal notes for a few days. Instead, they should use that time to browse through all of the information they can find on their general topic of interest.

5. Be available to guide students through the same process of exploration, discovery, and delight that Rahul experienced.

   Some students may already know their way around the library, the internet, and other resources. Others may need help discovering the wealth of information available to them. Give everyone a copy of the Resource Suggestions list on page 176. Even experienced researchers might not think of contacting online travel agencies or seeking out a historical reenactment group. Students can use the blank lines to add other resources and websites they believe will be helpful.

6. After students are finished browsing the resources, meet with them and help them choose subtopics on which to focus their ongoing research.

⭐ STRATEGY

The Resident Expert Planner

Once students choose a subtopic they want to study in depth, they're ready to move on to the next stage of the Personal Interest Study Project: becoming a "resident expert." A reproducible Resident Expert Planner is found on pages 179–180. A simpler version for primary students is on page 181. See also the Independent Study Option for the Primary Grades: The 4C Booklet on page 183. For more information on resident experts, refer to chapter 3, pages 73–98.

How to Use the Resident Expert Planner

1. Help students identify a topic they want to pursue in depth. Explain that they will have the opportunity to really get into their topic, and they will be expected to share some of what they learn with the class or other appropriate audience.

   Identifying the topic is simple. The specific subtopic from the Topic Browsing Planner becomes the main topic for the Resident Expert Planner.

   For example, let's say a student is interested in the general topic of life in other countries around the world. He might browse his way through various countries,

then decide he's most interested in learning more about life in China. Eventually he may choose to focus on life as a child in China. That becomes the specific subtopic of his Topic Browsing Planner and the topic of his Resident Expert Planner.

2. Have students break down their main topic into six subtopics. For each subtopic, they should come up with three questions to ask. (If you're using the primary version of the planner, your students will come up with four subtopics and two questions each.)

   Conduct mini-lessons on writing questions that are designed to elicit specific information. Give students a few days to think about and write their subtopics and questions. This might take more browsing time, during which students may return to some of the sources they consulted earlier. They might also consult other sources they listed on their Resources Record Sheet.

   For example, the student who chooses to focus on life as a child in China might come up with these subtopics and questions:

1. **Daily Life**

   a. What are children's routines at home?

   b. What are their chores and responsibilities?

   c. What types of foods do they usually eat and when?

2. **Family Life**

   a. What might their parents do for a living?

   b. How many brothers and sisters might they have?

   c. Do extended family members live nearby or far away?

3. **School**

   a. What days and times do they go to school?

   b. What subjects do they study?

   c. What kinds of teaching methods are used in Chinese schools?

text continues on page 177

Topic Browsing Planner

Student's name: Rahul   **Date:** 10/18

General topic to explore: Antarctica

On a separate sheet of paper, list the things you already know about this topic. Staple that list to this form.

Subtopics I may want to learn more about:

Animals of Antarctica   Plants of Antarctica

Scientific Expeditions   Female Antarctic explorers

Penguins   Movies about Antarctica

How global warming affects icebergs and how that affects other bodies of water

Professionals I might interview:

Dr. Carlos DeMarco, scientist, Shedd Aquarium, Chicago

My mom's friend's son Tim, who just returned from 6 months on a science team in Antarctica

Experiments or surveys I might conduct:

Effects on stationary objects of changes in water levels

Differences in resistance to cold of men and women

Specific subtopic I will focus my project on:

How the increased rate of the melting of the polar ice caps is affecting bodies of

water—and people—all over the globe

Teacher's signature: Judy Lynch

Student's signature: Rahul Patel

Topic Browsing Planner

Student's name: _____ Date: _____

General topic to explore: _____

On a separate sheet of paper, list the things you already know about this topic. Staple that list to this form.

Subtopics I may want to learn more about:

_____   _____

_____   _____

_____   _____

Professionals I might interview:

_____

_____

_____

Experiments or surveys I might conduct:

_____

_____

_____

Specific subtopic I will focus my project on:

_____

_____

Teacher's signature: _____

Student's signature: _____

Resources Record Sheet

Sources of Information	Specifics (call number, author's name, publication date, internet address, etc.)	Title	Where I Found It
Books (reference books, biographies, histories, first-person accounts, etc.)			
Periodicals (magazines, newspapers, newsletters, etc.)			
Internet Resources (websites, newsgroups, blogs, professional networks, government agencies, etc.)			
Other Sources (TV, radio, news shows, critical reviews, interviews, etc.)			

Topic Browsing Planner for Primary Grades

Student's name: _____ Date: _____

General topic to explore: _____

On the back of this paper, list the things you already know about this topic.

Subtopics I may want to learn more about:

_____

_____

_____

_____

_____

Specific subtopic I choose to learn more about:

_____

_____

_____

_____

How I will share what I've learned with the class:

_____

_____

_____

_____

Teacher's signature: _____

Student's signature: _____

Resource Suggestions

(Refers to both actual and online resources)

Books

Almanacs
Atlases
Biographies
Dictionaries
Encyclopedias
First-person accounts
Histories
Nonfiction books
Reference books
_____
_____

Internet Resources

Blogs
Chat rooms
Internet magazines
Newsgroups
Online encyclopedias
Websites
_____
_____

Libraries and Archives

Company libraries/archives
County records
Indexes to free materials
Indexes to periodicals
Library archives
Maps
Newspaper files/archives
Public libraries
Reference libraries
School libraries
Specialized bibliographies
Specialized encyclopedias
Specialized libraries
State, national, and world
   records

Websites, e.g., ancestor.com
_____
_____

Organizations

Chambers of Commerce
Groups
Professional associations
Social and professional clubs
Teams
Troops
_____
_____

Other

Documentaries
Field trips
Films
Videos
_____
_____

People

Experts in the field
Faculty members
Family members
Friends
Friends' parents
Government officials
Historical reenactment
   groups
Neighbors
Parents
Professionals in the field
Senior citizens
Teachers
Youth group leaders
_____
_____

Periodicals

Brochures
Catalogs
Diaries
Journals
Magazines
Newsletters
News reports
Trade magazines
_____
_____

Places

Antique shops
Art galleries
Businesses
Cemeteries
Colleges and universities
Historical sites and societies
Houses of worship
Living history sites
Museums
Schools
Smithsonian Institution
Travel agencies
Weather stations
_____
_____

Digital Resources

CD-ROM encyclopedias
Databases
Digital notetaking websites
Simulation programs
Online or device apps
_____
_____

4. Religion

    a. What are the main religions in China?

    b. What type of religious education might a child have?

    c. What religious holidays are celebrated?

5. Government, Laws, and Economy

    a. What type of government does China have? How has it changed in recent years?

    b. What are some rules and laws in China that are different from the laws you live by?

    c. What are the country's main imports and exports?

6. Recreation

    a. What do families do together for fun?

    b. What are the main government or state holidays?

    c. How do Chinese people like to spend their vacations?

3. Once students have their subtopics and questions, it's time for them to start taking notes. Teach them a note-taking method (see the following box).

4. You may want students to keep track of the resources they use and prepare a bibliography. If so, teach them your preferred format in a mini-lesson and provide websites for further exploration.

Cornell Note Taking is currently a preferred note-taking method. This method is employed through the college years. For more information, visit lsc.cornell.edu/notes.html. Graphic organizers are preferred by visual and tactile-kinesthetic learners, and auditory learners often find notes taken in outline form to be more satisfying.

Tell students to record only those resources they actually use, not those they simply read or consult. Explain that even when they take a lot of notes from a single source, they only need to make one card for that source.

IMPORTANT Be sure not to make this requirement too tedious. We don't want kids spending hours recording reference source information and preparing lengthy, detailed bibliographies. You might ask younger students to record only two books, one encyclopedia (or other reference book), one article, and one website. Older kids will be relieved if you allow them to limit the number of sources that require formal citations.

5. Work with students to identify the materials and supplies they need. They may already have good ideas from the time they spent browsing their general topic.

6. Help students plan how they will report on their project. Give them copies of the Product Choices Chart on page 87.

7. Have students keep track of the work they do on their personal interest projects. The Daily Log of Extension Work on page 92 is an excellent tool for this purpose. It also makes students accountable for being productive. Provide class time for this.

You may decide to let students do part of their project at home, as a way to differentiate their homework. They should note this on their Resident Expert Planner and use a separate Daily Log to record their progress at home. The home part of the project may be shared, but is not formally graded, since some students have advantages over others regarding how much assistance is available to them at home.

You might also use the Check-Off Sheet for Resident Expert Project on page 182. Students fill in each square with a brief description of part of their project. As each part is completed, they mark an X in the box for that square and record the date they finished that task.

Don't insist that they do the parts in any particular order. As long as they get them done, it really doesn't matter. Global learners may actually do better if they plan their project backward from the last step to the first.

Don't set a time limit for any part or step. As long as students follow the working conditions and are faithfully entering data in the Daily Log, the amount of time they spend on a project isn't important. The most important goal is to foster excitement about doing the research.

8. Work with the students to identify any potential problems they might encounter while working on their projects. Help them brainstorm possible solutions.

⭐ STRATEGY

The Note Card Method

Some gifted students are not efficient or effective notetakers. They tend to write down too much, and they may have trouble organizing their information. The Note Card method can help them stay organized and be more selective about the information they will record.

When students try to research one subtopic at a time in several sources, things can quickly become very confusing. They may have trouble remembering which books they've consulted, and there is no way to record interesting information about other subtopics they notice along the way.

With the Note Card method, it's okay if one source yields information about several subtopics. Students can easily switch cards and keep taking notes from that one source without interruption. The best part may be that they only have to use each source once. When they put it aside, they are done with it, because they have pulled everything from it that they need for whichever note cards are needed. Students can then have a master list of all the resources they have actually used in their research.

You'll need a supply of 5" x 7" note cards in six different colors (or four for primary students). *Note:* This method can also be used with a digital device.

1. Give each student 18 cards—three each of the six different colors. Have them decide which color goes with which subtopic on their Resident Expert Planner. They might choose yellow for subtopic one, green for subtopic two, and so on.

2. Tell them to label each card with a subtopic and a question. *Examples:* For a study of the solar system, the subtopics might include planets, meteors and meteorites, black holes, interplanetary travel, etc.

3. Explain that whenever they come across information about the first question under their first subtopic, they should record it on the card with that label. For example, if a student finds information from three sources about black holes, the information would be recorded on that subtopic's card. Students are therefore using only one source of information at a time, but moving freely between making their notes on the appropriate cards. *Tip:* Prepare some sample cards in advance and display and demonstrate them as you explain this process. It's easier to show this than to tell about it.

4. Tell students that each note should be one or two lines long—no longer. Each note should be a phrase—no capital letters on the first word, no ending punctuation.

These simple instructions minimize copying. (Be very clear that nothing should be copied word-for-word from another written source.) Kids are more likely to make notes selectively and put information in their own words. Teach them how to write phrases; sometimes just subjects and verbs are enough.

5. Remind students to check each note carefully to make sure it belongs on a particular card. They should pay close attention to the subtopics and questions written at the top of each card.

text continues on page 183

Resident Expert Planner

continued →

Student's name: _____

My topic: _____

Date project work begins: _____

I am contracting for a grade of: _____

My 6 subtopics and 3 questions for each:

1. _____
   a. _____
   b. _____
   c. _____

2. _____
   a. _____
   b. _____
   c. _____

3. _____
   a. _____
   b. _____
   c. _____

4. _____
   a. _____
   b. _____
   c. _____

5. _____
   a. _____
   b. _____
   c. _____

6. _____
   a. _____
   b. _____
   c. _____

Resident Expert Planner continued

Materials or supplies I need for my project:

What I need:	Where to get it:
_____	_____
_____	_____
_____	_____
_____	_____

The format I will use for my report: _____

The part of the project I will complete at home (optional): _____

_____

Potential problems:	Possible solutions:
_____	_____
_____	_____
_____	_____

Student's signature: _____ Teacher's signature: _____

Resident Expert Planner for Primary Grades

Student's name: _____

My topic: _____

Date project starts: _____

My 4 subtopics and 2 questions for each:

1. _____

   a. _____

   b. _____

2. _____

   a. _____

   b. _____

3. _____

   a. _____

   b. _____

4. _____

   a. _____

   b. _____

Materials or supplies I need for my project:

What I need: _____   Where to get it: _____

How I will give my report: _____

Student's signature: _____   Teacher's signature: _____

Check-Off Sheet for Resident Expert Project

Student's name: _____

Project topic: _____

□ _____
DATE COMPLETED _____

□ _____
DATE COMPLETED _____

□ _____
DATE COMPLETED _____

□ _____
DATE COMPLETED _____

□ _____
DATE COMPLETED _____

□ _____
DATE COMPLETED _____

□ _____
DATE COMPLETED _____

□ _____
DATE COMPLETED _____

□ _____
DATE COMPLETED _____

The Personal Interest Study Project Agreement

The Personal Interest Study Project Agreement on page 185 is similar to the Independent Study Agreement on page 90. It is an official contract between you and the student, designed to teach kids how to behave responsibly while working independently.

Hold a meeting for all kids who have decided to become resident experts. Give everyone a copy of the agreement and have them follow along as you read it aloud. Make sure students understand that if they fail to meet the conditions, the logical consequence is that they will have to return to the teacher-directed group for the remainder of the unit.

You may share the agreement with students' parents, but their signatures aren't required, since most of the work will be done in school. Students should bring their agreements to workplaces outside the classroom (the library, media center, resource room, other classrooms) but should never take them home until their project has been completed. If they leave the classroom to work, they should always leave their record-keeping forms in the classroom. Students and supervising adults should know that students are required to return to class for the last five minutes to hear any important information.

Keep the signed agreements and the completed Daily Logs from both school and home in the students' compacting folders.

Independent Study Option for the Primary Grades: The 4C Project[1]

For beginning researchers, fold a large sheet of drawing paper into four sections, or prepare a four- or five-page booklet, perhaps with lines for writing. The fifth page will be the cover. Label the top-left section COLLECT, the top-right section COMPARE, the bottom-left section CREATE, and the bottom-right section COMMUNICATE. See details in the box at the bottom of this page.

Students work on their projects while you teach grade-level content to kids who need direct instruction. This project is not homework. It replaces the regular schoolwork that is not challenging for some students. Kids working on a 4C Project can record their progress on a Daily Log of Extension Work (see page 92).

Assessing: Independent Study Work

If students are intrinsically motivated to work on personal interest independent study projects without receiving grades, encourage that attitude. However, it is very likely that kids (or their parents) will want grades. If they do, use the Evaluation Contract described in chapter 3 (page 96) and have students choose the grade they plan to work for. The only two choices available should be A or B. Why would anyone want to do an independent study project for a lower

The 4C Booklet	
COLLECT facts, words, ideas, and pictures about your topic.	**COMPARE** your topic to something else. Look for similarities and differences, advantages and disadvantages, relationships, ways to classify or categorize, or something else you can compare.
CREATE a way to express what you have learned about your topic.	**COMMUNICATE** your findings by sharing them with the class or other appropriate audience.

[1] Used with permission from Connie Webb, McMinnville Public Schools, McMinnville, Oregon.

Internet Options for Independent Study

Freerice (freerice.com) is a website where users play various educational, multiple-choice games in order to fight world hunger. For every question the user answers correctly, 10 grains of rice are donated to hungry people. There are several interesting categories, and the program keeps track of the rice the player earns.

Glogster (edu.glogster.com) enables users to create a "glog" (short for graphical blog)—an interactive multimedia image that looks like a poster, but allows readers to interact with the content. Glogster's goal is to provide an outlet for unlimited creative expression online.

Google Earth (earth.google.com) is a critical resource to include in your social studies, history, geography, or language arts curriculum, to name a few. While reading any book, news, or political or historical event, students can visit the actual place on the internet.

Khan Academy (khanacademy.com) is a dynamic site where curious students can learn almost anything for free. Includes thousands of videos on everything from arithmetic to physics, finance, and history, and offers hundreds of skills to practice.

Prezi (prezi.com) is a digital presentation tool using a map layout that zooms to show contextual relationships in a nonlinear format. It allows users to incorporate not only text and pictures, but videos and other presentation objects.

My Wonderful World (test.mywonderfulworld.org) is part of National Geographic's campaign to expand geographical learning. The site provides high engagement and interactive, geography-based activities for both kids and teens.

See chapter 8 and the references and resources section for more ideas for digital learning.

grade? Remember that the difference between a B or an A is one of depth and complexity, rather than amount.

Letting Students Evaluate Their Own Work

Whether or not a grade is attached to a personal project, you might ask students to complete a self-rating every two weeks or so. Several methods are available for doing this.

1. Create a checklist of desired project behaviors and abilities and ask students to complete it every two weeks or so. The rating scale should be a simple two-value process. A "1" or frowning face for "not yet done," a "2" or smiley face for "keeping up."

2. Use the Self-Evaluation Checklist on page 186. Ratings should be simple pluses (+) and minuses (–). You may always add a place for your feedback.

3. Develop a rubric with your students. Having your students contribute their ideas to the evaluation tool is very motivating for them

and they generally create more detailed and thorough projects.

Discrepancies between a student's self-evaluation and a teacher's evaluation can lead to better understanding about the expectations for future projects and improved performance on current projects.

See chapter 8 for more information on assessment strategies.

QUESTIONS ★ ANSWERS

"What if a student who needs to do an independent study can't find a topic to work on?"

Suggest that he spend a few days writing down questions that pop into his head for which he doesn't know the answers. Those questions can become topics for study. Provide him with several websites to peruse online or send him to the library to browse the books in the nonfiction

text continues on page 187

Personal Interest Study Agreement

Read each condition as your teacher reads it aloud. Write your initials beside each condition to show that you understand it and agree to abide by it.

Learning Conditions

_____ I will spend the expected amount of time working on my Personal Interest Study Project.

_____ I will complete all required forms and keep them at school.

_____ If I want my project to be graded, I will complete an Evaluation Contract and work at the agreed-upon level.

_____ I will leave my project to participate in designated whole-class activities or lessons as the teacher indicates them—without arguing.

_____ I will keep a Daily Log of my progress.

_____ I will share progress reports about my project at regular intervals with the class or other audience. Progress reports will be five to seven minutes long. Each will include a visual aid and a question for the class to answer.

Working Conditions

_____ I will be present in the classroom at the beginning and end of each class period.

_____ I will not bother anyone or call attention to the fact that I am doing different work than others in the class.

_____ I will work on my project for the entire class period on designated days.

_____ I will carry this paper with me to any room in which I am working on my project, and I will return it to my classroom at the end of each session.

_____ **I understand that I may keep working on my project as long as I meet these learning and working conditions.**

Student's signature: _____

Teacher's signature: _____

Date: _____

Self-Evaluation Checklist

	Student	Teacher

During My Research:

I selected a topic that held my interest.

I understood the working conditions.

I followed the working conditions.

I worked well independently.

I asked for help when I needed it.

_____

_____

_____

For My Report to the Class:

I created an interesting question for the class to answer.

I had someone listen to my report before giving it to the class.

I was able to explain what I learned to others.

My report had an attention-grabbing beginning.

My report was well-organized.

I spoke loudly and clearly with good expression.

I made frequent eye contact with others.

I held the class's attention during my report.

I answered questions clearly.

_____

_____

_____

section. Any books he finds interesting can lead to possible topics. Also, have him take the Interest Survey on page 168.

"What if a student decides that she doesn't want to pursue her subtopic after finishing a Topic Browsing Planner?"

Simply file the completed planner in her compacting folder and let her move on to something else. Or, if this makes you uncomfortable, tell your students that you expect them to study one subtopic in depth for every three planners they complete. If they resist, try to find out why. Perhaps they are reluctant to get up in front of the class to make progress reports. Find a mutually acceptable way for them to share their information. For example, you might allow them to create a digital project and present the information digitally.

"Won't other students also want to browse and share what they learn with the class?"

Of course they will. Select a time in your weekly schedule and let everyone browse through some topic. Leave time near the end for students to share what they have learned, briefly and informally. Or use those mini-reports as mini-rewards for when the class finishes a session early, or the kids have been particularly wonderful on a given day during that week. Most kids love to do a mini-photo share talk, sharing only one picture that describes what they have learned.

"What should I do if students who are working on these special activities become disruptive?"

You probably already know what to do. The response to this situation is always the same. Ask the students to rejoin the class and participate in the regular activities. Tell them that their behavior indicates that they would be more productive in teacher-directed situations.

Whenever students take advantage of an opportunity to do alternate activities, whether it's a Learning Contract (chapter 2), Study Guide (chapter 3), or Personal Interest Study Project (this chapter), start by making sure they know what to do and have adequate resources and

skills for the task. Decide in advance on the working conditions and explain them in careful detail. Have students sign an agreement to abide by the working conditions. Attach the agreement to their contract, guide, or planner so they can refer to it often.

For ideas and examples of working conditions, see Julie's Learning Contract on page 54, Working Conditions for Alternate Activities on page 57, either Independent Study Guide Agreement in chapter 3 (pages 90 or 91), and the Personal Interest Study Project Agreement on page 185. Please be selective. Even though Working Conditions is a reproducible form, don't simply photocopy it every time one of your students chooses a special activity or independent study. You may find that some of your students need fewer or different working conditions to stay on track.

Sometimes, if gifted students find themselves working alone on a project, they will misbehave on purpose to manipulate themselves into a position where they won't appear so "different." Most kids prefer not to be singled out by having to work alone. Allow kids working on personal interest projects to work together, even if their topics are different.

"What happens if students refuse to work on their planners and insist on just sitting and doing nothing during their choice time?"

As the teacher, you must make it clear that they have only two choices: Either they can develop an independent study project of some kind, or you can assign them more "regular work." Doing nothing isn't an option. Our response to this is, "My job is to teach, and your job is to learn. If you are done learning what I am teaching, then it is your job to learn something new and my job to help you."

"What if a student never finishes the project related to his personal interest topic?"

Celebrate! Why would you want the project to be finished? You and the student would then have to go through the process of choosing another topic!

Real expertise is an endless journey, and gifted kids are often driven to become experts on a topic that interests them passionately. People who make their living as researchers often spend many years on a single project. So relax. There's nothing wrong with a project that goes on forever, as long as the student demonstrates mastery of the required standards, meets the working conditions, remains invested in the research, and is willing to share progress reports now and then.

"How can I justify using the time it takes to create and monitor independent study activities when there's so much pressure on me to bring below-level students up to par?"

Imagine how much less guilty you'll feel when you're no longer holding back fast learners to the same pace required by students who don't find learning easy. When gifted kids are working on independent projects, you'll actually have more time to work with needy students. Any time you spend teaching gifted kids to work well independently pays off in large dividends. It reduces the stress you may feel because gifted students and their parents are so frustrated with the learning pace of the classroom. When you know all kids are really learning, you can feel better about your own effectiveness as a teacher.

Chapter Summary

When we excuse gifted kids from regular class activities so they can pursue topics that interest them, we must trust that they will use that time productively—provided we have taught them the expected behaviors. Students will be more successful at independent study if procedures and expectations are clearly explained before they begin their work. Gifted kids are usually so relieved and happy to discover that there is a place in school for their passionate interests that they are eager to meet the required working conditions.

CHAPTER 7
Grouping Gifted Students for Learning

Grouping practices have long been a hot topic and highly debated issue in education. One of the challenges is that our educational system has been trying to find the one grouping practice that is best for all students. Historically, every time educators search for the *one* best practice that will meet the needs of all students, the search is futile. The present attempt at finding the "right" practice is the Common Core State Standards. Although optimism is high for this initiative as of this writing, we must be constantly alert to facets of its implementation that require compacting and differentiation opportunities for gifted students.

Gifted students require different considerations than their age peers. This becomes especially evident when students are grouped for learning according to ability levels. Throughout this book, we have shown examples of ways that gifted students choose to pursue more challenging work when it is made available for them. We have also seen that teachers are more likely to plan and provide for gifted students when there are more than one or two in their class. When very small numbers of gifted kids are in classrooms, they often decide to fade into the background to look more "normal," which is likely to impede their ongoing achievement.

The practice of grouping high-ability students has been challenged in an educational climate that opposes ability grouping in general. However, the research of James Kulik, Chen-Lin Kulik, John Feldhusen, Marcia Gentry, and this book's coauthor, Dina Brulles, clearly demonstrates that gifted students consistently benefit from learning with students of similar ability. The good news is that research shows that grouping gifted students together in the same classroom does *not* have a negative impact on students who have not been identified as gifted.[1]

We can accomplish our goal of allowing gifted students to work together through the careful use

[1] Brulles, et al, 2011.

189

of two practices: cooperative learning and cluster grouping. This chapter describes both strategies in detail. Although their benefits are similar, they are distinct practices, and therefore discussed separately.

Cooperative Learning

Cooperative learning has been suggested as one response to the challenges inherent in teaching a class with a wide range of ability. In some classrooms, gifted students who have already mastered grade-level curriculum are expected to mentor their peers. This is grossly unfair to the gifted students, who are then being denied the opportunity to make forward progress in their own learning.

Cooperative learning is an educational practice that can provide achievement gains and improve social interaction. Just as the demands of the adult workplace often require all people to work in groups from time to time, cooperative learning skills are valuable for all students, including those who are gifted. It is important to note, however, that on-the-job groups are rarely totally heterogeneous in nature. In most cases, team members have common training and experience.

Gifted students may have much to lose and little to gain from traditional cooperative learning practices. As you will see, it's not difficult to create appropriate cooperative learning experiences for your gifted students.

It's not difficult to create appropriate cooperative learning experiences for your gifted students.

Scenario: Kim Liu

Kim Liu was a very unhappy sixth grader. His science teacher used cooperative learning almost all of the time, and Kim Liu had exhibited some decidedly uncooperative behaviors in his group. Most often, he insisted on doing his work alone, sulked when he was forced to join the group, and refused to carry out the jobs to which he was assigned.

Sometimes, he would act as though he had decided to participate in the cooperative learning activity, but he would soon take over the group, regardless of his assigned job, and try to boss the others into doing things his way. At other times, he simply told his teammates the solutions so he could get some relief for a few minutes at the end of science class. Kim Liu's teacher was using a lot of energy trying to come up with ways to convince him to cooperate. No strategy seemed to work, and almost everyone involved was totally frustrated.

During this period, his teacher attended one of Susan's workshops on teaching gifted kids. She was startled to hear Susan describe children whose reactions were similar to Kim Liu's. Using guidelines presented in the workshop and detailed in this chapter, she was able to help Kim Liu and her other gifted students develop a more positive attitude about cooperative learning. They were especially thrilled with the regular opportunities to work with each other on more advanced tasks in their own cooperative learning group, which made everyone concerned much happier.

Cooperative Learning and Gifted Students

Imagine yourself at the first class meeting of a graduate course you need to take. Your professor announces that a major course requirement, which will count for 51 percent of your grade, will be a group project. To save time, she has divided the class into groups based on your majors. She will be providing a few minutes during class for the group members to get acquainted.

Visualize yourself at the first meeting of your group when you immediately discover not only one, but two students in your group who give every indication of behaving like slackers. If you are a student who is proud of your perfect 4.0 graduate record, you know you will be doing everything you can to make sure your record is not threatened by these two people who are already enumerating the various reasons why they can't or won't work very hard on this project.

Nod your head if you know that you are probably going to be taking over the management of your group. Nod if you realize that you are most likely going to end up doing much more than your fair share of the work. With cooperative learning, we often create situations in which some students have to do just what we would try to avoid. Imagine that! There are, however, more effective and productive methods for structuring your cooperative groups.

Most training in cooperative learning directs teachers to set up completely heterogeneous groups. Cooperative learning trainers teach that a group of four students would ideally include one high achiever, two average achievers, and one low achiever. Many experts in cooperative learning contend that all students, regardless of their ability, realize achievement gains from participating in heterogeneous cooperative learning groups. They claim that high-ability students don't suffer, and actually understand concepts better when they explain them to other students.

Author, educator, and researcher Robert E. Slavin has observed, "Gifted students working in heterogeneous cooperative learning groups are no worse off than they are in more traditional classrooms." Statements such as this imply that it's perfectly acceptable to place gifted students in heterogeneous groups for learning. But consider this little-known fact about Slavin's research: It systematically excluded the top 5 percent of the student body, meaning that his studies never actually included gifted students. His data, then, may be accurate for high achievers, but not necessarily for gifted kids. One must also question how much learning typically happens for gifted students in traditional classrooms. "No worse off" is not synonymous with "better off."

When gifted students are questioned about their attitudes toward cooperative learning, the majority typically say that they do not really dislike cooperative learning per se. They just resent being taken advantage of in cooperative learning groups and having to do most of the work. Many adults can surely relate to that sentiment.

When the learning task requires lots of drill and practice, or when some students are having significant trouble learning new standards, it's highly likely that gifted students in heterogeneous cooperative learning groups will spend most of their time tutoring the other students. They may actually do more teaching than learning. With the increased pressure to bring the least capable students up to the levels of learning required by standards, the practice of using gifted kids to teach others may appear even more attractive. Parents do not send their children to school to teach others. All parents have a belief that school is a place where their children can make measurable academic progress and that outcome should be available for *all* students.

It's highly likely that gifted students in heterogeneous cooperative learning groups will spend most of their time tutoring the other students.

The implied message gifted students receive from always being placed in heterogeneous cooperative learning groups is that once they master the grade-level content, nothing is left for them to learn. Most teachers would not consciously choose to send such a message.

Dr. Karen Rogers has studied for many years which instructional practices actually produce learning growth for gifted students. According to the data she has gathered, traditional mixed-ability cooperative learning groups in which students are mixed purely heterogeneously with no special attention paid to gifted students do *not* lead to measurable forward progress for gifted kids.[2] However, when the cooperative learning tasks are problem-based and open-ended, and the teacher has enough training to make sure gifted kids are not being taken advantage of in any way during the cooperative group work, heterogeneous cooperative groups may be defensible for part of the learning time.

Gifted students can benefit from learning how to work cooperatively with other students. Cooperative learning experiences can specifically teach them the important social interaction skills they sometimes lack, while allowing them to enjoy the company of their age peers. The real question is not whether gifted students belong in cooperative learning groups. Rather, the question

---

[2] Rogers, 1993.

is under what conditions can they most benefit from cooperative learning and be motivated to learn the social skills they need to succeed later in life?

⭐ STRATEGY

Cooperative Learning Groups for Gifted Students

When gifted students are removed from heterogeneous cooperative learning groups and placed together in their own group with an appropriately challenging task, their experience with cooperative learning is much more positive than when they are forced to tutor or coach other students in heterogeneous groups. Especially for tasks that focus on drill-and-practice, it is desirable to place gifted students in separate groups to work on more difficult tasks. The rest of the class is arranged in heterogeneous groups, with the high-achieving students in the group being very capable students, although not necessarily gifted. Another method that works well is to place two gifted students in a group with two students of average ability. This represents a mixed-ability learning group, yet still allows the gifted students to work together.

Teachers may fear that when the gifted students are working in their own groups, the other groups will lack appropriate role models. Nothing could be further from the truth. Educational researcher, author, and professor Dale H. Schunk from Purdue University has documented that for one person to serve as a viable role model for another, there can't be too much difference in their abilities. This concept makes sense when you compare it to almost any other learning process. For example, if you're learning to downhill ski, you're more likely to gain confidence by watching novices fall and get up unharmed than by watching expert skiers fly down a treacherous slope.

It is usually true that high-achieving kids make much more patient coaches than highly gifted students. When gifted students in heterogeneous cooperative learning groups try to explain something to the others, it's as if they are speaking a foreign language. Their listeners may nod their heads in agreement, but they may also feel intimidated, and they won't ask questions for fear of looking foolish or dumb. Additionally, many gifted kids cannot explain things in a way that others understand. This is because gifted kids make intuitive leaps in their thinking process, and therefore cannot explain things in the sequential way that other students learn. This results in the gifted students feeling frustrated about how long it takes the others to understand an idea they grasped at once. In frustration, they may resort to tyranny—"Just write down what I told you and don't ask any questions. Trust me!" Since the gifted students have not been trained in how to teach (nor should they be) they commonly resort to just giving the answers. Since the other kids may feel daunted in the presence of gifted kids, they may rely on the gifted students to simply tell them the answers, thus feeling even more inadequate. No one benefits from this experience.

You may have seen ample evidence in your own classroom that heterogeneous cooperative learning can be problematic for gifted students. They are the students who are most likely to complain about having to do cooperative learning. It is their parents who tend to be most negative about cooperative learning because they worry that their children's own learning time will be severely limited.

After one second-grade teacher placed her gifted students in their own cooperative learning group, it took her class several days to adjust. One group approached her and declared they couldn't do any work that day because, "We need Josephine and she's *absent!*" The teacher verified that Josephine was one of her gifted students. Finally, the teacher's firmness and confidence in the students paid off. As the students realized they were not going to be saved by the return of the most capable students, all of the groups got to work, completed their tasks, and began cooperating to learn, instead of counting on the gifted students to lead them to success.

Most teachers who have removed gifted students from heterogeneous groups report that they are very pleased with the results. They observe their gifted students moving quite happily through the more difficult material, learning to cooperate on tasks few can do alone. Teachers are especially thrilled when they see new academic leadership emerging in other groups.

IMPORTANT Not all gifted students enjoy working in groups and it's okay to let them work alone at certain times. When you think about it, most adults seek out cooperation only when they need assistance. We prefer to work alone on tasks we can do easily without help from others. If we want gifted students to learn how to cooperate, we must make sure they are working on tasks difficult enough to create a need for cooperation. The students must perceive that cooperation is necessary. Forcing students to work together in groups without providing a reason for collaboration is not a good practice and will hinder their success.

Gifted Student Groups vs. Heterogeneous Groups: Which Is Better?

How can you decide when it's best to place your gifted students in their own cooperative learning groups, and when heterogeneous groups would probably be better for everyone? Here are two approaches you might try.

1. Assess the type of cooperative learning task that has been assigned. When the task is drill and practice (math computation, studying for a recall-type test, answering comprehension questions about a story or novel the class is reading), and you have evidence that some students have mastered that material, place those kids together in their own group and assign them a more complex task. *Examples:* They might read an advanced novel, work on advanced problem-solving techniques in math, write story problems

for the rest of the class, use the content to produce an interactive activity for the class, create a digital documentary on the topic, or work on resident expert projects in small groups.

For tasks that focus on critical thinking, the development of concepts and generalizations, or problem-based learning, placing gifted students in heterogeneous groups may be appropriate from time to time. Such experiences may be richer when a variety of viewpoints is represented. Any open-ended activity with many possible answers or solutions lends itself to heterogeneous grouping. So does any subject in which the content is new for everyone, including the gifted students. Hands-on science experiments and current events discussions are other good choices for cooperative learning experiences with heterogeneous groups.

2. Ask yourself three key questions.

- "Does the task require input from different types of learning modalities and different perspectives?"

- "Is the subject matter new for all students?"

- "Is it likely that the gifted students will be engaged in real learning rather than continuous tutoring?"

If you can answer yes to all three questions, then heterogeneous cooperative learning groups are probably appropriate. If you answer no to one or more of the questions, then it will probably be better to place the gifted students in a separate group to work on the same kind of content from a more challenging perspective. All other students would work in heterogeneous groups comprised of one of the strongest remaining students, one student who may find the task difficult, and one or two students of average ability. As you circulate among the cooperative groups at work, let your observational skills tell you whether your gifted students have been placed where they belong for optimal learning for everyone.

Cluster Grouping

You have probably asked yourself questions such as these numerous times while reading this book:

- "How am I ever going to find the time to implement these strategies when I have the complete range of students in my class?"

- "Is it fair to create learning extensions for just one or two students who need this kind of attention? After all, their grades seem to indicate that they're doing just fine in school."

- "Isn't it more important that I spend my time with the kids who really need me since my principal is telling me to focus on helping my struggling learners master the required standards?"

In most schools, when teachers and principals meet to set up classes for the following year, the gifted students are separated from each other so all classes can have one or two of the "best students," and erroneously, they commonly believe that the gifted identified students are those "best students." So they separate them. This practice creates the troublesome dilemmas previously described.

It is extremely difficult for gifted students to work at their levels of potential when they are a minority of one or two in a heterogeneous classroom. For many gifted students, being in a classroom in which they are always the smartest one, with no one else working at their level, becomes an excruciating experience. They sometimes pretend to be less capable than they really are just to fit in with the other kids. This situation arises in almost all socioeconomic conditions, within all cultures, and in all geographic areas. If very smart kids perceive it's not cool to be smart, their potential contributions to our society may be lost forever.

For many gifted students, being in a classroom in which they are always the smartest one becomes an excruciating experience.

As educators dedicated to ensuring academic progress for all students, many of us wonder why so many education practices appear to force us to choose between meeting the needs of one group while sacrificing the needs of another. School district mission statements promise to serve all students. Yet, in daily practice, gifted kids often get less teacher attention and less opportunity to work on challenging curriculum than anyone else in the class. Their parents may take their children out of our schools to place them in alternate learning environments. Since the state reimbursement for these students also disappears from your school when these families leave, this problem is both ethical and economic.

One increasingly popular solution is to group gifted students at each grade level into a cluster group within an otherwise heterogeneous classroom. The teacher of this class is one who has some understanding of the social, emotional, and academic needs of gifted students and training in compacting and differentiation strategies. All of the arguments used earlier about cooperative learning apply to the logic of purposefully clustering gifted kids together.

Scenario: Third Grade at Adams School

Six children at Adams Elementary School had been identified as gifted at the end of second grade. As the teachers and principal met to set up the classes for the three third-grade sections, they considered how to group the gifted students. The traditional method called for them to divide the six gifted students evenly, placing two in each of the three classes so all teachers would have their "fair share" of the brightest students. Under this system, all three teachers would have to develop appropriate compacting and differentiation opportunities to challenge their few gifted students.

The staff at Adams decided to try something different. Instead of separating the gifted students, they formed a cluster group of all six students and placed them in the otherwise heterogeneous class of one teacher who had some training in differentiated instruction. Knowing that at least six students would benefit from any compacting and differentiating opportunities she created, the teacher felt justified in taking the time to develop and use them.

When the gifted kids found themselves in a group of others with similar abilities, they started taking risks to experience learning activities that were different from what the rest of the class was doing. They were also more willing to take advantage of the differentiation opportunities because they would have learning companions for those tasks.

Students placed in the classroom with the gifted cluster had been formally identified as gifted. This included gifted students who were of primary age, twice-exceptional, culturally or linguistically diverse, and underachievers or nonproductive students. Productivity was not a factor in identifying a student as gifted. This grouping method includes gifted students who have advanced abilities, even if they don't demonstrate those abilities by consistently completing their schoolwork. This represents a unique difference from many types of gifted programs: it allows us to enfranchise gifted students who may not have previously been served.

The Schoolwide Cluster Grouping Model (SCGM)

Cluster grouping works best when it's a schoolwide initiative. It's not enough for individual teachers to simply cluster gifted kids together. It is essential that a principal or gifted program coordinator carefully monitor the clustering to ensure that consistent compacting and differentiation are taking place.

Schools that implement gifted cluster grouping are providing something that sounds almost impossible to achieve in our current educational climate: attention to gifted education that requires only minimal funds for its support. This is because the model's structure becomes part of the school's system and utilizes many of the same materials purchased for other learners at that particular school. When cluster grouping models are implemented with fidelity, gifted kids can have their learning needs met every day, in every subject area. Best of all, it prevents gifted kids from becoming the group that benefits *least* from heterogeneous grouping practices.

A three-year study of cluster grouping at an elementary school documented improved achievement at all grade levels in which clustering was done, including classes where there were no gifted clusters. One factor that accounted for that improvement was the unique way in which students were grouped into classes. In the spring, when class placements were made, students were sorted into the following five groups:

1. Gifted

2. High Achieving

3. Average

4. Below Average

5. Significantly Below Grade Level

Classroom A, taught by a teacher with some training in gifted education, was assigned the cluster group of gifted students (1) and some students from groups 3 and 4. Classes B and C had

Example of a Classroom Composition for the SCGM
(For a Single Grade Level)

30 Students in 3 Classes	Group 1: Gifted	Group 2: High Achieving	Group 3: Average	Group 4: Below Average	Group 5: Far Below Average
Classroom A	6	0	12	12	0
Classroom B	0	6	12	6	6
Classroom C	0	6	12	6	6

Benefits of the SCGM*

Schools implementing the SCGM have reported a number of benefits. The way in which the model is implemented and supported determines the benefits realized by the school community. The school's population, demographics, size, and other gifted services available can influence the outcomes of the model. Schools that effectively support the model commonly report the following benefits:

- Gifted students receive full-time attention to their exceptional learning needs, allowing them to progress at their own pace in an inclusionary setting.

- The gifted education program in the district can move from part to full time without major budget implications.

- Gifted students who may not have participated in traditional gifted programs, including English language learners, twice-exceptional students, and underachieving gifted students, become enfranchised in this model.

- Although all teachers still have heterogeneous classes, the student achievement range in each class is slightly narrowed, which facilitates effective teaching.

- Achievement tends to rise for *all* kids across the grade levels being clustered because of the narrowed range of ability and achievement levels in each class, and due to the emphasis on training cluster teachers to provide and manage differentiated instruction in their classrooms.

- When not placed with identified gifted students, high-achieving students often emerge as new academic leaders in their own classes.

- Parents of gifted students support schools that provide appropriate services for their gifted children. Some districts find that families who have left their home school return when the district implements the model.

* Winebrenner and Brulles, 2008

---

students from Groups 2–5. Thus, Teacher A had no students from Group 5, and Teachers B and C had no identified gifted students. See the chart on page 195 for a visual model of this arrangement.

The SCGM reduces the range of achievement in each classroom. It frees the gifted cluster teacher to spend more time with the gifted kids instead of being pulled away by the needs of those students who are significantly below grade level. Likewise, the other teachers have a slightly narrowed range of achievement, and along with support from the special education teachers, they also appreciate the narrowed range of abilities and achievement levels in their classes. And yet, all classes still have a range of achievement levels and all classes still have students who are positive academic role models.

QUESTIONS & ANSWERS

Following are some selected questions and answers regarding cluster grouping for gifted students. For more detailed information on how to create gifted cluster classes and implement a schoolwide model, please refer to the references and resources on page 238. In particular, our book, *The Cluster Grouping Handbook: A Schoolwide Model*, addresses this issue thoroughly.

"What does it mean to place gifted students in cluster groups?"

Cluster grouping occurs when a group of identified gifted students is purposefully clustered in a mixed-ability classroom. Gifted students are clustered and placed with a teacher who participates in ongoing professional development in gifted education and differentiated instruction. If 10 or more gifted students are in one grade level, an additional gifted cluster class may be designated.

"How should gifted students be identified for the cluster group?"

Identification should be conducted each spring with assistance from someone with training in gifted education. Standardized ability tests, using both verbal and nonverbal measures, are recommended to identify students for placement into the gifted clusters. If there will be more than one gifted cluster class in one grade level, the gifted identified students can be separated into the classes by their areas of strength, such as math or reading. This works especially well at the middle school level. See chapter 1 for more information about identifying gifted students.

"Isn't cluster grouping the same as tracking?"

No, there are several important differences between cluster grouping and tracking. In a tracking system, all students are grouped by ability for much of the school day and usually remain in the same track throughout their school years. When tracked, students are assigned a set curriculum based on their ability level. They generally do not veer from that curriculum; making it unlikely they would move to a different track in future years. In cluster classes, students work at different levels for different subjects. All classes in the grade level have students with a range of learning abilities; all classes have high-ability or high-achieving students. In a cluster model, extended learning opportunities are open to all students in the class. Teachers use students' entry points, or readiness, to determine levels and pace of curriculum. Student placements change yearly, so only the gifted students remain grouped together yearly. However, since classroom placements change every year, the gifted students continually interact with different grade-level peers every year.

"Why should gifted students be placed in a cluster group instead of being assigned evenly to all classes?"

When placing gifted students evenly among all classes, each teacher still has the full range of abilities. Teachers trying to meet the diverse learning needs of all students, from levels of very advanced to very low, have difficulty providing adequately for everyone. Often, the highest ability students are expected to "make it on their own." However, when a teacher has a cluster of gifted students, taking the time to make appropriate provisions for several gifted students seems more realistic. Gifted students learn more when grouped with other gifted students. When gifted students have opportunities to learn together they are more comfortable working at extended levels of depth and complexity in a given area. Gifted students' willingness to take risks in learning experiences increases when they spend time learning with peers who have similar interests and abilities.

"Will the clustered gifted students inhibit the performance of the other students in that class?"

When the gifted cluster group is kept to a manageable size, cluster teachers report that there is general improvement in overall achievement for the entire class. This suggests the exciting possibility that when teachers learn how to provide for what gifted students need and offer modified versions of the same opportunities to the entire class, expectations and the levels of learning are raised for all students. Therefore, the cluster grouping model can actually increase achievement for many students when the placement recommendations of the model are closely followed.[3]

"Do gifted clustered students always work together?"

Gifted students have varying levels of achievement, interests, and experiences. Therefore, their need for acceleration or extensions will also vary depending on the content being learned. There are times when some students in the gifted cluster group will be experiencing differentiation or acceleration, and times when they won't. There

---

[3] Gentry, 1999, 2008.

are also times when students who have not been identified as gifted can benefit from available differentiated learning opportunities. Opportunities for moving faster or going deeper into the curriculum are routinely offered to the entire class.

"Is clustering feasible at all levels— elementary, middle, and high school?"

Cluster grouping may be used at all grade levels and in all subject areas, but the structure will vary when incorporated at the middle school and high school levels. Gifted students may be clustered into one section of any heterogeneous team, especially when there are not enough students to form an advanced section for a particular subject. Variations of cluster grouping are also a welcome option in small rural settings, and in almost any grade level configuration.[4]

"Should cluster grouping practices replace our district's current program components in gifted education?"

Not at all. Cluster grouping can supplement existing program components. The complaint many teachers (and parents) have about most gifted programs is that they comprise only a small percentage of the student's learning time. Adding cluster grouping to a comprehensive program already in place is a beneficial, cost-effective option. The program makes the job of the gifted specialist easier since she has fewer teachers' schedules to work with and is therefore more available for the gifted cluster teachers.

If your school must choose between resource-room programs or cluster grouping, our recommendation is to go with the cluster grouping. This greatly improves the chances that gifted students will receive appropriate learning opportunities on a daily basis. If your district has full-time, self-contained classes for gifted students, their composition should be limited to highly gifted students. If there are not enough highly gifted students for an entire class, grades may be combined. The gifted students who are not considered highly gifted become the gifted cluster students at their schools. Therefore, cluster grouping easily co-exists and complements other components of your comprehensive gifted education program. If your school has a teacher who serves as a gifted education coach or leader, that person's time helping teachers who have gifted students in their class is spent much more efficiently and effectively when cluster grouping is used. That person's presence also allows cluster teachers access to additional coaching and assistance to help provide the best possible classroom program for their gifted kids.

Chapter Summary

This chapter has pointed out how gifted students need special considerations when grouping students for the most effective learning outcomes in heterogeneous classes. It should now be easier to understand that the same grouping practices are usually not equally effective for gifted students as they are for average and below-average students. Since a critical goal of all educators is to provide documentation of academic progress for all students every year, the techniques described in this chapter are designed to help you attain that goal for all students in your class.

---

[4] Gentry and Kielty, 2004.

CHAPTER 8
Assessment and Technology

In today's world, so much overlap exists between technology and assessment that it seems natural to combine them into one chapter. Of course, some aspects of assessment have nothing to do with technology, and vice versa, but the two topics relate and can be used together. The essential elements of instruction and assessment are enhanced by the use of technology. Technology makes learning more active and productive, which makes students more likely to learn the required standards, which makes assessment results more positive and satisfying. As we strive for positive achievement outcomes, we know that technology enhances the learning experiences for the majority of students and teachers, thus improving their self-confidence and assessment outcomes.

Technology has become an essential link in our approach to judging the quality of our schools, and it helps us align all essential elements within that process. Testing companies make many assessments available online. Students are often very savvy about using technology as a tool in their learning experiences. Some school districts have transitioned to full electronic access and integration with all of their courses, classes, and programs. And student achievement is measured much more accurately with the use of technology.

A growing number of testing and learning experts argue that technology can dramatically improve assessment—and teaching and learning. Research projects demonstrate how information technology can both deepen and broaden assessment practices in elementary and secondary education, by assessing more comprehensively and by assessing new skills and standards. And all of these can strengthen national standardized test results.

These new technology-enabled assessments offer the potential to understand more than simply whether a student answered a test question correctly. Using multiple forms of media that allow for both visual and graphical representations, we can present complex, multi-step problems for students to solve, and we can collect detailed information about an individual student's approach to problem solving. When these elements are assessed, there is more incentive for schools to pay attention to problem-solving experiences in their curriculum.

A report by the International Society for Technology in Education (ISTE) asserts that technology has a positive effect on student achievement and that correct implementation is key to its success. This includes:

- Effective and ongoing professional development in the integration of technology and instruction
- Alignment of technology-linked work to required standards
- Incorporation of technology into daily learning experiences
- Individualized feedback to students to tailor experiences to individual needs
- Multiple opportunities for student collaboration
- Frequent use of project-based learning and real-world simulations
- Awareness that many students' only access to computers is at school[1]

As interaction with technology is an everyday experience in more and more schools, so is the focus on ongoing assessment. All students benefit from the same practices. We start by assessing a student's entry level with targeted curriculum. We apply learning strategies that are designed to move students forward in their learning. We check to see how the strategies worked, and repeat the

entire process over as needed. Technology can help manage the data we collect in this process, see trends and patterns, and share accurate information with our community.

Effective Assessment Practices

Assessment should not merely be done *to* students; rather, it should also be done *for* students, to guide and enhance their learning. The National Council of Teachers of Mathematics (NCTM) defines the role of assessment:

- To assist student learning
- To identify students' strengths and weaknesses
- To assess the effectiveness of a particular instructional strategy
- To assess and improve the effectiveness of curriculum
- To assess and improve teaching effectiveness
- To provide data that assist in decision making
- To communicate with and involve parents[2]

To make the best use of instructional time for all students, *assessment must drive instruction.* That means, simply, not teaching a concept or standard if your students are not ready for it or if they have already mastered it. There is an abundance of educational research and articles about how to teach students who are not ready for the required standards. Assessment helps us determine exactly which interventions are needed and how to measure their effectiveness.

Effective curriculum planning for all students is built around the following questions:

- What do my students need to know? (*Learning objectives*)
- What kinds of learning activities will best present the required knowledge and prepare students for the required assessment? (*Instructional strategies*)

[1] ISTE, 2008.
[2] Kellough, et al, 2002.

- What kinds of assessment will document if the required learning has been accomplished? (*Assessment*)

- What are the most useful tools to help me in all of these areas? (*Instructional technology*)

There are two general categories of assessment: formative and summative. *Formative assessments* provide information to teachers about the effectiveness of their methods and pacing to inform their ongoing instruction. Formative assessments, such as pretests, are never formally graded. Rather, the diagnostic information they provide is used to adjust subsequent instruction. *Summative assessments* are used to evaluate growth within particular standards when mastery is expected. Summative assessments are generally experienced as chapter or unit tests, entrance exams, and state or national required assessments. Teachers must focus on what will be assessed at the end of a learning unit in the summative assessment in order to choose effective formative assessments on the way to assuring mastery.

Attributes of formative assessment:

- *Learning progressions*—"How do I know what my students already know?"

- *Learning goals*—"Have I clearly determined and stated expected outcomes to my students?"

- *Descriptive feedback*—"Am I providing authentic and relevant feedback on my students' work?"

- *Self and peer reflection*—"Are my students involved in authentic, reflective, and collaborative assessment of their work?"

Formative assessments answer critical questions that guide instruction, such as:

- Should you reteach using different methods that may have a higher likelihood of leading to successful outcomes?

- Should you consider longer or shorter pacing of instruction?

- Should you move the entire class forward more quickly when many students do very well on the formative assessments?

- Which students need consistent compacting and differentiation experiences?

You need accurate information and documentation to make these decisions. As a wise saying goes, "You can't manage what you don't measure."

Formative Assessment for Gifted Leaners

Formative assessment is a collaborative process that relies on constructive feedback and creates a partnership between the student and the teacher. Effective implementation of formative assessments for the gifted students in your class who are working on extension activities may require a shift in your normal assessment strategies.

Ultimately, these assessments should emphasize *learning,* not grading. This may be a challenge for some gifted students who are accustomed to their schoolwork being easy. It may be uncomfortable for you, as well. If so, remember that getting good grades does not constitute learning. Learning involves working at a challenge level. This quite often involves academic struggle for the gifted child who has rarely struggled before.

Ultimately, these assessments should emphasize *learning,* not grading.

Since gifted students learn new content very quickly, you should pay close attention to document that they are conceptualizing the content as opposed to simply remembering it. Ask yourself, "Can they transfer their ideas? Can they relate what they have learned to new contexts?" The assessment challenge with gifted students is that they may show evidence that they need to work with advanced-level standards. When students can prove they already know what will ultimately be included in a summative assessment, some of the formative assessment process becomes unnecessary.

Formative Assessment Strategies

These formative assessment strategies are simple to use, easy to assess, require very little writing for the students, and convey accurate information for you. The results of formative assessment strategies can be used to form flexible groups for ongoing instruction, as well as to inform you about the most effective ways to move the students through the content.

For these strategies to be effective with gifted students, you will want to have your extension activities prepared even before you begin your instruction. That way, you will feel much more positive about seeing kids emerge who need advanced learning experiences and you won't wonder what to do with them.

⭐ STRATEGY
One-Pagers

One favorite method used to find out what students know about a topic is called One-Pagers. A One-Pager is basically a blank sheet of paper sectioned into five parts: four equal quadrants with a fifth section in the center of the page. This strategy can be used with almost any topic.

Let's use the topic of literary elements to illustrate the strategy. Designate the topics for each quadrant of the paper. For example, to assess what students know about the essential elements of literature, the topic headings could be Setting, Characters, Plot Details, and Theme. Have students write one of these topics in each of the four quadrants. Then, have them write a category title in the middle section; in this case

it might be Literary Elements. Announce to your students, "Tell me everything you know about these elements under each heading on this piece of paper." By limiting it to one page, the students know to just jot down important thoughts that describe each element. If all students do a quick One-Pager before and after each story or novel, it will be easy to see which students are ready for more complex work, and which need more review of the basic story components. This provides valuable information you may use to create learning groups for instruction and to match tiered lessons to the needs of each flexible group.

⭐ STRATEGY
Show Me

This strategy demonstrates a quick way to assess students' readiness to move on to more advanced content. It relies on group signaling methods. As a quick assessment regarding content that has just been taught, use questions you have prepared in your lesson plans to determine how much has already been understood by which students. The students response should be simply yes or no, true or false, or a number from 1 to 10.

Model how students should use their hands to signal their responses. The most critical part of this method is to train students *not* to show their response until you give a verbal signal—often asking a question and then saying, "Show me." At that point, students use their fingers to show their answer. The real beauty of this is you don't have to even notice their signals. When students know that they must all signal at exactly the same time, you just have to pay close attention to which students' heads whip around at the "show me" signal, as they try to get help from their classmates. Be sure to use plenty of variety including some signaling methods that allow students to stand up and even move around.

Give Me a Five

A variation of Show Me is called Give Me a Five. After finishing a lesson, ask your students, "Where are you with this material? Can you give

Give Me a Five

Signal	What It Says	Action Required
1 finger	"I'm completely lost."	Invite student to join tomorrow's direct instruction group.
2 fingers	"I'd like some additional help from you."	Invite student to join tomorrow's direct instruction group.
3 fingers	"I'm pretty sure I have it, but I think more practice would help."	Invite student to join tomorrow's guided practice group.
4 fingers	"I've got it and I'm ready to move on."	Invite student to join tomorrow's extension activity group.
5 fingers	"I'm ready for more difficult content."	Explore possibilities for content acceleration.

me a one through five?" With a fist held in front of their chest, students show one through five fingers to indicate their level of comfort with the material. You can easily get visual information about how to group students for instruction at the time of the next lesson.

As you can see, this formative assessment method makes it very easy for you to look around at the students' responses and use them to form your flexible groups for the next day's lesson. You will easily know which students to group together for extension work, which for independent practice, which for additional review, and which for more direct instruction in a way that is more suited to their learning needs.

Quick Check

Yet another variation of Show Me is a quick homework check. Designate five problems for the Show Me response, and give the correct answers to the students. At your signal, students hold up the number of fingers that describe how many problems they got correct. This provides an instant way for you to know who needs another direct instruction lesson and who is ready for extension work.

⭐ STRATEGY

Student Observations

Quite a bit of formative assessment can be gleaned from simply watching and listening to students. Gifted students' responses may appear significantly advanced for their age group. You can direct the discussion in any way necessary, such as asking students to use vocabulary that was learned in previous lessons.

Dr. Bertie Kingore has designed a unique, accurate, and teacher-friendly method to identify gifted students through guided observations.[3] The tool, called the the Kingore Observation Inventory (KOI), actually trains teachers to recognize gifted behaviors, whether or not a student is also productive. Unlike some other instruments that require you to rate all your students on many behaviors, the KOI does not. Instead, teachers are trained to observe their students for "gifted" behaviors, which are recorded on a special form the teacher carries.

During active teaching and learning time, teachers systematically observe their students for a week or two looking for students who exhibit behaviors that indicate they are advanced in a particular category of learning. There are several

[3] The Kingore Observation Inventory (professionalassociatespublishing.com).

other categories as well, including underachievers and students who are not fluent in English.

⭐ STRATEGY
Ticket Out the Door

During the last five minutes of class, rather than asking students if they have any questions, try the Ticket Out the Door strategy. Give students a slip of paper or an index card—which are uniform in size—and have them write their name on it. Then ask a question that will provide you with feedback to determine the level of understanding each student has achieved from the day's lesson. Have students write their answer to the question on the card. Reassure them that the information will not be graded, just used to create flexible learning groups for the next lesson. (See page 40 for more on flexible grouping.) Collect these "tickets" as students leave the classroom. Use the information to flexibly group students for the next day's lesson. Students who obviously have a clear understanding can work on extension activities the next day. Other students will return to the same required standards using various methods of reteaching. You may also identify students who need intensive assistance.

⭐ STRATEGY
Journaling

A simple way to informally learn what students know about a specific topic you are planning to teach is by asking them to write about that topic in their journals. Journaling allows students who have a lot of background knowledge on a particular subject to really elaborate on it. This provides you with valuable information about students' readiness levels.

First, pique their interest by introducing the topic. Prior to providing the prompt, you could show a video clip, explore a website, or read a brief piece of literature on the topic. Then, give a prompt and have your students write on the topic in their journals.

When reading through the journal entries, you can create your flexible learning groups based on the students' background knowledge and readiness levels. Record your students' names in three separate lists: those with little or no knowledge of the topic, those with some knowledge, and those with significant knowledge. When you begin the unit, these three learning groups will work on the same material but at different levels of complexity.

Summative Assessment for Gifted Learners

The second major type of assessment is summative. Summative assessments are used for evaluation or grading after a particular section of content is expected to have been mastered. You'll recall that with formative assessments, formal recorded grading is discouraged because we are measuring students' competencies *while* the material is being learned. We want the grades that will be formally recorded after summative assessment to reflect student success with mastering the required standards.

While formative assessments can provide achievement information at a time when classroom interventions may have an impact on learning outcomes, many summative assessments cannot. We commonly receive the results of "high-stakes" summative assessments during the summer or early fall of the following school year. These assessments are mostly used to evaluate the effectiveness of curriculum and instruction for an entire class or grade level. They also evaluate the effectiveness of various school programs to determine the extent to which school improvement goals have been met.

Typical summative assessment experiences include:

- End of chapter or unit assessments
- End of quarter, semester, term, or year exams
- District benchmark or interim assessments
- Report card and transcript grades

- Formal state or national exams

- AYP (adequate yearly progress) scores or other indicators of a school's yearly achievement growth

- College entrance exams

Because there is such a wide variance in the ways summative assessments are used in various states, we recommend that you contact your local office of assessment to get the particulars for your school or district.

Grading for Gifted Students

Grading gifted students' work requires careful attention and consideration. Many of your gifted students and their parents have been conditioned to believe that high grades guarantee that new learning is taking place. You may also have thought this to be the case. However, we know this is simply not true. Quite frequently, gifted students would be able to earn a high grade even before you have "taught" them the material. Has real learning taken place?

Imagine you are using one of the compacting and differentiation strategies included in this book. Then you learn that your principal will be doing an observation on this lesson. You may be concerned that your principal does not understand the newly learned method you were planning to use. If this feels like too great a risk, you might change the lesson to something more traditional. In much the same way, if we expect gifted students to embrace highly challenging work that is difficult for them, we cannot attach assessments to it that might bring down their grades in any formal manner.

Gifted students must experience two conditions in order to be convinced it is safe for them to try more challenging work.

1. First, they must be reassured that they will not have to do a larger amount of work than their classmates. As an adult, you probably would not volunteer for work that was simply more than what others were doing without any tangible benefit.

2. Second, they need to know that their extension work will not lead to lower recorded grades. If you cannot guarantee those outcomes, students may refuse to take advantage of the available Extension Menus, saying something like, "No thanks. I'll just do what the other students are doing."

All the strategies described in this book provide those two guarantees, and that is why gifted students are very likely to choose to take advantage of them.

When we create challenging learning situations for gifted students, they will probably stop having an "easy time" in school. While they'll likely still be getting high grades, they'll also be required to engage in and often struggle with difficult projects. This may upset them, as well as their parents. You may need to reeducate some parents so they understand the importance of their children experiencing frustration and struggle so that true learning can take place. Chapter 10 (in the digital content) provides information and reassurance for parents who may be alarmed that their children are no longer breezing through school.

Our goal in grading should be to record successful outcomes that document actual learning results, even for those who are working with advanced material. Students and parents want to know how progress is being documented. As long as they understand why an actual letter or percentage grade will *not* be the way that documentation is recorded, they can rest assured that the availability of the advanced work does not present an insurmountable risk that would make gifted students reject opportunities to move ahead.

Our goal in grading should be to record successful outcomes that document actual learning results, even for those who are working with advanced material.

When students are working above grade level, or with content that is much more rigorous academically, we need to document their progress in a different way than with simple letter or percentage grades. Here are a few options:

- As a separate document or on the student's report card, add a box marked "Curricular Adjustments." Then make note of the student's progress, such as, "In math, Samantha has fully mastered the fourth-grade material and is currently working at the fifth-grade level. The evidence of her success is her ability to continue to work at that advanced level. This quarter she has excelled in the standards: Operations, Algebraic Thinking, and Geometry. She has encountered more challenge in the standard in Measurement and Data." This assessment method allows close ongoing observation of this student's progress in math.

- Address and document the student's working habits in the appropriate section of the report card, progress report, or other reporting tool. An example of a narrative statement might be, "Esteben is currently working two grade levels ahead in math. He eagerly attempts new and challenging material." Or, "Alicia is working above grade level in reading. She becomes very frustrated when she does not understand what she is reading. She is learning different strategies to make her comprehension more dependable."

- For accelerated work, such as placement in a higher grade's math or reading work, the recorded grade would come from the actual grade earned with that advanced content, since it represents the student's full-time curriculum in that subject area. You might add a note on the reporting form that states the student is being graded on advanced-level work.

As discussed in chapter 1, the research of Dr. Carol Dweck and others has proven that some students lose courage when they get high grades easily and then resist seeking out more challenging tasks. For decades, this situation has been very confusing to parents and teachers. We wonder why these very smart kids stop being willing to take the high-level classes in favor of classes at more average levels. This research finally answers the perplexing questions adults have about this issue.

How to Grade Students with Learning Contracts and Study Guides

As we discussed in chapters 2 and 3, grades are handled a little differently when a student is on a Learning Contract versus Study Guide. With Learning Contracts, the A's a student earned on the pretest are entered into your grade book at the same time you enter grades for other students for a particular assignment—as long as they follow the expected working conditions on the days they are working on extension activities. When students don't follow a working condition, you might discuss with them how to make better choices. However, when they continue to ignore the Essential Rules for Independent Work described on page 44, expect them to rejoin the direct instruction group for the remainder of the unit.

With the Learning Contract strategy, students are therefore receiving their A grade for two reasons: they demonstrated mastery on the pretest on this particular standard, and they followed the working conditions on the day you actually taught that standard to students who needed to learn it. Their extension activities are *not* formally graded. Nor is a student expected to finish one extension activity per day. If they were, students would choose only easy activities, and the differentiated opportunities would not provide the intended outcomes.

Things are quite different when using the Study Guide method for new content, as described in chapter 3. When many of the standards are unfamiliar to the student, we don't recommend a pretest for the reasons explained in that chapter. However, if there is no pretest, there is no evidence of which standards the students may have previously mastered. In that case, we compact and differentiate the pace at which the students work and the amount of time they must spend working with grade-level standards.

Their grades come from a combination of content checkpoints as shown on the Study Guide and the grade they choose to earn for their extension project. An Evaluation Contract may be used to assess a student's extension work, and this

---

What About Extra Credit?

Most gifted students do not need extra credit work. "Extra" credit implies that students have completed their "regular" work. However, since gifted students buy time for extension work by successfully completing compacted work, and are working on other activities to replace the grade-level work, they do not need to do anything more to demonstrate mastery. The extra credit issue becomes moot. Instead, if they receive credit for their extension work, it is called "replacement" or "equivalent" credit, and is in no way "extra."

---

grade is recorded in the grade book in place of a grade for work associated with the required grade-level standards. See chapter 3 for details on Evaluation Contracts.

How to Spend Less Time Grading

While grades are important, most teachers struggle with the amount of time they spend grading, wondering about its effectiveness but feeling guilty if they don't consistently grade all student work. According to researcher Lee Jenkins, there are no studies that prove any correlation between the amount of time a teacher spends grading and student achievement. However, Jenkins also documents there *is* a direct correlation between student achievement and the amount of time a teacher spends doing lesson planning that is based on formative assessments.[4]

The following formative assessment methods encourage students to do high-quality, legible, and accurate work while decreasing the amount of time you spend grading and entering the grading data in your grading records.

⭐ STRATEGY
Roll the Die

Use a regular die with large numerals of one through six. Working on a selected topic area, small groups of students complete six separate activities and are expected to keep their dated work. On the seventh day of work, a student from each group rolls the die, and whichever numeral comes up represents the activity that was completed on that specified day. That is the only

activity that is graded, and that grade represents each group's grade for the total number of activities done for a topic area. Of course, you can make this sequence take fewer days of study. Students, however, will value accuracy with all their work since no one knows ahead of time which day's activity will represent the entire grade for that topic area.

Variation: To select the actual problems that will be used for the grade for the entire assignment of 15 problems or examples, use a 15-sided die. One student throws the die three times. The numbers that show up are the only three problems that will be graded from that assignment. After the answers are shared, students receive their grade by the number of designated problems they have correct. Again, no one knows ahead of time which problems will "count," and you get measurable results without grading all the problems for all students.

Students who have been excused from having to complete the entire assignment through compacting opportunities as described in earlier chapters will not have to participate in this event. We caution you to be certain you never assume any proficiency exists until you have documented evidence of that fact. It is a disservice to gifted students to place them in situations where they are asked to learn something for which they have never learned the required framework. In other words, just because a student is very smart, we can never assume that "he must know this or that." Only formative or summative assessments can document that mastery has actually been achieved.

---

[4] Jenkins, 2003.

⭐ STRATEGY

Scoring Rubrics

Rubrics contain specific sets of criteria that demonstrate various ratings regarding students' work products. Every project can be assessed by using a rubric. Rubrics can be generated by you or by your students. If students provide input into how their projects are developed, they should also help develop the rubric for assessment. Make sure all students clearly understand the language it uses, as well as the role of individual students in using the rubric. Rubrics help make assessments and grading procedures more objective than subjective, more informative than punitive, and more descriptive than a single letter or number grade.

Rubrics are effective for all students, but gifted students find their use particularly satisfying. Gifted kids often hate surprises—especially unpleasant ones! Typical grading practices are very arbitrary. Students may try to predict the grade they will receive, but their guesses are often way off the mark. Rubrics allow students to know in advance which specific criteria will be used to assess their work. Not only can the rubric be used to figure out the grade a product will probably earn, it can also be used for students to edit their products during the production process in order to satisfy more challenging criteria. Rubrics are also a very helpful tool to use in peer editing, a practice that allows students to deeply analyze the purpose and the content of a lesson. Finally, rubrics can help students at various schools within the same district produce higher-quality products that are more consistent among schools. There is abundant information online for creating rubrics. See pages 238–239 in the references and resources for suggestions.

Using Technology to Challenge Learners

Along with the recent increased attention to assessment has come the rapid emergence of technology use in school. Formal assessment now is commonly administered online, and a tremendous amount of differentiation and content acceleration occurs through digital tools.

Students love using technology to learn. It is easy for us to observe that students are more actively engaged using technology than they are during some teacher-directed lessons, and we know that active engagement leads to much better learning outcomes.[5] Today's students naturally want technology to continue to be an essential part of their learning, since most have been accustomed to using it since they were very young. Students in technology-rich environments have been shown to experience positive effects on achievement in all subject areas and improved attitudes toward learning and their own self-concepts.[6]

Present-day students are noticeably different from the types of learners many of us were trained to teach since they are accustomed to getting most of their knowledge and information from digital sources. If you are equally savvy, you might offer assistance to any colleagues who are not as comfortable with the instructional technology currently in use. We must model both how to access worthy information as well as ethical ways of using it.

When today's kids want to talk to someone, they want to communicate instantly so they text their mom or dad, Skype with their grandparents, or chat with friends on a social network. Today's kids even perceive email as obsolete and too slow. As educators, we want students to experience and understand that technology can be just as exciting at school as outside of school, and that we will facilitate their already-mastered technology skills into their daily learning experiences.

Gifted Kids and Technology

Gifted kids, in particular, benefit from using technology in the classroom because of the endless possibilities for research and collaboration with others, including academic leaders in a particular field. Providing gifted students opportunities to learn with technology gives them an outlet for their creativity. Instead of simply writing a story

---

[5] ISTE, 2008.
[6] Sivin-Kachala, 1998.

about a boy who can fly, they can create a digital project that enables them to depict their character actually flying! They thrive on the opportunities technology provides to enhance their creativity. Today's software and digital programs provide an endless array of possibilities for kids to create whatever they envision. Twice-exceptional students are freed from their learning restrictions to express their special brand of creativity in ways that help them overcome their learning challenges. Gifted students can get lost in sites such as NASA, National Geographic, the Smithsonian Institute, and countless others. It is intuitive for students to jump into one of these sites to explore ideas, find topics for study, and then proceed with their research projects. It is a rabbit-hole phenomenon, in which you don't know where you are going to end up once you start. Exploring topics in such an environment can be highly engaging for gifted kids because it is fast-paced and appeals to all the senses. They are also excited by the limitless content they can find.

The classroom is a place where kids can collaborate, create, assess, build, and apply. Gifted kids want to find value or reason to come to the classroom beyond learning facts and getting information. They can get facts anywhere, anytime. Making learning meaningful and relevant for gifted kids in our classrooms involves stepping into their digital world.

Making learning meaningful and relevant for gifted kids in our classrooms involves stepping into their digital world.

Gifted children thirst for more and more information about topics in which they are interested. Instantly, technology provides students with an abundance of resources from different perspectives, which gives them opportunities to consider all viewpoints and learn to evaluate resources. They can then construct their own understanding about what they are learning and how that information fits into their world.

You may have some concerns about kids' fascination with technology and whether it might be isolating them. Consider that instant messaging *is* having a conversation; online gaming *is* collaborating and playing; social networking sites *do* expand communication. Through Facebook, Twitter, texting, and gaming, kids are communicating and collaborating more now than ever before. What has changed, however, is whether kids actually participate with each other in the same physical space! We must be willing to teach kids the way they learn and try to keep up with their facility with technology.

The Teacher's Changing Role in the Age of Technology

Your role as a teacher has changed more in the last decade than perhaps at any other time in your teaching career—required standards, assessments, curriculum alignments, and of course, technology. One thing you learn from teaching gifted students over time is never to "fake it." If you don't know the answer to something, have the good sense to admit it. Some of your students know much more than you do. Learn to feel okay responding to a question with, "I really don't know this. I would appreciate your assistance in explaining this software, technology, or app." Your honesty might actually encourage your students to have similar courage when they need to tell you about what *they* don't know.

The amount of technology you will use for instructional purposes depends on your comfort level and experience with it, availability of various programs and software, and opportunities for professional development. Most teachers currently use computers for lesson planning, record keeping, grading, projection systems, music, and class presentations. In this new era, you will find numerous opportunities to become a student again and enter a world that can help reinvigorate your teaching and your students' learning.

The good news is there are many options for you to improve or share your technology skills. Ask the person in charge of technology at your school or in your district to help you access whatever training you need. Look for grants to help

Helpful Websites for Students' Creative and Critical Thinking

Kahoot! (kahoot.com) is a game-based learning site teachers can use in the classroom to create, play, and share engaging quizzes on any topic.

Baamboozle (baamboozle.com) is a game-based learning site that received a 2017 Best Website for Teaching & Learning award from the American Association of School Librarians.

Cite This for Me! (citethisforme.com) is a popular citation website that includes Harvard, APA, MLA, and other styles.

Wizer (app.wizer.me) is a teacher-made, intuitive spreadsheet platform that has grading, sharing, and individual student assignment capabilities.

Buncee (app.edu.buncee.com) is a presentation app that can be used by teachers and students for effective and fun communication and collaboration.

Mysimpleshow (mysimpleshow.com) is a website for making "explainer videos" that can be used for professional, educational, or personal purposes.

Seesaw (web.seesaw.me) is a website for teachers to help students create digital portfolios.

GoNoodle (gonoodle.com) is a video platform that engages children through movement to introduce new topics in the classroom or hone skills at home.

Zoom In (zoomin.edc.org) is an online platform that helps kid dive deeper into historical content through primary and secondary sources.

Tween Tribune (tweentribune.com) is a free resource from the Smithsonian Institution that contains articles, videos, and historical stories for K–12 students.

OER Commons (oercommons.org) is a website that has free higher education resources.

CommonLit (commonlit.org) is a free resource for reading passages and literature exercises for grades 3–12.

Newsela (newsela.com) is an instructional content platform that includes differentiated texts grouped by subject area.

MediaSmarts (mediasmarts.ca) is a K–12 platform that educates children about the issues in "traditional" media as well as the arising issues in digital media.

Poets.org (poets.org) is a database that includes poems by and biographies about poets throughout history as well as some contemporary poets. You can sign up for Poem-a-Day to receive a daily poem by email.

Duolingo (duolingo.com) is an app-based platform that first gauges and tests your knowledge of a language you would like to learn. It then provides daily activities to grow your knowledge and tests your skills as you learn. Available in multiple languages and on most phones.

Bloomz (bloomz.net) is a free app that can be downloaded by teachers and parents to effectively communicate with one another securely and privately.

Khan Academy (khanacademy.org) is a personalized learning platform that utilizes videos and articles to teach subjects from kindergarten to college.

Freckle Education (freckle.com) is a differentiation platform for grades preK–12 in multiple subjects. It claims to be the first differentiation platform to exist for these ages.

See more ideas for digital learning in chapter 6, page 184, and in the references and resources, pages 238–239.

pay for what you need. Use the Khan Academy yourself. As with anything we need to learn, start with one topic or program of interest to you, and concentrate on that until you reach a comfort level with its use. Then branch out—one new technological device at a time.

Technology in your classroom can benefit you tremendously. Your preparation time is minimal, since many kids are so computer and internet savvy. The use of technology can deepen and broaden the learning for students who have compacted out of the regular curriculum. Depending on the availability of computers and other digital teaching tools, you may group students into pairs or small groups so they can interact with the technology on preapproved websites. The goal is to find websites that are aligned with the required or advanced standards and with students' personal areas of interest.

Teacher Online Resources

The following are websites that provide teacher resources to help you improve the interest level of your curriculum for your students. Since hundreds of new programs and applications are made available daily, this list serves simply as an example of the types of resources that are available. You can search on your own and we encourage you to do so on a regular basis. An excellent topic for staff, department meetings, professional learning communities, or gifted cluster teacher meetings is to share any websites colleagues are finding interesting and helpful.

Bertie Kingore's website (bertiekingore.com) hosts the marvelous collection of Dr. Kingore's materials that assist in identification of and educational interventions for gifted students of all ages.

Hoagies' Gifted (hoagiesgifted.org) includes easy access to a treasure trove of articles, books, studies, and suggestions for parenting and teaching gifted students.

Khan Academy (khanacademy.org) is as good for you as it is for your students. This fabulous, free resource presents short tutorials for anyone who needs to know just about anything.

Teachertube (teachertube.com) provides a free, safe, focused online community for teachers to share instructional videos with their students or other teachers.

Moodle (moodle.com) is a free virtual learning environment that has become popular among educators as a tool for creating online dynamic websites for their students.

Free Technology for Teachers (freetech4teachers.com) supplies teachers with free resources and websites they can use in their classrooms. Includes a link to Fakebook, where kids can create fake Facebook pages as learning aids.

Class Tools (classtools.net) has tools you can use to create free game formats for your curriculum.

TED Talks (ted.com) hosts a series of TED (Technology, Entertainment, and Design) conferences dedicated to "ideas worth spreading." Short, high-interest lessons cover a variety of topics.

The G Suite for Education (edu.google.com) provides a free collection of services to enable digital teaching to flourish in classrooms around the world. The core services in G Suite include Calendar, Classroom, Drive, Docs, Forms, Gmail, Hangouts, Keep, Sheets, Sites, Slides, and Vault. Google Classroom (included in G Suite) is an online platform that allows teachers and students to connect with ease and confidence. Assignments, videos, and discussion forums are all at a teacher's fingertips. Other services provide the ability to create and share documents, spreadsheets, and slideshows for an authentic learning environment. Add to the mix Google Forms to simplify data collection and Google Keep, a note-taking and organizational tool to support learners in the classroom.

School Website Resources

Another great way you can use technology in teaching is to start housing some of your curriculum on your school's or district's website or intranet. Create areas where students can go to access their extension work. Even if no computers are available at the time, students can access the extension lessons through any handheld device, such as a smartphone or tablet, the same way they would on a laptop. Housing your curriculum in this way serves numerous purposes and solves many logistical challenges for teachers. Primarily, the practice eases accessibility for the students who are working at different levels. Students access what they need, when they need it. If you put your extension lessons online, you can build in hyperlinks that lead kids straight to the sites you want them to visit. This also reduces the amount of time and material you need to put into the lesson plan.

In addition, if your staff wants to do a study of this book, or other books of interest to teachers, your school or district website can be used as an "online" course so some of the face-to-face meetings can be replaced by a digital format.

Also, visit the website of your state's or college's education department, as well as those of the publishers of your adopted materials.

Making Differentiation Easier

Using technology in the classroom makes differentiation much easier. For example, in math, if one student is working two years above grade level and another is working four years above grade level, you can find online math programs they can both use independently. You can do a search to find an abundance of challenging, already prepared materials, including lessons, games, competitions, and so much more. Applications or software for this purpose can be accessed not only through computers, but also through handheld devices such as iPads, smartphones, or tools that haven't even been invented or marketed yet!

Google Classroom, in particular, aids differentiation by giving teachers the ability to customize lessons for specific groups of learners. For example, in Mrs. Brown's fifth-grade classroom, students are getting ready to engage in a lesson on the use of figurative language in literature. When Mrs. Brown pretested her learners on their knowledge of figurative language, she discovered that her students exhibited a range of understanding. To accommodate for this range, she has uploaded several different lesson formats onto Google Classroom. Class begins with a discussion of the value of figurative language, and

then students take out their laptops and log into Classroom. Every learner finds an assignment tailored to her or his learning needs:

- One group will watch a video selected by Mrs. Brown that goes through a variety of different figurative language elements and then will respond to a poem, identifying the different figurative language elements in it.

- A second group has been given three poems, each containing different figurative language elements. Working together through a shared document, group members will identify each element and share the imagery they think the language choice is portraying.

- The students in the final group have a strong understanding of figurative language and are given the opportunity to create their own poems or short stories using multiple figurative language elements. They may choose to create a shared presentation, work together on a shared document, or create individual works.

Mrs. Brown now has the freedom to move from student to student and provide the individual support that each needs.

Digital learning is not exclusive to gifted students; all students enjoy it. So it is important to make certain all students in your classes have equal access to available technology. Using technology as a regular part of your classroom instruction is an excellent way to engage other students when you are meeting with your advanced students who are working on extension projects, or vice versa.

⭐ STRATEGY

Using Technology for Collaborative Learning

Think about how your gifted students get excited about collaborating on meaningful projects with like-minded learners. In this section you will learn a number of ways your students can collaborate in their learning experiences through the use of technology. Web 2.0 allows students to interact with the content and with each other both inside and outside their own classrooms. Collaborating digitally with other gifted students motivates them to work on projects and build off each other's ideas to make the work even more meaningful. And don't forget to help students connect with professionals in fields in which the students are interested.

Interactive Whiteboards

Interactive whiteboards, when used to their capacity, get learners out of their seats and involved in hands-on learning experiences. They provide numerous advantages that fit with inquiry, problem solving, and project-based learning by helping students go beyond a traditional mode of getting information to an integrated mode of using, manipulating, and sharing information as they interact with it.

Although all students seem to benefit from interaction with technology, it is especially beneficial for students who are twice-exceptional (see page 22) so they can visually access the information they need to keep up with their gifted peers. Other types of assistive technology products and websites can also help with the challenges of teaching twice-exceptional students.

Technology-Assisted Problem-Based Learning

Problem-based learning (PBL) focuses classroom projects in ways that are intended to bring about deep learning. Students use technology and inquiry to engage with issues and questions relevant to their lives. Student learning is then assessed through their projects rather than traditional testing methods. Through cross-curricular projects and individual exploration, students move beyond the learning of data to shaping the areas in which they choose to expand their knowledge base. PBL is essential in today's student experiences because the problems students will face during their careers cannot be predicted yet. The best training they can get now is learning how to figure out what to do when they don't know what to do.

The basic features of problem-based learning include:

- Personally meaningful, real-world situations
- Complex and challenging questions that apply creative and critical thinking
- Interaction and collaboration on relevant, engaging, hands-on projects
- Choice in content, process, resources, and product
- Research and investigation skills
- Positive and productive collaborative skills
- Interdisciplinary long-term projects
- Metacognitive skills: self- and peer-assessment of a product
- Discovery and development of unique perspectives
- Real-world audience beyond the teacher and other students

Gifted students get excited about figuring out solutions to challenging problems as well as using technology to share what they have learned in very creative and innovative ways. Problem-solving opportunities start by connecting your students to an overarching big question or problem to solve, ideally one that is actually challenging their school or community. They will need to do online research, come to some consensus on a solution, and then create a digital product that shows the steps they took to solving the problem or to an illustration or demonstration of the proposed solution. With technology-assisted PBL, their final project is going to be so much better, deeper, and more complex than more traditional products. A Google search on "Problem-Based Learning Strategies Using Technology" will lead you to many helpful ideas and even lesson plans, similar to the following one.

Sample Lesson Plan

Your class is learning about a situation that has been experienced by many countries: civil war. Using the tools in earlier chapters of this book, you determine that some of your students are ready to learn about the required standards with added depth and complexity. Your advanced students can refer to the Tiered Lesson Plan you have created for the unit and choose to participate in digital forums where the viewpoints of people from both sides of the conflict are provided. Students might then take on the roles of character prototypes from that period in the country's history. Perhaps they create an imaginary blog to create a dialogue about the events they have "witnessed." If the civil war in which they are interested is more recent, students can access media materials from that time period to participate in a blog as it might have been structured during the event. Students will be using modern tools to learn about the past in much more realistic detail than is possible to glean from textbooks.

Graphical Blogs

As discussed in chapter 6, a "glog" (short for graphical blog) is an interactive multimedia image that looks like a poster, but readers can interact with the content. Students start with a large digital screen that resembles an actual large poster or bulletin board. They can pin up images, pictures, texts, and other "objects" using interesting fonts, placements, and orientations. Therefore, parents, friends, students from other schools, and others can view the project if permission is given. Visit edu.glogster.com.

Sample Lesson

When teaching characterization, have students depict a character from a novel they are reading by creating a glog. On their glog they will include pictures of their character, important events experienced by the character, and other relevant elements. The final project will actually be a "digital poster."

Technology-Based Tiered Assignments

When preparing tiered lessons, use the internet to find information on the same topic at several different reading levels. Websites (such as webpagefx.com/tools/read-able) check the readability levels of various internet texts you are considering. In this way, students learn similar content at levels they can read and comprehend,

and everyone is better prepared to participate in class discussions, simulations, Socratic Seminars, and other activities. Other tools that help students combine their individual research are shared Google documents or Dropbox folders, through which they are able to continually add information, collaborate with their teachers or peers, and continue their search for newly discovered relevant websites and other resources.

Set up a digital forum with preset parameters for each level of activity you create: entry level, advanced, and most challenging. Before starting the unit, determine which activities you want to assign to which students. Some kids may watch pertinent video, take quizzes, and answer questions that give automatic feedback on the accuracy of their answers. Students who need higher-level challenges may be asked to compare and contrast the perspectives of information from two different resources. Gifted kids operating at a very high level can be directed to online forums where experts in the field can respond to questions that come up from their research. To increase students' active participation, you might also require your students to respond to students' postings from other classes or other school years.

Sample Activity

If your class is studying the respiratory system of the human body, you can differentiate the instruction for your advanced learners. While you are giving the regular direct instruction to your class, students who are experiencing compacting can discover websites their classmates might use for the projects they will do later in the learning process. Students prepare a brief description of the content from these sites. Then they add these sites and a brief description of their content to the Google document or Dropbox file in the appropriate categories.

⭐ STRATEGY

Using Mobile Devices

Many schools now allow students to use their own smartphones or other handheld devices in the classroom. Be sure to establish and explain the ground rules for using these devices safely and ethically (see pages 217–218 for more information on this). Mobile devices help students explore, research, and create wherever they are. Their learning and productivity are not limited to the classroom. These devices often have cameras, which is extremely helpful for creating digital projects, because students can interview others, take pictures and video clips of things going on around or outside the school, and record their own thoughts and messages in digital files.

Mobile devices help students explore, research, and create wherever they are. Their learning and productivity are not limited to the classroom.

Some of the many benefits to using handheld devices:

- They are powerful research and production tools, yet inexpensive compared to computers.

- Many students already have them and know how to use them so their use does not take up much of your instructional time.

- They start up quickly (since there is no hard drive).

- They are able to connect to the internet so students can store and access files anywhere and on any device.

- When storing data on an online server (in the "cloud") or similar storage system, you no longer have to use USB flash drives or email files back and forth. This is very useful for the disorganized student!

Cheating issues are a concern for teachers when deciding whether or not to let their students use handheld devices to learn, even though students do not need technology to cheat. Some strategies can help you avoid those possibilities, and they all lead to better instruction. For example, teachers who allow mobile devices as instructional tools learn how to teach at a higher level, so students' responses require significantly more complex answers than students just giving simple answers they can easily look up on their smartphones. The advanced tasks require students to search for information, synthesize that information, draw their own conclusions, and then offer their own informed opinions. You can even tier your assignments according to the amount of technology the kids are using. *Example:* "If you are using a smartphone, then _____ is expected of you."

A number of apps are also available for taking quizzes on the iPad. The teacher generates the quiz by loading the questions into the program using an app. Students enjoy clicking their answers on an iPad instead of using paper and pencil. The best part is that your students receive instant feedback—they can see their scores immediately and you don't have to grade papers. You can sort the results in different ways. You can see which problems everyone answered correctly and which ones you need to reteach. You can also use these as quick formative assessments to see who doesn't need to spend time learning this material. If you have only four or five devices available, you can rotate students through the quizzes. You can also use internet question banks to change the questions on the quiz.

Sample Application

Consider the common scenario of a gifted student who has compacted out of some of the material but may need to practice one or two skills before moving on. It may be that the skills this student is missing you plan to address at a later time. Instead of waiting until you address those skills with the class, using a handheld device, the student can click onto a relevant math app, select that particular skill, learn and practice it, and then be ready to move on with her or his extension work. ***Note:*** The student would still be expected to take the chapter or unit post-test to demonstrate mastery of grade-level standards.

⭐ STRATEGY

Webquests and Cyberhunts

Webquests

A webquest is an inquiry-oriented lesson format in which most or all of the information learners work with comes from the internet. Teachers provide multiple websites to use as reading content, allowing students to use the resource that works best for their level of understanding. A webquest generally includes an introduction, a task, resources, a process, an evaluation, and a conclusion. For more than a decade, many teachers have used webquests in independent study for their gifted students, as well as in demonstrating how all students can locate and use online information to enhance their learning.

A webquest about alligators might include the following:

Introduction: "Congratulations! You have been selected to work with a team of scientists in the Florida Everglades to learn about alligators. You will learn as much as you can and then present your findings at a scientific reptile conference."

Task: "As part of your study you will learn about where the alligator is on the food chain, historical facts about alligators, and important vocabulary words that describe alligators and their behavior. You will also illustrate an alligator."

Resources: List appropriate sites students can use during a webquest to keep them on task and focused, and to lessen the likelihood of them stumbling upon an inappropriate website, which is always a risk, even with filters.

Process: Have students create a KWL (What I **K**now, What I **W**ant to Know, What I've **L**earned) chart or similar graphic organizer in this step. They will look at photos of whatever they are studying, take notes, find facts, and so on. Explain that all scientists need to keep a journal of their investigations.

Evaluation: Offer some choices for products to be evaluated, which might include:

- Write an informational page for a textbook about reptiles.
- Write a factual poem about alligators.
- Write a letter to the Florida Department of Tourism asking questions about alligators.
- Draw a detailed picture of an alligator, labeling the body parts.

Conclusion: This is often the presentation of the final project to an appropriate audience. Possibilities:

- Create a keynote presentation about alligators.
- Film a factual movie about alligators.
- Build a realistic model of an alligator.
- Record a podcast about alligators that might be played on public radio.

Create a scoring rubric for the webquest to include a variety of factors. Always show the students the rubric at the beginning of the project so they understand the expectations. The rubric might include ratings for how well the students:

- Answered the questions.
- Defined the vocabulary.
- Used effective presentation skills.
- Demonstrated effective work habits by staying on task, working well with others, and keeping accurate records of their progress.

Throughout the entire process, be sure the tasks represent a variety of thinking levels, including the most challenging levels. Some basic comprehension and definition work will be included, usually near the beginning of the project. Further into the project, students might be required to make a prediction, write a persuasive letter, compare several items or events, or prepare an eye-catching summary. The final part of the webquest includes demonstrations of creativity, such as making a movie, creating a podcast, or enacting a dramatization.

Cyberhunts

A cyberhunt (short for "cyber scavenger hunt") is a much shorter and more basic activity than a webquest. It might be as simple as sending kids to different websites to answer questions about a particular topic. A cyberhunt is more of a reading comprehension and fact-finding activity, but it also builds internet navigation skills, which are important especially for the younger students who may not have had much exposure to certain concepts or topics. There might be some extension activities at the end of a cyberhunt, but not a big final project like a webquest.

It's helpful to use online sources that store all of the data students gather in a cyberhunt. This way they can update and store all of their information in one location. Such an organizational piece is key to academic success for some students, especially those who jump around from one idea to the next and those who tend to lose their work.

Sample Cyberhunt

You might conduct a cyberhunt by taking a virtual fieldtrip to the Louvre in Paris, France (louvre .fr/en). Try to put students in the mindset that they are really there. Have them take notes, like, "What I really enjoyed doing during the fieldtrip was . . ." or make it like a scavenger hunt, "Find a _____ painting" or "Compare _____'s painting of flowers with _____'s painting of flowers."

See the references and resources on pages 238–239 for suggested sources for webquest and cyberhunt ideas.

> **NOTE** Often the most useful internet sources for gifted kids are ones that house primary source documents. These documents allow students to read directly from an original source instead of interpreted versions. This helps them construct their own interpretations of the material.

Acceptable Use Policies

The biggest concern you may have when you begin using digital instruction is determining what is acceptable and what is not. Most schools and school districts are realizing they must have policies in place to reflect the rapidly changing digital world. Administrators and parents will want to know your safety procedures and how you are teaching netiquette (see below). Share this information in your newsletters and on your class website.

Net Smarts and Online Safety

To be smart internet researchers, students need to be taught how to evaluate websites. Set up a station in your classroom with a rubric that shows kids how to do this. The students use this rubric for assessing the websites they want to add to their class resource bank. These rubrics are available online so you can either do a search yourself or ask your students to do it. When posting website resources, have students list the link, the title, a brief description, and the readability score. This can be an activity for gifted students who have compacted out of your lesson. Your entire class will benefit.

Netiquette

Netiquette (short for "network etiquette" or "internet etiquette") is a set of social conventions that facilitate interaction over networks, ranging from user groups and mailing lists to Facebook, blogs, and other forums. Like other forms of etiquette, netiquette is primarily concerned with matters of courtesy in communications.

Sample Netiquette Lesson

At the beginning of the year, conduct a brainstorm activity to have students answer the questions:

- Do you have concerns about using technology? If so, what are they?
- What are the concerns of your parents?

Have students tweet their responses if they have smartphones or post their responses in a Google document, or you can list the students' answers on an interactive whiteboard.

From there, go through the concerns, addressing issues such as:

- bias
- discerning truth

- credibility
- advertising
- respect
- inappropriate content
- digital footprints

Other topics to discuss:

- How is a paper journal entry different from a blog?
- What might the concerns be about wikis?
- How might information be different on a blog versus on a video log (or "vlog")?
- What is the common language of netiquette?
- What are some ways to evaluate a website?
- When is it appropriate to use informal versus formal communication styles (e.g., in blogs, tweets, chats, wikis, websites, emails, etc.)?

Discuss with students how all of these topics fit under the netiquette umbrella. Teach them how to know if something is acceptable or not, how to discern the real and possible dangers of using technology, and the importance of being considerate and respectful in the digital world. Discuss also what should be done if they become aware that some peers may not be following the expected guidelines.

QUESTIONS ⭐ ANSWERS

"It seems that we are constantly testing (assessing) our students. Why?"

Assessment serves many purposes: to guide instruction, to ensure quality teaching is occurring, and to document academic growth, to name a few. Using formative assessment helps us plan instruction and using summative assessment monitors students' progress. We use assessments as accountability measures to make sure we are using all the information available to us to help our students learn.

"Is the use of assessment different for gifted students than for others?"

The use of assessment is critical for *all* students. Gifted students are more likely to have mastered grade-level content, and they learn more quickly than age peers. Therefore, the use of formative assessment is especially important for them so that teachers can document continuous progress in all the content areas.

"What is the teacher's responsibility when using technology to teach?"

The teacher's role is to locate reliable and reputable resources that help students explore and expand on the information being learned in the classroom. The teacher must monitor student usage and create classroom systems that allow for safe and productive use of technology.

"How can parents be certain that their children will not be able to access objectionable material online at school?"

Schools have established systems in place, often called acceptable use policies (AUPs), that clearly define the ways students can access online information. They also use strong filters to block questionable sites. Some teachers have built into the experience methods or rubrics for students to judge the value of websites they visit. However, even with the filters teachers find it necessary to continue careful monitoring of students' internet use to ensure appropriate time on task. Teachers should be trained in monitoring technology use. If they need help, they should ask a person in the school district who is responsible for technology how they can acquire training.

Chapter Summary

This chapter has explained how to appropriately assess all students, with particular attention to the assessment of gifted students. We have also described how technology impacts learning and assessment. Since the world of technology changes so rapidly, we encourage you to work with a group of colleagues to keep track of newer technologies and websites.

CHAPTER 9
Gifted Programming

This chapter provides information pertaining to a few topics that are important to meeting gifted students' learning needs. You are invited to conduct further research on the topics that are of interest to you.

- What types of gifted program options are available?

- How can we manage differentiated instruction for gifted students and keep useful records?

- Under what circumstances is acceleration recommended? What types of acceleration are effective?

- How is the role of the gifted education specialist changing?

- How can gifted education advocates work with parents to improve gifted services?

Gifted Program Delivery Options

Identifying gifted kids and providing appropriate services for them has always been a "chicken-egg" situation. Should we still identify gifted students if programming is not available? How can we design programming for gifted kids if we don't know the needs of the gifted students we find? Should we identify all of our gifted kids, or only those who will benefit from programs we can actually offer?

Above all, gifted programming should lead to optimum learning for *all* ability groups. If students in the advanced-level classes are simply getting more work in class and significantly more homework, golden opportunities have been missed for bringing into their learning experiences the qualities of depth, complexity, and novelty in all possible forms.

Above all, gifted programming should lead to optimum learning for *all* ability groups.

Over the years, gifted education programs have been delivered through various models with varying degrees of effectiveness. This section briefly describes some of the most prevalent program delivery systems and discusses the pros and cons of each model. They include self-contained programs, content replacement classes, pull-out classes, cluster grouping models, and enrichment programs that occur outside of regular school hours. Each of these models, as described here, has benefits and challenges.

In any of these regrouped classes, the most important consideration for success at all levels is whether the methods used for each ability group and learning levels have been correctly matched to the students' strongest learning modalities and the teachers' preferred teaching styles. Grouping advanced learners together is only the first step in providing what they need. The second, and most important step, is making certain that the learning experiences in these advanced classes provide all the elements of depth, complexity, and novelty described in detail in chapter 5.

The purpose of these classes is to provide opportunities for gifted students to work in more homogeneous groups at certain times during their school day. When this happens, these kids often become comfortable enough to really be themselves and to stop hiding their natural abilities for fear of peer censure.

Option 1: Self-Contained Full-Time Classes

Pros:

- Gifted students receive full-time attention to their differentiated learning needs in the company of peers with similar abilities and with a teacher who has had specialized training in gifted education.

- The curriculum in these self-contained classes is expected to be more rigorous and challenging than might be found in totally heterogeneous classes.

- Opportunities for accelerated learning are usually more prevalent in these classes.

Cons:

- Only a small percentage of identified gifted students can be served in the self-contained model. Typically, only the top 1 to 2 percent of gifted students is invited to attend these

classes, and it is generally expected that those chosen are also highly productive in the classroom.

- Self-contained classes rarely serve highly gifted students who are not also high achieving, which include English language learners, twice-exceptional students, and those who underachieve.

- Often, the classes are held in only certain schools in the system, and students and their families must find transportation to and from the classes daily.

- Students who continue to be placed in self-contained classes over several years are insulated, having few opportunities to interact with the general school population. At times, the class composition does not reflect the ethnic and socioeconomic diversity present in the district.

Option 2: Content Replacement Classes or Switching Groups for Various Subject Areas

Pros:

In these classes, gifted and high-achieving students receive advanced and accelerated curriculum, most commonly in mathematics and reading. Their curriculum is expected to focus on more complex and engaging learning experiences toward the goal of engaging and challenging all students.

Cons:

Often, in the advanced sections, students simply experience *more* work, which is not necessarily focused on providing appropriate rigor to gifted students' curriculum. When this is the case, students may develop distaste for having to do so much more work and may ultimately opt out of advanced courses in high school. Of course, if teachers who teach advanced sections have gifted education training, they have learned the principles of depth, complexity, and novelty and will be much more effective with advanced learners.

Option 3: Honors and Advanced Placement (AP) Classes

Pros:

- Gifted students tend to gather together in these classes because they enjoy the benefits of working with a more homogeneous group of their learning peers.

- Their families perceive these courses will give their children certain advantages in college.

Cons:

- Honors classes may focus on *more* work instead of *different* work unless teachers have had gifted education training.

- AP classes are dedicated to making sure students learn the exact content of specific college-level courses to enable them to get college credit for a particular course. This may limit the percentage of time most AP teachers can spend in activities that allow students to really learn in depth.

Option 4: Pull-Out Programs

Gifted pull-out programs have been disappearing from many school districts all across our country for various reasons. In most places, attempts to replace these programs center on a belief that gifted students will receive the differentiation they need in mixed-ability classes. Unfortunately, that is more likely to happen when teachers get the training that is necessary to help them work successfully with their gifted students in these settings.

Pros:

- Gifted students at least have some time on a regular basis when they can just "be themselves"—very smart, highly competitive, and eager to show off their exceptional abilities.

- Sometimes the activities in the pull-out class are very enjoyable and provide a needed break from the repetitious classroom learning situations so often experienced by gifted students.

Cons:

- When provided as the sole programming model, pull-out programs serve gifted students only on an intermittent basis, ranging anywhere from an hour a day to an hour or less a week. The model does not acknowledge that gifted students are gifted throughout the school day, and in one or several content areas.

- Pull-out classes vary widely in the quality of instruction and in the degree to which students' experiences meet the curricular expectations of depth, complexity, and novelty.

- Classroom teachers may resent the interruptions in their teaching time.

- Classroom teachers often insist that gifted students, returning from the pull-out class, must make up all the work they missed while they were gone. This gives very little value to the work these students did in the pull-out class, and causes them to have more work than other students.

- Classroom teachers may become complacent about challenging gifted students during the time they spend in their classrooms, since they are already "getting gifted education" in that program down the hall every Wednesday morning, for example. For a pull-out model to be effective it is critical that the classroom teachers *also* have an understanding of the social, emotional, and academic needs of gifted students, so they are able to consistently make differentiation opportunities available in the students' regular classrooms.

Option 5: Acceleration

In the document titled *A Nation Deceived: How Schools Hold Back America's Brightest Students,* the preferred method of intervention is acceleration. In *subject acceleration,* highly advanced students are placed into the classes at a higher grade level in one or more subjects, while the balance of that student's program may be taken with age peers. *Grade acceleration* moves students ahead in all subject areas so they actually complete their K–12 program in less than 13 years.

NOTE Please don't form an opinion about whether pull-out programs for gifted kids should continue until you have taught or observed one. It is difficult to overstate how differently gifted kids behave when they are surrounded by like-minded peers and can be their wonderfully competitive and knowledge-loving selves without fear of censure.

When considering the merits of a pull-out program, the critical question is related to what students are *doing* in these classes: "Could all students do this work, and would all students want to do it?" The content and activities gifted students experience in a pull-out class should be more advanced, sophisticated, and rigorous than their age peers could handle. If everyone could benefit from a particular activity, then everyone should experience it.

Gifted students who attend a pull-out class should never be sent back to the regular classroom with required homework, unless the teacher of the pull-out class and the classroom teacher have agreed that the homework will *replace* the grade-level work they have compacted out of. Likewise, classroom teachers should not expect gifted students to make up all they missed once they return. Offering the Most Difficult First option in chapter 2 is a good compromise for all. The classroom teacher gets the evidence he or she needs that the student is competent with the material, and the gifted students do not feel they are getting lots of extra work just because they are highly capable.

The research on acceleration has found that the long-term benefits of acceleration far outweigh any disadvantages for highly gifted children. When gifted kids are grouped with their learning peers, instead of solely with their age peers, they often find themselves feeling understood and validated for who they are. Although some of these kids may experience a difficult time in adolescence, when they are physically smaller and perhaps less socially adept than their peers, by the time they reach college most have adjusted quite well.

A student may be accelerated in several ways: through early entrance to kindergarten, grade skipping (or double promotion), completing curriculum for two grade levels in one year, or working ahead in a particular subject.

Early Entrance to Kindergarten

Some gifted children are ready to start kindergarten at age 4. Schools that support this practice develop procedures and guidelines to help determine if early entrance is appropriate for the child. Criteria include a specific birth date and achieving a certain score on an achievement test.

Recalling the bell curve from page 5, you will discover that a child can be considered gifted if the IQ score is near 130. However, some gifted students have IQ scores of 160. It is important for parents to know their child's actual IQ so they can advocate properly for the best type of intervention. Testers can be found in the psychology departments of colleges. Children with scores of 135 or higher are more likely to benefit from early entrance to kindergarten and other methods of acceleration than those who score below that level. Students who score at or above 150 are considered profoundly gifted and will need to experience acceleration several times throughout their school careers.

Dr. John Feldhusen researched the effects of early entrance to kindergarten in the 1980s, and his findings have been validated by Nancy Robinson, et al., in 1991.[1] Feldhusen and his team recommended that a child being considered for early entrance should:

- Be within six months of the approved entering age.

- Have been tested and evaluated by a trained psychologist for IQ and readiness.

- Be more mentally mature than is expected for his or her age.

[1] Robinson, N. & Weimer, L., 1991.

- Have the necessary academic skills for kindergarten entrance.

- Be physically healthy and well-adjusted socially and emotionally when observed with her or his learning peers rather than age peers.

- Want to go to school at this time.

- Not come from a family that puts a high value on competitive sports, since the child might always be too small or not strong enough to earn a place on teams. (This is not a concern if the child is large for his or her age.)

Note: Schools that allow for early entrance generally have a provisional period of the first quarter of the school year to make sure the placement is appropriate.

Grade Skipping

When considering grade skipping, keep these guidelines in mind:

- The students themselves should be part of the acceleration plan and should want the change to happen.

- Acceleration into the same grade level of an older sibling generally is not successful unless there are many sections of that grade level. Siblings should not be placed in the same classroom unless there is no alternative.

- Concern over physical characteristics, motor coordination, and social-emotional development are a consideration, but not a priority. Students who are good candidates for acceleration generally can compensate in these areas with great success.

- A written implementation plan is essential and must have the input of the receiving teacher as well as the present teacher.

- Use the Iowa Acceleration Scale for concrete methods to identify which students are good candidates for grade acceleration.

- If your school is small, and the student's out-of-grade placement will be noticed, ask a gifted education or cluster group teacher, a social worker, or a counselor to visit the class at the beginning of the school year to discuss the matter of grade skipping in such a way that it appears to be okay and natural.

If it's clear that a student would benefit from grade skipping but isn't given the chance, don't be surprised if his or her motivation and productivity in school are adversely affected. Kids who are rarely challenged in school become less willing to work hard. Furthermore, if the primary reason for keeping the student with his or her age peers is concern about social adjustment, this sends the message that peer relations are more important than academic achievement. This can put pressure on the student to conform to peer attitudes, behaviors, and values. In the words of Sylvia Rimm, "No one expects an average child to repeat skills after they've demonstrated competence. Why should an intellectually gifted child be punished with such meaningless learning tasks?"

Completing Two Grades in One Year

Some schools prefer this method to the more typical practice of having a student skip an entire grade. Here's an example of how it might work in a first-grade and second-grade combination class:

Ben begins first grade already very mature and sociable and with exceptionally high skills in all subject areas. It soon becomes obvious that he has mastered most of the first-grade curriculum. The teacher recognizes that Ben is bored. The teacher and principal determine that it would be appropriate for Ben to complete first-grade and second-grade curriculum in the same calendar year. Since he is placed in a first-/second-grade combo class, he does it without missing any significant portion of either year and without cutting himself off from social contact with age peers from either grade. After completing his first year in this class, Ben proceeds to the third grade with the second graders who are moving forward at the same time. The entire process is seamless and feels very natural to all concerned.

Acceleration in One Subject

More frequently, we find students who are precocious in one or two subject areas but only slightly above average in others. For these students, accelerating the curriculum only in their areas of strength is more appropriate than skipping a grade. This is most easily done in a cluster grouping model. The second-grade students who are working at a fourth-grade level in math should be grouped in a classroom with other second graders who are also accelerated. This way, the teacher can bring the more challenging curriculum to the student(s) who need it.

To ensure success, all those who will be affected by this schedule change should be involved in the planning stage. For some teachers, this will mean facilitating the continuation of the plan into the next grade level and beyond. For some parents, it may mean providing transportation when the student goes to a middle school for math each morning and returns to the elementary school for the rest of the day.

Option 6: Out of School Time Services

Sometimes gifted education opportunities are only provided outside of regular school hours. This system is fraught with inconveniences and questionable objectives.

Pros:

When formal gifted programs are not available, teachers can implement some of the same instructional strategies and auxiliary opportunities that many programs routinely provide. Some schools offer extension programs after school, before school, or on Saturdays. Possible extension program activities include chess, spelling bees, science fairs, and online activities.

Cons:

- When gifted services require that students attend school before or after the regular instructional day it sends the message that their learning needs are auxiliary to the school's priorities.

- These services also require that families schedule schooling (and related transportation needs) outside of the regular school schedule.

- These services negate the expectations of many state departments of education that provisions for gifted students should be included in the regular instructional day.

Option 7: Supplemental Activities

Supplemental activities are great experiences that enrich learning and stretch the imagination of all students, not only the gifted. These activities should be open to your entire class, or to all students at certain grade levels. None of these represents a valid gifted education component that can stand on its own merits.

- field trips
- working with mentors
- career exploration
- academic competitions
- digital media immersion
- dual enrollment/early entrance to college
- digital learning opportunities
- programs designed to engage high-ability students

Option 8: International Baccalaureate (IB) Classes

IB classes focus on developing students' abilities for conceptualization, data analysis and interpretation, uncensored curiosity, and problem solving with actual issues. IB students demonstrate what they have learned with exhibitions, portfolios, extended essays, and other types of assessment. More and more schools are attracted to IB as a way to keep their local populations satisfied so they won't seek out greener pastures in other schools or educational settings.

Pros:

- Classes are more interesting and relevant than typical honors or AP classes.

- Classes connect students with the topics and discussions being studied worldwide and provides a good transition to studying abroad.

- The required extended essay gives high school students an opportunity to explore a self-selected topic in depth and gain experience with the type of required work done at the college level.

- Writing and oral presentation skills often improve.

- In some schools, IB grades are weighted.

- Some IB classes and certificates are possible without doing the full IB diploma.

- IB work that earns specified high grades can translate into college credit.

- The program is well-rounded since it expects students to complete community service.

Cons:

- The program requires serious dedication to academics, and IB students may have to significantly curtail their social experiences. (However, students often have more in-depth interaction with their IB friends.)

- The program is not available in some locations or at all grade levels.

- The program is costly. All involved teachers are required to attend special IB training.

Option 9: Cluster Grouping Programs

Cluster grouping models have been used in various formats for several decades. In the Schoolwide Cluster Grouping Model (SCGM), gifted identified students are clustered together in otherwise heterogeneous classes. Their gifted cluster teacher is expected to provide consistent compacting and differentiation opportunities in that classroom for all students who need them.

Pros:

- Because teachers have a noticeable group of these kids, it is more likely that their exceptional learning needs will be noticed and met.

Gifted students receive full-time services by teachers trained in gifted education

- Gifted students have other gifted students to learn with.

- Achievement rises for all students in the grade level that uses the SCGM. Gifted students' test scores rise as well.

- Success in this model requires monitoring by an administrator to ensure that gifted students experience differentiated learning opportunities when needed.

Cons:

- One challenge with cluster grouping models occurs when schools group the identified high achievers into the same classes as the identified gifted students, another long-standing practice.

- This practice may lead to other classes having no potential academic leaders, which causes strife with staff members and parents.

- Another issue is that some principals have not been successful in keeping students who score below proficiency levels out of the same classes in which the gifted cluster group is placed.

See chapter 7 for more information on the cluster grouping model.

So . . . what is the best gifted program for our students?

Knowing that one single gifted service model cannot fully provide for the differentiated learning experiences gifted children need, school administrators should strive to implement services that are more inclusive than exclusive, have the potential to provide full-time gifted services on existing budgets, and can improve learning outcomes for identified gifted students.

Many districts are finding that a gifted education program that combines cluster grouping and pull-out classes or cluster grouping with self-contained classes for the top 2 percent of the school population is the most beneficial for their schools. So if your school presently uses pull-out classes, self-contained classes, or any other component and wants to keep them going, consider supplementing them with cluster grouping.

Program Management and Record Keeping

Although only a few states require Individualized Education Plans (IEPs) for identified gifted students, it's a good idea to keep track of differentiation opportunities and outcomes over time. Careful record keeping is vital whenever you do something new and different. Each chapter in this book has various forms designed to be used to keep accurate records of students' compacting and differentiation experiences.

The Differentiated Learning Plan

When working with gifted students, consider using a Differentiated Learning Plan (DLP) if your state or district does not provide any IEP for gifted students. Page 227 shows one version of a DLP. In some schools, this form is used as a group DLP for all students who are placed in a gifted cluster group. For ideas on what to record on the form, consult the section on differentiating content, process, products, environment, and assessment in chapter 1. For information about cluster grouping gifted kids, see chapter 7.

The Meeting Record Sheet on page 228 may be printed or copied on the back of the DLP or stapled to it. Use it to record information from every meeting about a student's Differentiated Learning Plan.

The Gifted Student's Cumulative Record Plan

The Gifted Student's Cumulative Record Form on page 229 provides an ongoing record of the alternate activities in which gifted students are engaged. Teachers can learn about the projects students have completed in previous grades and use this information to plan for the current year.

The form helps teachers provide consistency and continuity from one grade level to the next, and it also gives some assurance that appropriate compacting opportunities will be available for students as they move through the grades.

1. Prepare one form for each gifted student. If your school uses cumulative record folders, this form should be kept there. If not, it should be passed along from one teacher to the next. Middle and high school teachers should know where these records are stored in their buildings, and also have access to them to see what strategies and projects have been successful in previous years.

2. Use the form to briefly describe all compacting opportunities, personal project work, and other differentiation provided to the student during the year. Record what strategies were successful for you with each student.

3. Consult the form several times each year to assist with your planning to ensure that the students continually study new or expanded topics every year.

The Changing Role of the Gifted Education Specialist

If you are in the rare position of being employed as a gifted education specialist, you may be called on to:

- Monitor the learning needs of gifted students.

- Provide leadership in equitable identification methods and practices for gifted students and those who are twice-exceptional.

- Find ways to offer differentiated learning opportunities to more than just the identified gifted kids.

- Provide ongoing consulting services to classroom teachers about compacting, differentiation, and content acceleration.

- Demonstrate compacting and differentiation strategies, coach classroom teachers, and provide extension materials.

- Help teachers use alternate methods of assessing the work students do on extension activities and projects and show them how to document whether gifted students are actually making forward progress in learning.

text continues on page 230

Differentiated Learning Plan

Student's name: _____ Grade: _____

Teacher's name: _____ Date plan begins: _____

Student's Learning Strengths	Student's Areas of Interest

Learning Goals and Needs	Extended Learning Experiences	Resources	Results/Comments

Student's signature: _____ Teacher's signature: _____

Parent's signature: _____ Date: _____

Meeting Record Sheet

Student's name: _____

Grade: _____

Teacher's name: _____

Date plan begins: _____

Date	Topic(s)	Suggested Change(s)

Gifted Student's Cumulative Record Form

Student's name: _____

Date of birth: _____ Year/age/grade student was identified as gifted: _____

Grade Level	Year and Teacher	Compacting Opportunities	Independent Project Work

- Provide ongoing opportunities for staff development on issues related to gifted education.

- Help parents understand their role in seeking out and obtaining appropriate learning opportunities for their children.

- Advocate for cluster grouping of gifted students. For a discussion of this topic, see chapter 7.

How to Gain Parent Support

Some parents are confused by their gifted child's advanced abilities. They become uncomfortable when people call attention to the ways in which their child is different from age peers. They may actually say something like, "I only want my child to be normal!" Gifted children need to know that they are normal. They are not, and never will be, average. They simply are behaving in ways that reflect their advanced abilities.

Parents sometimes make the same mistake as educators in assuming that if their child is gifted, consistently high grades will be the norm. Many parents expect their gifted kids to be doing lots of work, all of which should be graded by you. In order for them to support your efforts on behalf of their children, you will need to reeducate them about what it means to be gifted, and also what it means to provide appropriate school experiences for gifted children. The following guidelines may be helpful as you teach the parents of the gifted kids in your classroom.

- Take time to explain your plans regarding compacting and differentiation. Parents need reassurance that you are not just assuming that their children have mastered certain standards. Explain how you will be carefully assessing what their children know on an ongoing basis.

- Be aware that parents are concerned about their children's popularity. Most will be happy to learn that their children are part of a gifted cluster, especially if they understand that clustering has positive effects on the social acceptance of gifted children. If you have no

cluster, explain to parents that compacting and differentiation opportunities are routinely offered to other students, so their children will not appear so unusual or always be expected to work by themselves.

- Recognize that parents are concerned about their children's grades. You will need to reassure them that gifted kids and A's don't always go together. Parents need to understand how your efforts to provide meaningful learning experiences and opportunities for real struggle are more important than perfect report cards.

- Invite parents to share information about their children, anything that will help you know and understand them better. For example, you'll want to find out about children's areas of interest, hobbies, and collections as possible topics for resident expert projects. Use the Interest Survey on page 168.

- Be a source of information for parents. Refer them to appropriate articles and books on parenting gifted children. For suggestions, see the references and resources for chapter 10 in the digital content.

- Encourage parents to read chapter 10 included in the accompanying digital content. Invite them to come in for a conference when they have finished the chapter. If you read it, too, you will have more information in common, which will lead to better communication.

Chapter Summary

This chapter has touched briefly on several topics related to programs for gifted students. Greatly expanded information is available from many other sources, including those described in the references and resources section. What's really exciting is that the internet has become an excellent source of information, research, findings, suggestions, insights, ideas, and more about gifted kids. There are so many wonderful websites that didn't previously exist that any teacher, administrator, or parent who wants information about virtually any topic can access it quite easily.

Conclusion

You may recall that in the introduction of this book you were asked: "Of all the students you are teaching in a given class, which group do you think will probably learn the *least* this year?" The answer is that the most able, rather than the least able, will make the least forward academic progress than any other group *unless appropriate compacting and differentiation interventions are used.* Of course, the italicized phrase was missing in the introduction, but its presence in this conclusion reflects our confidence that you are now much more skilled in your abilities to:

- Challenge all of your students.

- Give your students opportunities to demonstrate that they already know what you are about to teach or can learn it in much less time than you have allotted.

- Use compacting methods with all required standards.

- Create instructional groups that are flexible and change their composition depending on the content that must be learned and the learning needs of the students.

- Allow students whose abilities exceed grade-level expectations in any area of learning to be grouped together for work on appropriately differentiated activities.

- Offer meaningful choices whenever possible regarding content, process, products, environment, and assessments.

- Focus on open-ended tasks.

- Encourage independent research on topics in which students are passionately interested.

- Make technology options available as actual learning tools.

- Understand and apply differentiated assessment and grading options.

- Be sensitive to what gifted kids need in cooperative learning situations.

- Understand and support cluster grouping.

- Take advantage of opportunities to learn more about gifted students and their exceptional learning needs.

Gifted students whose teachers make opportunities available for compacting and differentiation in all subject areas are generally happy, productive students. They enjoy school and learning. They don't feel bored or like their learning time is being stolen from them.

And when you, their teachers, reach out to your colleagues to share what works with your gifted students, and then coach other teachers in successful implementation of these differentiated learning opportunities, your school's abilities to serve the exceptional learning needs of its gifted students is greatly enhanced. That type of peer coaching is what makes a significant, positive, long-term difference in the willingness and

---

Teaching Gifted Kids in Today's Classroom Professional Development Multimedia Package

A multimedia package is available for teachers who are using these strategies as part of a professional learning community or book study group. The package contains a copy of the book, a video that shows the strategies being used in actual K–8 classrooms, and a *Study Group Leader's Guide* that helps teachers lead a book study group over the course of a school year. Visit freespirit.com for more information.

---

abilities of teachers to make necessary changes in their teaching methods. And because the methods in this book are potentially accessible to most students, many more students than those formally identified as gifted can benefit from getting that book study group going!

We hope you are as excited about using these strategies as we are about sharing them with you. Writing this revised edition of *Teaching Gifted Kids in Today's Classroom* has allowed us to bring the 21st-century into the book, especially in the topics of assessment and technology. We are so grateful for the ongoing support for this book from teachers like you who easily use its content to challenge gifted students and prevent their families from leaving your schools to seek better challenges elsewhere. You have our endless gratitude for taking the necessary risks to give your gifted students what they need.

We would love to hear from you. Please send your feedback about this book and your experiences with the strategies presented here. You can reach us in care of our publisher:

Free Spirit Publishing
6325 Sandburg Road, Suite 100
Minneapolis, MN 55427-3674
help4kids@freespirit.com

Susan Winebrenner, M.S.
Dina Brulles, Ph.D.

References and Resources

Chapter 1: Characteristics of Gifted Students

Giftedness

Clark, Barbara. *Growing Up Gifted: Developing the Potential of Children at Home and at School.* Upper Saddle River, NJ: Pearson, 2012. The definitive textbook for parents and teachers.

Colangelo, Nicholas, and Gary A. Davis. *Handbook of Gifted Education.* Boston: Allyn & Bacon, 2003.

Dabrowski, K. *Theory of Positive Disintegration.* Anna Maria, FL: Maurice Bassett, 2016. See Bill Tillier's website (positivedisintegration.com), which includes an introduction to Dabrowski's psychological model, a glossary of terms and concepts, bibliographies, links, and more.

Kingore, Bertie. *Developing Portfolios for Authentic Assessment, PreK–3.* Thousand Oaks, CA: Corwin Press, 2008. Using portfolios to identify gifted students and document learning progress for all students.

———. *The Kingore Observation Inventory, KOI.* Austin, TX: Professional Associates Publishing, 2016. A unique and highly effective tool for identifying gifted students through their school behaviors. This has been my favorite method of identifying gifted students in grades K–6. Using the tool helps teachers gain more knowledge about the characteristics of gifted and advanced learners.

———. *Recognizing Gifted Potential: Planned Experiences with the KOI.* Austin, TX: Professional Associates Publishing, 2017. Accompanied by a binder and flash drive, this resource empowers teachers to use the KOI to its full potential.

Lee, Seon-Young, Paula Olszewski-Kubilius, and Dana Turner Thomson. "Academically Gifted Students' Perceived Interpersonal Competence and Peer Relationships," *Gifted Child Quarterly*, 56(2), 90–104, 2012.

Smutny, Joan Franklin, ed. *The Young Gifted Child: Potential and Promise: An Anthology.* Creskill, NJ: Hampton Press, 1998. Joan Smutny has collected a wealth of information from numerous sources in this comprehensive examination of the issues and practices surrounding the topic of young children who are gifted.

Smutny, Joan Franklin, Sally Yahnke Walker, and Ellen I. Honeck. *Teaching Gifted Children in Today's Preschool and Primary Classrooms.* Minneapolis: Free Spirit Publishing, 2016. The companion to this book, for teaching gifted kids ages 4–9.

U-STARS~PLUS by Mary Ruth Coleman. Provides high-quality science and literature instruction using popular children's books, allowing teachers to respond to children's strengths with challenging, advanced educational experiences. Contact the Council for Exceptional Children at 888-232-7733, www.cec.sped.org.

Perfectionism

Greenspon, Thomas S. *Moving Past Perfect: How Perfectionism May Be Holding Back Your Kids (and You!) and What You Can Do About It.* Minneapolis: Free Spirit Publishing, 2012. Explains perfectionism, where it comes from, and what parents can do to help their children, and themselves, move past it.

———. *What to Do When Good Enough Isn't Good Enough: The Real Deal on Perfectionism.* Minneapolis: Free Spirit Publishing, 2007. Helps kids understand what perfectionism is, how it hurts them, and how to learn to accept themselves as they are.

Creativity

de Bono, Edward. *Six Thinking Hats.* Boston: Little, Brown and Company, 1999. Teaches kids how to see any situation from several different perspectives. From the creator of Lateral Thinking.

Draze, Dianne. *Creative Problem Solving for Kids.* Waco, TX: Prufrock Press, 2005.

Eberle, Bob, and Bob Stanish. *CPS for Kids: A Resource Book for Teaching Creative Problem-Solving to Children.* Waco, TX: Prufrock Press, 1996. Activities for students in grades 2–8.

Khatena, Joe. *Enhancing the Creativity of Gifted Children: A Guide for Parents and Teachers.* Cresskill, NJ: Hampton Press, 1999.

PRIDE, GIFT, and GIFFI creativity identification instruments by Sylvia Rimm (sylviarimm.com).

Torrance Tests of Creative Thinking. Available from Scholastic Testing Service (ststesting.com).

Twice-Exceptional and Underachievers

AEGUS (Association for the Education of Gifted Underachieving Students) focuses attention and research efforts on able learners whose potential may be unrecognized, undeveloped, or not nurtured (aegus1.com).

Armstrong, Thomas. *ADD/ADHD Alternatives in the Classroom.* Alexandria, VA: ASCD, 1999. Describes nonmedical interventions for children with attention deficit disorders.

Baum, Susan M., Robin M. Schader, and Steven V. Owen. *To Be Gifted and Learning Disabled.* Waco, TX: Prufrock Press, 2017. Helps parents and teachers understand twice-exceptional students.

Dweck, Carol S. *Mindset: The New Psychology of Success.* New York: Ballantine Books. 2016. The source of the new research on the importance of praising kids for their effort and hard work rather than for their intelligence.

Edu-Kinesthetics, Inc. (braingym.com). Publishes and distributes materials for kinesthetic learners. Their Brain Gym program has been used successfully by parents and teachers to significantly improve learning attitudes and achievement.

Hoagies' Gifted Education Page (hoagiesgifted.org). Everything you need to know about the social, emotional, and academic needs of gifted persons.

Kay, Kiesa, ed. *Uniquely Gifted: Identifying and Meeting the Needs of the Twice-Exceptional Student.* Gilsum, NH: Avocus Publishing, 2000. Chapters by 43 authors consider all types of situations in which gifted students also have significant learning difficulties.

Lavoie, Richard. *How Difficult Can This Be? The F.A.T. City Workshop.* In a 70-minute video, Lavoie leads a group of parents, educators, psychologists, and children through a series of exercises that cause frustration, anxiety, and tension, feelings familiar to children with learning disabilities. Available from PBS Video (shop.pbs.org).

——. *Last One Picked . . . First One Picked On*. Lavoie addresses the social problems that children with LD face and offers practical solutions in this 62-minute video (shop.pbs.org).

Lovecky, Deirdre V. *Different Minds: Gifted Children with AD/HD, Asperger Syndrome, and Other Learning Deficits*. London: Jessica Kingsley Publishers, 2004. Provides an insight into the challenges and benefits specific to gifted children with attention difficulties.

NLDline (nldline.com) provides references and resources to help increase public awareness and understanding of nonverbal learning disorders.

Reis, Sally M., Terry W. Neu, and Joan M. McGuire. "Case Studies of High-Ability Students with Learning Disabilities Who Have Achieved." *Exceptional Children* 63, no. 4 (1997): 463–479.

Rimm, Sylvia. *Why Bright Kids Get Poor Grades and What You Can Do About It*. Scottsdale, AZ: Great Potential Press, 2008. Helps parents and teachers get underachieving students back on track.

Tanguay, Pamela B. *Nonverbal Learning Disabilities at School*. Philadelphia: Jessica Kinsley, 2002. Addresses issues related to the academic education of the child with NLD and related conditions.

2E Twice-Exceptional Newsletter (2enewsletter.com) is an online resource for parents and teachers of twice-exceptional learners.

Uniquely Gifted (uniquelygifted.org) is a collection of resources for families with gifted and special needs children and for the professionals who work with them.

Videos on gifted students with learning disabilities:

- "Susan Baum on Twice-Exceptionality" (youtu.be/_R7OqJ14ST8).

- "What Is Twice-Exceptional and Gifted? By Dr. Dan Peters, Summit Center" (youtu.be/PlQ4z-1OVw4).

- "Maureen Neihart's Workshop: Helping Twice-Exceptional Students Succeed— What Works?" (youtu.be/sYaQuo08MO8).

West, Thomas G. *In the Mind's Eye: Creative Visual Thinkers, Gifted Dyslexics, and the Rise of Visual Technologies*.

Amherst, NY: Prometheus Books, 2009. A compelling argument for the importance of visual thinking and visual technologies as well as the high creative potential of many individuals with dyslexia or other learning difficulties.

Willard-Holt, Colleen. "Dual Exceptionalities." ERIC Digest E574, April 1999, ERIC #430344.

Winebrenner, Susan. *Teaching Kids with Learning Difficulties in Today's Classroom*. Minneapolis: Free Spirit Publishing, 2014. Ways to help "slow," "remedial," and other struggling students learn and achieve.

Yale Center for Dyslexia & Creativity (dyslexia.yale.edu), founded by Bennett and Sally Shaywitz, serves as a nexus for research on dyslexia and is a leading source of advocacy and information to better the lives of people with dyslexia.

Diverse Populations

Cline, Starr, and Diane Schwartz. *Diverse Populations of Gifted Children*. Upper Saddle River, NJ: Prentice Hall, 1999.

Ford, Donna. *Multicultural Gifted Education*. Waco, TX: Prufrock Press, 2011. Helps bridge the gap that exists between educating advanced learners and educating culturally different learners.

Peterson, Jean Sunde. "Gifted—Through Whose Cultural Lens?" *Journal for the Education of the Gifted* 22:4, 354–383, 1999.

Intelligence Testing and Identification

Gifted Development Center (gifteddevelopment.com) in Denver, Colorado, provides comprehensive testing, referrals to testers in other states, and referrals to counselors who have experience working with gifted kids and their families.

Johnsen, Susan. *Identifying Gifted Students: A Practical Guide*. Waco, TX: Prufrock Press, 2011. Designed for practicing professionals, addresses definitions, models, and characteristics of gifted students and provides a complete summary of all major assessment instruments, including scoring information, reliability, and validity.

Kingore, Bertie. *The Kingore Observation Inventory (KOI)*. Austin, TX: Professional Associates Publishing, 2016. An observational tool for identifying gifted kids in the primary grades.

Osborn, Julia. "Assessing Gifted Children." Davidson Institute for Talent Development (www.davidsongifted.org). A version of this article originally appeared in *Understanding Our Gifted* (Winter 1998).

Standardized Tests. Standardized assessments that are culturally and economically bias-free:

- *Cognitive Abilities Test (CogAT)* by David Lohman and Elizabeth Hagen. Rolling Meadows, IL: Riverside Publishing.

- *Naglieri Nonverbal Ability Tests* by Jack Naglieri. Upper Saddle River, NJ: Pearson.

- *Otis-Lennon School Abilities Test (OLSAT)*. Upper Saddle River, NJ: Pearson.

- *Peabody Picture Vocabulary Test (PPVT)* by Lloyd M. Dunn and Leota M. Dunn. Upper Saddle River, NJ: Pearson. Answers can be allowed in student's native language.

- *Ravens Progressive Matrices* by J. C. Raven. Upper Saddle River, NJ: Pearson. A group test of nonverbal ability.

- Slosson Educational Publications, Inc. (slosson.com). Sells intelligence and other diagnostic tests, including the *Slosson*, which can be administered by educators who are not trained psychologists.

Other Sources of Information

A.D.D. WareHouse (addwarehouse.com). Materials for teaching and parenting kids with learning challenges.

Council for Exceptional Children (cec.sped.org). A complete source for information, research, and interventions for helping children with all kinds of special educational needs.

Education Resources Information Center (ERIC) (eric.ed.gov). Digital library of education literature on topics including gifted education and twice-exceptional students.

The International Dyslexia Association (dyslexiaida.org). A nonprofit organization dedicated to helping individuals with dyslexia, their families, and the communities that support them.

LD OnLine (ldonline.org). Seeks to help children and adults reach their full potential by providing accurate and up-to-date information and advice about learning disabilities and ADHD.

Learning Ally (formerly Recording for the Blind and Dyslexic, learningally.org). The nation's educational library for people with print disabilities, with more than 75,000 titles. Many states have their own libraries.

PRO-ED, Inc. (proedinc.com). Publisher of standardized tests, books, curricular resources, and therapy materials for all categories of special education and gifted education.

Renzulli Center for Creativity, Gifted Education, and Talent Development, University of Connecticut (gifted.uconn .edu). Visit the website for research-based resources, links, and more.

Supporting Emotional Needs of the Gifted (SENG) (sengifted.org). Helps parents identify giftedness in their children and helps children understand and accept their unique talents. Provides a forum for parents and educators to communicate.

Chapter 2: Compacting and Differentiating for Skill Work

"Differentiation Using Curriculum Compacting" PowerPoint. (www.gifted .uconn.edu/wp content/uploads/sites/061 /2015/01/Curriculum_Compacting.pdf) from the National Research Center on the Gifted and Talented.

Gavin, M. Katherine, et al. "The Impact of Advanced Curriculum on the Achievement of Mathematically Promising Elementary Students," *Gifted Child Quarterly*, 53(3), 188–202, 2009.

Teaching Gifted Kids in Today's Classroom Professional Development Multimedia Package by Susan Winebrenner and Dina Brulles (freespirit.com). Everything needed to conduct comprehensive professional development for teachers of gifted students, including a DVD (100+ minutes) showing actual classroom teaching sessions and a *Study Group Leader's Guide* that directs users through the book and video.

Extension Activities

ETA hand2mind (hand2mind.com). Source for VersaTiles, Cuisenaire Rods, and other hands-on materials for math, science, and reading/language arts.

Highline Advanced Math Program (home .avvanta.com/~math). Math enrichment for grades 5–7. Also has activities for Math Olympiad competitions.

Marcy Cook Math (marcycookmath.com). Materials extend standards and problem-based learning.

The Math Forum (nctm.org/mathforum). This online math education community center features interactive projects, links, learning materials, and an online library.

Math Solutions (mathsolutions.com). Founded by Marilyn Burns, Math Solutions is dedicated to improving students' learning of mathematics by providing the highest-quality professional development services, products, and resources to educators.

McGraw Hill Education (mheducation .com). A great source of extension materials including from Glencoe, Wright Group, and Jamestown.

Mrs. Roberts' Calculus Class (mrsroberts .com/MrsRoberts/Calculus/calculus .htm). Beginning online lessons to learn calculus.

24 Game (24game.com). Published by Suntex International Inc., the 24 Game and other products at the site can be used for math extension.

Distance Learning

Redbird (mheducation.com/prek-12 /explore/redbird). Developed by Stanford University, *Redbird* offers advanced multimedia computer-based distance-learning courses in math, language arts, and writing for students in elementary, middle, and high school.

Virtual High School (vhslearning.org). Offers online classes in art, science, language arts, and more.

Chapter 3: Compacting and Differentiating for New Content

General

Black, Kaye. *Kidvid: Fun-Damentals of Video Instruction*. Tucson, AZ: Zephyr Press, 2000. Helps kids produce their own videos.

Brulles, Dina, Karen Brown, and Susan Winebrenner. *Differentiated Lessons for Every Learner: Standards-Based Activities and Extensions for Middle School*. Waco, TX: Prufrock Press, 2016.

Lee, Seon-Young, and Paula Olszewski-Kubilius. "A Study of Instructional Methods Used in Fast-Paced Classes," *Gifted Child Quarterly,* 50(3), 216–237, 2006.

Smutny, Joan, and Sarah E. von Fremd. *Teaching Advanced Learners in the General Education Classroom: Doing More with Less!* Thousand Oaks, CA: Corwin Press, 2011. Guides readers toward existing resources to use in differentiating instruction.

——. *Differentiating for the Young Child: Teaching Strategies Across the Content Areas, PreK–3.* Thousand Oaks, CA: Corwin Press, 2010. Offers differentiated strategies with examples and classroom applications.

The Timetables of… series. These books help students see history and other disciplines from a chronological point of view. Each one serves as a rich menu for independent study topics.

- Bunch, Bryan, and Alexander Hellemans. *The Timetables of Technology: A Chronology of the Most Important People and Events in the History of Technology.* New York: Simon & Schuster, 1994.

- Cule, John. *The Timetables of Medicine: An Illustrated Chronology of the History of Medicine from Prehistory to Present Times.* New York: Black Dog & Leventhal Publishers, 2000.

- Grun, Bernard. *The Timetables of History: A Horizontal Linkage of People and Events.* New York: Simon & Schuster, 2005.

- Greenspan, Karen. *The Timetables of Women's History: A Chronology of the Most Important People and Events in Women's History.* New York: Simon & Schuster, 1994.

- Harley, Sharon. *The Timetables of African-American History: A Chronology of the Most Important People and Events in African-American History.* New York: Simon & Schuster, 1995.

- Hellemans, Alexander, and Bryan Bunch. *The Timetables of Science: A Chronology of the Most Important People and Events in the History of Science.* New York: Simon & Schuster, 1991.

Social Studies

Abby's Resource Page for Social Studies Teachers (home.windstream.net/abbys resources). Hundreds of links to social studies, history, and education websites.

American Memory. Historical Collections for the National Digital Library (memory .loc.gov). Multimedia collections of digitized documents, photographs, recorded sound, moving pictures, and text.

National Council for the Social Studies (socialstudies.org). Lesson planning help for social studies teachers.

National Geographic Education (nationalgeographic.org/education). Source for teaching world geography and national geography standards.

NewsCurrents Online (knowledge unlimited.com/newscurrents.html). A weekly current events background and discussion program, available on the website 35 times a year by subscription. The same content is also available in nonelectronic form, including a filmstrip and teacher's discussion guide, from Knowledge Unlimited, Inc. (thekustore .com).

Debate

Debate.org (debate.org). Kids can choose a debate topic and weigh in online, or see how others feel about the topic.

Opposing Viewpoints series. New York: Greenhaven Publishing. Each book explores a controversial issue from all angles.

Science

Kinetic City (kineticcity.com). A crew of virtual kids takes visitors on science-related adventures. Also contains information about experiments to do at home and school.

MadSci Network (madsci.org). High-interest science extension activities.

NASA Education (nasa.gov/offices /education/about/index.html). This site features many activities related to the study of astronomy and space, as well as information for educators.

Neuroscience for Kids (faculty .washington.edu/chudler/neurok.html). Experiments, activities, games, links, and more about the nervous system.

Science Project Ideas series. Books by Robert Gardner include *Science Project Ideas About Animal Behavior, Science Project Ideas About Rain,* and *Science Project Ideas About the Moon.* Berkeley Heights, NJ: Enslow Publishers, Inc.

Catalogs

Delta Education (deltaeducation.com). Their catalog offers hundreds of products for K–8 science teaching.

Enslow Publishing (enslow.com). Publishes many educational series.

Social Studies School Service (socialstudies.com). A mind-boggling collection of multimedia resources in social studies. Although designed for secondary students, some materials are suitable for younger gifted students.

Chapter 4: Extending Reading and Writing Instruction

Reading and Vocabulary

American Classical League (aclclassics.org). Learning materials on Latin and Greek classical literature for kids of all ages.

Be a Better Reader (BABR) series from Pearson Education (pearsonschool.com). A program of reading skills that is not attached to any basal series. Works very well in a self-selected literature-based reading program.

Bergman, Olivia. *Reading for the Gifted Student* and *Vocabulary for the Gifted Student.* Separate books for grades 1–6. Find them online at flashkids.com.

Funk, Charles Earle. *Thereby Hangs a Tale: Stories of Curious Word Origins.* New York: HarperCollins, 2002. Provides the origins of hundreds of words.

Great Books Foundation (greatbooks.org). Their K–12 programs provide courses and materials for kids of all ages to study great literature from complex, higher-level perspectives.

Green, Jonathon. *Chasing the Sun: Dictionary Makers and the Dictionaries They Made.* New York: Henry Holt, 1996. Shares the history of the dictionary, including why dictionaries were created and what role the dictionary makers' bias plays.

Halsted, Judith Wynn. *Some of My Best Friends Are Books: Guiding Gifted Readers from Preschool to High School.* Scottsdale, AZ: Great Potential Press 2009. Helps guide parents and their gifted children toward fulfilling books.

International Literacy Association (literacyworldwide.org). Provides lists of books for various ages and interests; disseminates reading research; promotes literacy.

Khan Academy (khanacademy.org). Several hundred 15-minute video lessons, many in advanced math, that allow gifted students to teach themselves advanced concepts and allow you to keep up with them.

Language Arts Units for High-Ability Learners. Curriculum units for grades K–12 created by the Center for Gifted Education at the College of William & Mary (education.wm.edu/centers /cfge). Available through Kendall Hunt (kendallhunt.com).

Morris, William, and Mary Morris. *Morris Dictionary of Word and Phrase Origins.* New York: HarperTrade, 1988. A unique resource.

Reis, Sally. *The Joyful Reading Resource Kit: Teaching Tools, Hands-On Activities, and Enrichment Resources, Grades K–8.* San Francisco: Jossey-Bass, 2009.

Thompson, Michael, and Myriam Thompson. *Caesar's English: A Vocabulary Foundation for Elementary Scholars.* Unionville, NY: Royal Fireworks Press, 2000. Other books by Michael Thompson include *Classics in the Classroom, The Magic Lens,* and the Word Within a

Word series, which helps kids increase their vocabularies exponentially through understanding Greek and Latin stems or roots.

Winebrenner, Susan. *Super Sentences.* Bloomington, IN: AuthorHouse, 2013. Vocabulary building activities for ages 8 and up.

Wood, Patricia. "Reading Instruction with Gifted and Talented Readers: A Series of Unfortunate Events or a Sequence of Auspicious Results?" *Gifted Child Today*, 31(3), 16–25, 2008.

Prepackaged Units for Teaching Novels

Accelerated Reader software. Helps gifted readers K–12 with self-selected literature. Wisconsin Rapids, WI: Renaissance Learning, Inc. (renaissance .com).

Engine-Uity, Ltd. (engine-uity.com). Ready-to-use units in literature and other content areas based on Bloom's Taxonomy.

HMH Reading Inventory (hmhco.com). A reading motivation and management program that helps you encourage and monitor independent reading in students K–12.

Holt McDougal Literature, the Common Core Edition (hmhco.com). Helps students meet the demands of college- and career-level literacy.

Novel Units (ecslearningsystems.com). Student packets and teacher guides keyed to particular works of literature, currently available for more than 550 titles.

Primaryplots: A Book Talk Guide for Use with Readers Ages 4–8 by Rebecca Thomas (1993); *Middleplots: Ages 8–12* by John Gillespie et al. (1994); and *Juniorplots: Ages 12–16* by John Gillespie et al. (1993). Guides for book talks and independent reading. New Providence, NJ: R.R. Bowker.

Wordplay on the Web

FunBrain (funbrain.com). Free games, activities, and word games for K–8 teachers and kids.

OED Online (oed.com). The *Oxford English Dictionary* online.

Pun of the Day (punoftheday.com). Search for puns by category—the body, food, nature, and so on.

Vocabulary.com (vocabulary.com). Vocabulary explorations and puzzles.

Wacky Web Tales (eduplace.com/tales). Word games for grades 3 and up.

Word Central (wordcentral.com). Fun stuff for kids from Merriam-Webster.

Wordplay (fun-with-words.com). Anagrams, palindromes, spoonerisms, oxymora, mnemonics, etymology, word puzzles, and more.

Bibliotherapy

Bibliotherapy Education Project (cmich.edu /colleges/ehs/bibliotherapy). An introduction to assisting youngsters in overcoming emotional problems by reading about fictional characters with similar problems.

Writing

Bare Books. Racine, WI: Treetop Publications (barebooks.com). Several blank books are available for student authors to write in, including comic books and print and paste books.

Melton, David. *Written and Illustrated by . . . A Revolutionary Two-Brain Approach for Teaching Students How to Write and Illustrate Amazing Books.* Kansas City, MO: Landmark Editions, 2002. Old, but still a good writing resource.

Places that Publish Children's Writing

Creative Kids (ckmagazine.org). Magazine by kids, for kids, published by Prufrock Press.

Dunn, Jessica, and Danielle Dunn. *A Teen's Guide to Getting Published.* Waco, TX: Prufrock Press, 2006. Market and contest listings for teen writers.

Highlights (highlights.com). The popular magazine for children contains puzzles, craft pages, jokes and riddles, drawings and poems by kids, and more.

KidPub Press (kidpub.com). A site that publishes only children's work.

Knowledge Unlimited, Inc. (thekustore .com). Ask about their NewsCurrents Student Editorial Cartoon Contest.

Merlyn's Pen (merlynspen.org). A collection of juried, published fiction, poetry, and essays by students.

New Moon Girls (newmoon.com). A magazine by girls, for girls ages 8 and up, featuring positive messages and issues that matter to its readers.

Ranger Rick. National Wildlife Federation (rangerrick.org). A magazine for kids interested in animals.

Skipping Stones (skippingstones.org). An award-winning multicultural magazine for children ages 8–16.

Stone Soup (stonesoup.com). Publishes stories, poems, and art by children ages 8–13.

Young People's Press (youngpeoplespress .com). Resources for teachers: language arts, reading, social responsibility, and math.

Chapter 5: Planning Curriculum for All Students at the Same Time

General

Anderson, Lorin W., and David R. Krathwohl, eds. *A Taxonomy for Learning, Teaching, and Assessing: A Revision of Bloom's Taxonomy of Educational Objectives.* New York: Longman, 2001.

Bloom, Benjamin, et al. *Taxonomy of Educational Objectives: Handbook of the Cognitive Domain.* New York: Longman, 1984.

Brulles, Dina, and Karen Brown. *A Teacher's Guide to Flexible Grouping and Collaborative Learning.* Minneapolis: Free Spirit Publishing, 2018.

Coil, Carolyn. *Standards-Based Activities and Assessments for the Differentiated Classroom.* Marion, IL: Pieces of Learning, 2004.

The Curry/Samara Model (CSM) of Curriculum, Instruction, and Assessment. Teaches how to develop unit plans using Bloom's Taxonomy. (curriculumproject.com /curry_samara_model.php).

Kingore, Bertie. *Assessment: Time-Saving Procedures for Busy Teachers.* Austin, TX: Professional Associates Publishing, 2005 (kingore.com).

———. *Rigor and Engagement for Growing Minds: Strategies that Enable High-Ability Learners to Flourish in All Classrooms.* Austin, TX: Professional Associates Publishing, 2013. This book's content is designed to engage students so they are motivated to exert the effort required to reach higher achievement.

———. *Tiered Learning Stations in Minutes!* Austin, TX: Professional Associates Publishing, 2011 (kingore.com).

K–5 Arts Integration Curriculum Planning Kit by Susan Riley (educationcloset .com). This kit and related resources are available for free.

Tomlinson, Carol A. *How to Differentiate Instruction in Mixed-Ability Classrooms.* Alexandria, VA: ASCD, 2004.

VanTassel-Baska, Joyce. *Alternative Assessments with Gifted and Talented Students.* Waco, TX: Prufrock Press, 2008.

Extension Materials for Various Subject Areas

Engine-Uity, Ltd. (engine-uity.com). Ready-to-use units in literature and other content areas based on Bloom's Taxonomy.

J Taylor Education (jtayloreducation .com). This is the best source for materials that help you understand and use the Kaplan methods.

Royal Fireworks Press (rfwp.com). Request their catalog of materials to implement Bloom's Taxonomy in primary classrooms.

Social Studies School Service (socialstudies. com). Multiple catalogs of materials to support social studies learning.

ThinkTrix and Think-Pair-Share models laminated teaching guides to use with the Name Cards and Critical Thinking Methods (kaganonline.com).

Socratic Seminars

Augsburg Paideia Institute, Augsburg University (augsburg.edu/paideia /institute). Training in the Socratic teaching method.

Copeland, Matt. *Socratic Circles: Fostering Critical and Creative Thinking in Middle and High School.* Portland, ME: Stenhouse, 2005. Instruction on how to hold Socratic Seminars in the classroom.

Letts, Nancy (nancyletts.squarespace .com). Training in eliciting high-level thinking in all students through Socratic Seminars.

Metzger, Margaret. "Teaching Reading Beyond the Plot," *Phi Delta Kappan* 256 (November 1998), 240–246, 256. This teacher gives very specific guidelines for using the Socratic Seminar to make reading comprehension more interesting and complex.

Chapter 6: "I'm Done. Now What Should I Do?": Self-Selected Independent Study

Baum, Susan, R. Gable, and K. List. *Chi Square Pie Charts and Me.* Unionville, NY: Trillium Press, 1987.

Encyclopedia of Associations: International Organizations of the U.S. Farmington Hills, MI: Gale Cengage Learning, updated often. A fabulous resource for free material for student researchers from international headquarters of thousands of companies in the United States.

Encyclopedia of Associations: National Organizations of the U. S. Farmington Hills, MI: Gale Cengage Learning, updated often. The national version of the thorough encyclopedia.

Independent Investigation Method (IIM) (iimresearch.com). This method helps students of all ages research and present information on any subject.

Institute for the Advancement of Philosophy for Children (IAPC) (montclair. edu/IAPC). A curriculum that teaches reasoning and judgment to advanced thinkers of all ages.

Johnsen, Susan, and Krystal Goree. *Independent Study for Gifted Learners.* Waco, TX: Prufrock Press, 2005.

Kids' Vid (kidsvid.4teachers.org). Helps kids produce their own videos.

Pollette, Nancy. *Research Without Copying.* Marion, IL: Pieces of Learning, 2009. Using four types of students—the thinker, the mover, the nurturer, and the creator—the author shares strategies for student research.

Prufrock Press (prufrock.com). Their materials on research and thinking skills raise independent study into more complex and abstract realms.

Science Made Simple (sciencemade simple.com). School science projects and experiments for kids.

Teacher Created Materials Publishing (teachercreatedmaterials.com). Differentiated strategies in all subject areas for most grades.

WebQuest (webquest.org). A WebQuest is an inquiry-oriented activity in which some or all of the information that learners interact with comes from resources on the internet. The website includes an overview, readings, training materials, and examples.

Chapter 7: Grouping Gifted Students for Learning

Research and Practice on Cooperative Learning as It Affects Gifted Students

Cohen, Elizabeth. *Designing Groupwork: Strategies for the Heterogeneous Classroom.* New York: Teachers College Press, 2014. How to develop sophisticated, complex cooperative learning tasks that can challenge all students in cooperative learning groups.

Matthews, Marian. "Gifted Students Talk About Cooperative Learning." Educational Leadership 50:2, 48–49, October 1992. Dr. Matthews interviewed gifted students for their opinions about cooperative learning.

Rogers, Karen. 1999. "Research Synthesis on Gifted Provisions" (austega .com/gifted). Discusses instructional management services, instructional delivery services, and curricular services.

Research and Practice on Ways to Group Gifted Learners Together

Allan, Susan Demirsky. "Ability-Grouping Research Reviews: What Do They Say About Grouping and the Gifted?"

Educational Leadership 48(6), 60–65, March 1991.

Assouline, Susan, Nicholas Colangelo, and Joyce VanTassel-Baska. *A Nation Empowered: Evidence Trumps the Excuses Holding Back America's Brightest Students, Volume 1.* Iowa City, IA: University of Iowa, 2015.

Brigance diagnostic inventories of basic skills (curriculumassociates.com). Use the Brigance tools with students in the primary grades to document their advanced learning ability in order to place them in cluster groups and to know the level at which they need to be taught in almost all subject areas.

Brulles, Dina. "An Examination and Critical Analysis of Cluster Grouping Gifted Students in an Elementary School District." Doctoral Dissertation. Arizona State University, 2005.

Brulles, Dina, et al., "Schoolwide Mathematics Achievement Within the Gifted Cluster Grouping Model," *Journal for the Education of the Gifted,* 23(3), 200–216, 2012.

Coleman, Mary Ruth. "The Importance of Cluster Grouping," *Gifted Child Today* 18:1, 38–40, January–February 1995.

Gentry, Marcia L. "Promoting Student Achievement and Exemplary Classroom Practices Through Cluster Grouping: A Research-Based Alternative to Heterogeneous Elementary Classrooms," *Research Monograph* 99138. Storrs, CT: NRC/GT, 1999. (www.gifted.uconn.edu).

Gentry, Marcia L., and Bill Keilty. "Rural and Suburban Cluster Grouping: Reflections of Staff Development as a Component of Program Success." *Roeper Review* 26, no. 3 (March 2004).

Gentry, Marcia L., and Jamie MacDougall. "Total School Cluster Grouping: Model, Research, and Practice," Creative Learning Press, 2008.

Hoover, Steve, Michael Sayler, and John Feldhusen. "Cluster Grouping of Gifted Students at the Elementary Level," *Roeper Review* 16:1, 13–15, 1993. More evidence of the benefits of cluster grouping for gifted students.

Kulik, James A. "An Analysis of the Research of Ability Grouping: Historical and Contemporary Perspectives," Center for Gifted Education and Talent Development, 1992.

Olszewski-Kubilius, Paula. "Setting the Record Straight on Ability Grouping," *Education Week*, 2013.

Park, Gregory, David Lubinski, and Camilla Benbow. "When Less Is More:

Effects of Grade Skipping on Adult STEM Productivity Among Mathematically Precocious Adolescents," *Journal of Educational Psychology*, 105(1), 176–198, 2013.

Pierce, Rebecca, et al. "The Effects of Clustering and Curriculum on the Development of Gifted Learners' Math Achievement," *Journal for the Education of the Gifted*, 34(4), 569–594, 2011.

Rogers, Karen. "Grouping the Gifted and Talented," *Roeper Review* 16:1, 8–12, 1993.

———. *A Menu of Options for Grouping Gifted Students.* Waco, TX: Prufrock Press, 2006.

———. "The Relationship of Grouping Practices to the Education of the Gifted and Talented Learner." Research-Based Research Document (RBRD) 9102. Storrs, CT: NRC/GT, 1991.

Schuler, Patricia A. "Cluster Grouping Coast to Coast," National Research Center on the Gifted and Talented Newsletter, Winter 1997. Results of a research study examining the actual practice of cluster grouping in the United States.

Schunk, Dale H. "Peer Models and Children's Behavioral Change," *Review of Educational Research* 47, 149–174, 1987. Only study to prove that gifted students are not appropriate peer tutors for age peers.

Teno, Kevin. "Cluster Grouping Elementary Gifted Students in the Regular Classroom: A Teacher's Perspective," *Gifted Child Today* 23:1, 44–49, January–February 2000. A teacher documents the benefits of cluster grouping for gifted students, other students, and teachers.

Winebrenner, Susan, and Dina Brulles. *The Cluster Grouping Handbook: How to Challenge Gifted Students and Improve Achievement for All.* Minneapolis: Free Spirit Publishing, 2010. Explains how the Schoolwide Cluster Grouping Model (SCGM) differs from grouping practices of the past, and presents a roadmap for implementing, sustaining, and evaluating schoolwide cluster grouping.

Chapter 8: Assessment and Technology

Besnoy, Kevin D. and Lane W. Clarke. *High-Tech Teaching Success! A Step-by-Step Guide to Using Innovative Technology in Your Classroom.* Waco, TX: Prufock Press, 2010. Gives teachers advice from technology education experts on how the latest tools and software can be implemented into lesson plans to create differentiated, exciting curriculum for all learners.

Cross, Tracy L. "Technology and the Unseen World of Gifted Students: Social-Emotional Needs." *Gifted Child Today* 27:4, 1–3, Fall 2004.

International Society for Technology in Education (ISTE). "Technology and Student Achievement—The Indelible Link." Do a Google search for the title to find the PDF online.

Jenkins, Lee. *Improving Student Learning: Applying Deming's Quality Principles in Classrooms*. Milwaukee, WI: ASQ Quality Press, 2003. Teaches educators how to improve student performance through the use of quality principles.

Kellough, Richard D., and Noreen G. Kellough. *Secondary School Teaching: A Guide to Methods and Resources*. Boston: Allyn & Bacon, 2010. A comprehensive guide to instructional methods and contains many practical exercises for active learning.

Plucker, Jonathan, Nathan Burroughs, and Ruiting Song. *Mind the (Other) Gap! The Growing Excellence Gap in K–12 Education*. Bloomington, IN: Center for Evaluation & Education Policy, 2010.

Siegle, Del. "Gifted Students and Technology: An Interview with Del Siegle." Center for Talent Development, Northwestern University, 2005.

Sivin-Kachala, Jay, Ellen Bialo, and Jonathan Langford. *Report on the Effectiveness of Technology in Schools, 1990–1997*. Washington, DC: Software Publishers Association, 1998.

Tucker, Bill. "Technology and the Future of Student Assessment." *Reports & Briefs*. Education Sector, February 13, 2009.

Chapter 9: Gifted Programming

Acceleration

Assouline, Susan, et al. *Iowa Acceleration Scale Manual: A Guide for Whole-Grade Acceleration (K–8)*. Scottsdale, AZ: Great Potential Press, 2009.

Assouline, Susan, Nicholas Colangelo, and Joyce VanTassel-Baska. *A Nation Empowered: Evidence Trumps the Excuses Holding Back America's Brightest Students, Volume 1*. Iowa City, IA: University of Iowa, 2015.

Belin-Blank Center Institute for Research and Policy on Acceleration, National Association for Gifted Children, and Council of State Directors of Programs for the Gifted. "Guidelines for Developing an Academic Acceleration Policy," *Journal of Advanced Academics*, 21(2), 180–203, 2010.

Center for Talented Youth (CTY) at Johns Hopkins University. *Academic Acceleration: Knowing Your Options*. Baltimore: Johns Hopkins University Press, 1995.

DeLacy, Margaret. *Acceleration for Gifted Students*. Created for the Portland Public School District Talented and Gifted Advisory Committee, April 19, 1996.

Park, Gregory, David Lubinski, and Camilla Benbow. "When Less Is More: Effects of Grade Skipping on Adult STEM Productivity Among Mathematically Precocious Adolescents," *Journal of Educational Psychology*, 105(1), 176–198, 2013.

Renzulli, Joseph, and Sally Reis. *The Schoolwide Enrichment Model: A How-To Guide for Talent Development*. Waco, TX: Prufrock Press, 2014.

Robinson, N., and L. Weimer. "Selection of Candidates for Early Admission to Kindergarten and First Grade." In W. T. Southern and E. D. Jones (eds.) *The Academic Acceleration of Gifted Children*. New York: Teachers College Press, 1991.

Steenbergen-Hu, Saiying, and Sidney Moon. "The Effects of Acceleration on High-Ability Learners: A Meta-Analysis," *Gifted Child Quarterly*, 55(1), 39–53, 2010.

Extracurricular Team Activities (Often parents will take the coaching role)

Destination Imagination (destinationimagination.org). A nonprofit organization that provides educational programs for students to learn and experience creativity, teamwork, and problem solving.

Programming

Renzulli Learning (renzullilearning.com). Founded by Joseph Renzulli and Sally Reis, Renzulli Learning takes a strengths-based approach to understanding a student's interests, learning, and expression styles and provides an engaging educational environment with a personalized curriculum to help any student achieve academic success.

Robinson, Ann, Bruce M. Shore, and Donna L. Enersen, D. *Best Practices in Gifted Education: An Evidence-Based Guide*. Waco, TX: Prufrock Press, 2007. Provides the framework for effective planning and instruction in teaching gifted children. Topics include parent involvement, twice-exceptional students, gender differences, acceleration, and culturally diverse student populations.

Rogers, Karen B. *Re-Forming Gifted Education*. Scottsdale, AZ: Great Potential Press, 2002. Rogers explains the body of research in the field of curriculum for

gifted education, and for each educational option, delineates what the current research says about the benefit or lack of benefit to gifted children.

Additional Resources
Magazines and Journals

Gifted Child Today (journals.sagepub.com/home/gct). For teachers and parents of gifted kids.

Gifted Education Press Quarterly. Newsletter of unique articles by authors often not found in the larger journals (Gifted Education Press, giftededpress.com).

Imagine Magazine (cty.jhu.edu/imagine). Published by Johns Hopkins Center for Talented Youth, *Imagine* is designed to provide bright teens with the information and inspiration they need to make the most of their precollege years and beyond.

From the National Association for Gifted Children (nagc.org):

- *Gifted Child Quarterly*. Research and practice in gifted education.
- *Parenting for High Potential*. Tips for parenting gifted children.

Understanding Our Gifted (ourgifted.com). Quarterly journal for parents and teachers of gifted children.

Videos

Webb, James. *Parenting Successful Children*. A 52-minute DVD of tips on raising children in our high-speed society (Great Potential Press, greatpotentialpress.com).

Organizations

Talent search centers. A network of places in the United States through which gifted kids in grades 6–7 can take the high school–level SAT and possibly qualify for special learning opportunities. Google "Academic Talent Search" for information for your state.

Belin-Blank Center, University of Iowa (www2.education.uiowa.edu/belinblank). Talent searches, summer programs, scholarships, assessment, and workshops.

Center for Bright Kids (Regional Talent Development Center for the Rocky Mountain area) (centerforbrightkids.org). Offers K–12 enrichment and acceleration programming for high-interest and high-ability kids.

Center for Gifted Education, The College of William and Mary (education.wm.edu/centers/cfge). Contact the Center for information about summer institutes, talent searches, conferences, curriculum units, and more.

Center for Talent Development, Northwestern University (ctd .northwestern.edu). Talent searches, programs for gifted students during the school year (Saturday Enrichment Program, Gifted LearningLinks correspondence courses), summer programs, conferences, and more.

Duke University Talent Identification Program (TIP) (tip.duke.edu). Programs and services for academically talented students.

Johns Hopkins Center for Talented Youth (cty.jhu.edu). Conducts national and international talent searches; provides challenging and innovative learning opportunities in mathematics, science, and the humanities through summer programs, distance education programs, and conferences; publishes *Imagine,* a magazine for middle and high school students.

Midwest Torrance Center for Creativity, a Northern Illinois University partner (centerforgifted.org). Summer and weekend programs for gifted kids.

National Center for Research on Gifted Education, University of Virginia (curry. virginia.edu/research/centers/nrcgt). Conducts research on methods and techniques for identifying and teaching gifted and talented students and for using gifted and talented programs and methods to serve all students.

Summer Institute for the Gifted (giftedstudy.org). Information about U.S. summer programs for gifted kids.

Other Organizations

Association for the Gifted (TAG) (cectag .org). Promotes the welfare and education of children and teens with gifts, talents, and/or high potential. TAG is a division of the Council for Exceptional Children.

Council for Exceptional Children (CEC) (cec.sped.org). The largest international professional organization dedicated to improving educational outcomes for individuals with exceptionalities, students with disabilities, and/or the gifted.

Future Problem Solving Program International (fpspi.org). Provides students with necessary thinking and problem-solving skills that will serve them well throughout their lives.

Gifted Development Center (gifteddevelopment.com). Provides comprehensive testing, referrals to testers in other states, and referrals to counselors who have experience working with gifted kids and their families.

Hollingworth Center for Highly Gifted Children (hollingworth.org). A national volunteer resource and support network for highly gifted children, their families, schools, and communities.

International Baccalaureate Organization (IBO) (ibo.org). A nonprofit educational foundation that helps develop the intellectual, personal, emotional, and social skills of students ages 3 to 19 to live, learn, and work in a rapidly globalizing world. Founded in 1968, the foundation works with many schools in 140-plus countries.

Jacob K. Javits Gifted and Talented Students Education Program, U.S. Department of Education, Office of Elementary and Secondary Education (www2.ed.gov/programs/javits). Created by an Act of Congress in 1994, the Javits program funds grants, provides leadership, and sponsors the National Research Center on the Gifted and Talented.

Mensa International (mensa.org). The international association for children and adults with high IQs. In the United States, contact American Mensa (us.mensa.org).

National Association for Gifted Children (NAGC) (nagc.org). A national advocacy group of parents, educators, and affiliate groups united in support of gifted education. Join to receive the quarterly magazine *Parenting for High Potential,* discounts on other selected NAGC publications, and more. NAGC has affiliates in every state.

National Conference of Governor's Schools (ncogs.us). Summer programs for gifted and talented high school students.

Supporting Emotional Needs of the Gifted (SENG) (sengifted.org). Helps parents identify giftedness in their children; helps children understand and accept their unique talents. Provides a forum for parents and educators to communicate.

World Council for Gifted and Talented Children (world-gifted.org). An international organization that seeks to focus world attention on gifted and talented children and ensure the realization of their potential.

Websites

A to Z Home's Cool Homeschooling Website (a2zhomeschooling.com). A comprehensive collection of articles, links, and resources.

Gifted Child Society (gifted.org). This nonprofit organization provides educational enrichment and support services for gifted children, assistance to parents, and training for educators.

GT World (gtworld.org). An online support community for parents of gifted and talented children. Look for articles, links, testing information, definitions, and five mailing lists.

Hoagies' Gifted Education Page (hoagiesgifted.org). Much more than a "page," this is a wide and respected variety of resources for parents and educators of gifted youth, from research to everyday success stories, personal support groups, and links.

Homeschooling SIG of American Mensa (groups.yahoo.com/neo /groups/homeschoolingmensans). A SIG is a special interest group. The Homeschooling SIG is a support group for parents who are homeschooling their gifted children.

LD OnLine (ldonline.org). Seeks to help children and adults reach their full potential by providing accurate and up-to-date information and advice about learning disabilities and ADHD.

Index

Note: Page references in *italics* refer to figures; those in **boldface** refer to reproducible templates.

A

Accelerated learning
    approaches to, 221–224
    reading, 104, 142
    social adjustment and, 222, 223
Accelerated learning contracts, 62–64, *63*
Acceptable use policies (AUPs) for Web-based activities, 218
ADD/ADHD, *See* Attention deficit disorders (ADD/ADHD), children with
Advanced placement (AP) classes, 221
After-school programs, 224
Agreements with students, *See* Contracts and agreements
American Wars extension activities, **80, 81**
Animal stories, reading, **110, 111**
AP classes, 221
Apps for students, 50, 51, 210, 214–215
ASD, *See* Autism spectrum disorder (ASD)
Asperger's syndrome, 26
Assessment
    differentiating, 7–8
    Evaluation Contract, 93, 95, **96,** 183–184
    formative assessments, 201–204, 207–208
    grading options, 206
    identifying gifted students, 30–33
    of independent work, 183–184
    Learning Contract strategy, 67, 206
    purposes of, 200–201, 218
    scoring rubrics, 208
    self-evaluation by students, 184, **186**
    student sabotage of, 97
    Study Guide strategy, 93, 95, **96,** 206–207
    summative assessments, 201, 204–208
    use of technology for, 199–200, 214–215
    of young children, 33
    See also Grades/grading; IQ tests
Assistive technology, 213
Asynchronous development, 12
Attention deficit disorders (ADD/ADHD), children with
    characteristics, 24–25
    misdiagnosis, 25
    strategies for helping children, 26–29
Attribution theory, 18
Auditory learners, 144, 177
Autism spectrum disorder (ASD)
    characteristics, 26
    strategies for helping children, 26–29

B

Behaviors and characteristics
    ADD/ADHD, children with, 24–26
    autism spectrum disorder (ASD), children with, 26
    creative thinkers, 20, 22
    gifted children, 1–2, 11–14
    perfectionism, 16–17
    twice-exceptional students, 22, 23–24
    See also Problem behaviors
Bibliographies, 177
Bibliotherapy, 128, 136
"Big picture," providing, 27, 144
Biographies, reading, **112, 113**
Bloom's Taxonomy of Educational Objectives, 143, 145, **162,** 164
Blurting out answers, strategies for, 14–16
Book logos, making, 119, 123
Books, selecting, 102, 116–117, 123, 126
Book sharing, 119
Bookworm game, 51
Boredom, potential for, 1–2, 36
Brown, Karen, 7

C

Challenging behavior, *See* Problem behaviors
Challenging work
    need for, 2–3, 29–30, 102–103
    reassuring students about, 205
Cheating issues, 215
Checkers
    Learning Contract strategy, 58
    Most Difficult First strategy, 47
    parents as, 58
Choices for students, allowing, 6–8, 231
    See also Differentiation
Circle of Books, **120**
Class discussions
    domination of, strategies for, 14–16
    Socratic Seminars strategy, 161, 163
Class Tools website, 211
Cluster grouping
    benefits of, 196
    definition and overview, 164, 194, 197
    example scenario, 194–195
    frequently asked questions/teacher concerns, 196–198
    identifying students for, 197
    pros and cons, 196, 225
    Schoolwide Cluster Grouping Model (SCGM), 30, *195,* 195–196
    versus tracking, 197
    See also Grouping
Cluster Grouping Handbook, The (Winebrenner and Brulles), 195, 196
Cognitive Abilities Test (CogAT), 33
Collaborative learning
    cluster grouping, 164, 194–198, 225
    cooperative learning groups, 190–193
    technology for, 212–214
    See also Grouping
College
    college-level programs for students, 30
    difficulties in, 2
Common Core State Standards, 189
Compacting
    benefits of, 37–38, 72
    choice time versus free time, 39–40, 187
    Compactor Form, 39–40, **41,** 69
    definition and overview, 6, 37–38, 39–40, 72
    frequently asked questions/teacher concerns, 67–70
    grading considerations, 42, 48, 53, 67, 71
    Most Difficult First strategy, 42, 45–47, *46,* 67, 70–71
    need for, 38
    Pretest for Volunteers strategy, 48–50, *49, 50,* 53, 71
    qualifying for, 48, 53, 67
    in reading instruction, 103–104
    time budgeting and, 38, 39–40, 68, 70
    See also Differentiation; Learning Contract strategy
Compensation strategies, teaching, 26–27
Competitiveness, cultural differences and, 32
Content new to students
    differentiating and compacting, overview, 6, 73, 98
    example scenario, 74–75
    Study Guide strategy (*See* Study Guide strategy)
Content replacement classes, 220
Contracts and agreements
    Contract for Accelerated Learning, 62–64, *63*
    Contract for Expository Writing, *137*
    Contract for Permission to Read Ahead, 104, **105**
    Contract for Reading Skills, Grammar, and Language Mechanics, 106, *107*
    Contract for Reading Skills and Vocabulary, 106, **108**
    Contract with Problem-Solving Focus, 64, *65*
    Evaluation Contract, 93, 95, **96,** 183–184
    Independent Study Agreements, 86, 88–89, **90, 91**
    Learning Contract, 51, 53–55, *54,* **56,** 58–60
    Personal Interest Study Project Agreement, 183, **185**
Cooperative learning groups
    example scenario, 190
    gifted students groups, 190–193
    heterogeneous groups, 190–192, 193

About the Authors

Susan Winebrenner has an M.S. in curriculum and instruction and a B.S. in education. A former classroom teacher and gifted-program coordinator, Susan is an internationally recognized leader in the field of gifted education. She is the author of several books and teaching resources, including *Differentiating Content for Gifted Learners in Grades 6–12, Teaching Kids with Learning Difficulties in Today's Classroom* (with Lisa M. Kiss), and *The Cluster Grouping Handbook* and *Teaching Gifted Kids in Today's Classroom Professional Development Multimedia Package* (both with Dina Brulles). Through her consulting and workshop business, Education Consulting Service, Susan presents seminars nationally and internationally, helping educators translate education research into classroom practice. She has contributed articles to various educational publications and served on the faculty of New Leaders for New Schools. She lives in San Diego, California. Visit Susan's website at susanwinebrenner.com.

Dina Brulles, Ph.D., is a school administrator and the gifted-education director for Arizona's Paradise Valley Unified School District. Recognized for her expertise in creating and supervising schoolwide cluster grouping, she also assists districts throughout the United States in developing gifted-education programs, including those districts serving culturally and linguistically diverse gifted students. She is the coauthor with Susan Winebrenner of *The Cluster Grouping Handbook* and *Teaching Gifted Kids in Today's Classroom Professional Development Multimedia Package* and the coauthor with Karen Brown of *A Teacher's Guide to Flexible Grouping and Collaborative Learning*. She holds a Ph.D. in gifted education and an M.S. in curriculum and instruction and serves on the faculty of the Graduate College of Education at Arizona State University. Prior to becoming an administrator, Dina was an elementary classroom teacher, a bilingual teacher, an ESL teacher, and a gifted-cluster teacher. She lives in Peoria, Arizona. Visit Dina's website at giftededucationconsultants.com.